Swami
Dayanand Saraswati

Swami Dayanand Saraswati

Series Editor
M.A. Seewan

Editors
Saud Akhtar **R.K. Singh**

Himalaya Books Pvt. Ltd.
'Ramdoot', Dr. Bhalerao Marg, Girgaon, Mumbai - 400 004
Tel : (022) 23863863. Fax : (022) 23877178
Email : himpub@vsnl.com

First Edition : 2011

First Edition : 2011 **Edition : 2014**

Published by : **H.B.P.L.**
"Pooja Apartment", 4-B, Murari Lal Street, Ansari Road,
Darya Ganj, New Delhi-110 002
Phones : 23270392, 23278631 Reliance : 30180392 to 396
Fax : 011-23256286 Email : hphdel@vsnl.com

Sole Distributers : **HIMALAYA PUBLISHING HOUSE PVT. LTD.**

Branch Offices :

Mumbai : "Ramdoot", Dr. Bhalerao Marg, Girgaon, Mumbai - 400 004.
Phone: 022-23860170/23863863, Fax: 022-23877178
E-mail: himpub@vsnl.com; Website: www.himpub.com

Nagpur : Kundanlal Chandak Industrial Estate, Ghat Road, Nagpur - 440 018. Phone: 0712-2738731, 3296733; Telefax: 0712-2721216

Bengaluru : No. 16/1 (Old 12/1), 1st Floor, Next to Hotel Highlands, Madhava Nagar, Race Course Road, Bengaluru - 560 001.
Phone: 080-22286611, 22385461, 4113 8821, 22281541

Hyderabad : No. 3-4-184, Lingampally, Besides Raghavendra Swamy Matham, Kachiguda, Hyderabad - 500 027.
Phone: 040-27560041, 27550139

Chennai : 8/2 Madley 2nd street, T. Nagar, Chennai - 600 017.
Mobile: 09320490962

Pune : First Floor, "Laksha" Apartment, No. 527, Mehunpura, Shaniwarpeth (Near Prabhat Theatre), Pune - 411 030.
Phone: 020-24496323/24496333; Mobile: 09370579333

Lucknow : House No 731, Shekhupura Colony, Near B.D. Convent School, Aliganj, Lucknow - 226 022.
Phone: 0522-4012353; Mobile: 09307501549

Ahmedabad : 114, "SHAIL", 1st Floor, Opp. Madhu Sudan House, C.G. Road, Navrang Pura, Ahmedabad - 380 009.
Phone: 079-26560126; Mobile: 09377088847

Ernakulam : 39/176 (New No: 60/251) 1st Floor, Karikkamuri Road, Ernakulam, Kochi – 682011. Phone: 0484-2378012, 2378016;
Mobile: 09387122121

Bhubaneswar : 5 Station Square, Bhubaneswar - 751 001 (Odisha).
Phone: 0674-2532129, Mobile: 09338746007

Indore : Kesardeep Avenue Extension, 73, Narayan Bagh, Flat No. 302, IIIrd Floor, Near Humpty Dumpty School, Indore - 452007 (M.P.).
Mobile: 09303399304

Kolkata : 108/4, Beliaghata Main Road, Near ID Hospital, Opp. SBI Bank, Kolkata - 700 010, Phone: 033-32449649, Mobile: 7439040301

Guwahati : House No. 15, Behind Pragjyotish College, Near Sharma Printing Press, P.O. Bharalumukh, Guwahati - 781009, (Assam).
Mobile: 09883055590, 08486355289, 7439040301

Printed at : M/s. Aditya Offset Process (I) Pvt. Ltd., Hyderabad. On behalf of HPH.

Preface

Biography, is now a form of literature, very much in vogue. In fact, biography is a description or account of someone's life and the times, which is usually published in the form of a book. A biography is more than a mention of personal facts (life, education, work, relationships and death), it also portrays the subject's experience of events. Technically speaking, a work is biographical, if it covers, all of a person's life. Biography writing has a long history. A biography is real. Ancient Greeks developed the biographical tradition, which we have inherited, although until the 5th century AD, when the word 'biographia' first appeared, in Damascius' "Life of Isodorus," biographical pieces were called simply "lives". It is quite likely that the Greeks were drawing on a pre-existing eastern tradition. Certainly Herodotus' "Histories" contains more detailed biographical information on Persian kings and subjects. The earliest surviving pieces, which we would identify as biographical are Isocrates' "Life of Evagoras" and Xenophon's "Life of Agesilaos," both from the fifth century BC. "Parallel Lives" by Plutarch, a Greek writing under the Roman empire, is a series of short biographies of eminent men.

The Golden Age of English biography emerged in late eighteenth century, the century in which the terms "biography" and "autobiography" entered English lexicon. The classic works of the period were Samuel Johnson's "Critical Lives of the Poets" and James Boswell's "Massive Life of Johnson". Generally American biography followed English model. By World War I, cheap hardcover reprints had become popular. The decade of the 1920s witnessed a biographical 'boom'. Later, biographical writings developed a lot and today biographies are written and compiled in the finest form of the genre. In India too, biography, as a form of literature has been evolved, cultivated and polished over the years. Here is an effort to promote this tradition further.

This series of biographies of great men, great women and celebrities in all walks of life is an adventurous academic endeavour, in its own right. A team of researchers and compilers has worked for a good period of time to accomplish the project. For this purpose, hundreds of books by eminent authors and editors have been consulted and referred to. We have benefited from various works, liberally, in order to illustrate and enrich this effort of ours. Present book is devoted to the great personality of Swami Dayanand Saraswati.

Founder of Arya Samaj and Gurukuls for imparting Vedic education, Swami Dayanand Saraswati was one of the most radical socio-religious reformers in the history of India. He propagated egalitarian approach of the Vedas at a time, when widespread casteism was prevalent in the society. He was against idol worship. He underwent rigorous training under Swami Virjanand Saraswati. Dayanand Saraswati undertook a tour of the entire county, made fiery speeches condemning the caste system, idolatry, and child marriages. Dayanand Saraswati founded Arya Samaj to promote social service. He gave new interpretations to reform the stagnant Hindu thought through his book "Satyarthprakash" (The Light of Truth). He profusely quoted the Vedas and other religious texts to insist that salvation was not the only motto of a Hindu or Arya, as was believed. To lead a fruitful worldly life, working for a noble cause was important, and he preached that salvation was possible, through social service.

This is a compact and comprehensive account of the above mentioned great life, which is bound to attract the attention of scholars, researchers, students and the general readers, alike. Let's hope this humble effort would receive a warm welcome and due applause.

— *Editors*

Contents

1

An Illustrious Life

Introduction

Karshanji was a good and just man. He was generous in his dealings. He had faith in religious practices that had come down from times immemorial.

This happened about 200 years ago. Saurashtra of the present Gujarat State consisted of several small states. Among them was Morvi. Tankara was a town in this state. There lived a wealthy Brahmin, Karshanji Lalji Tiwari by name; he was also the tahsildar of Tankara. The ruler of Morvi had granted him a small troop of horses (cavalry) both for protection and as a mark of honour.

His wife, Amrithbai, was a beautiful and Virtuous woman. She was like a mother to all the villagers.

In 1825, a son was born to the couple. They named' him Moolashankar. According to the custom of the place, he was also called Dayaram. This child was to become famous as Maharshi Dayananda. When he attained the age of five, Moolashankar's education started. At the age of eight, his Upanayana Sanskara (being invested with the holy thread) was performed. The boy used to perform religious rites like 'Sandhyavandana' with devotion. He had a very good memory.

By the time he was fourteen he had learnt by heart the Yajurveda, the scriptures and the upanishads. Karshanji wished that his son should follow in his footsteps by becoming a devotee of Shiva. He, therefore, used to describe the greatness of Shiva every now and then. He would advise the boy to worship Lord Shiva and only then eat something on days of festivals. Moolashankar had an uncle whom he loved very much. His uncle himself was a simple man of great learning with a religious bent of mind. He influenced the boy deeply. Moolashankar had a sharp intellect and an extraordinary memory and so his uncle thought some day his nephew would become a great man.

Birth and Childhood

Swami Dayanand was born at Tankara (Morvi), a town situated on the bank of the Machhooka Mahanadi, in Kathiawar (Gujarat), in the Vikram era 1881 (1825 AD). His original name was Moola Shankar, and his father's Karsanji. He was the head of an eminent Brahman family of the village and was rich, prosperous and influential. Karsanji was in service, holding the position of Jamadar, which office was hereditary in his family. The post of Jamadar was one of great responsibility, being much like a Tehsildarhip, the principal duty of its incumbent was the realisation of State revenue. Karsanji had under him a number of sepoys to assist him in the discharge of his duties. The family over which he presided had lands of its own, and the income from these was largely supplemented by the interest on sums regularly lent to the neighbours in need of money.

Karsanji was man of stern disposition, having no faith in half measures. When he set his heart upon doing a thing, or when duty called upon him to undertake anything, he would set about his task with a will, and would not rest till it was accomplished, or till it was proved that, for some reason or other, it was in spite of the best he could do, impossible of accomplishment. He was a religious man, almost austere in life, and so thoroughly orthodox and uncompromising was he in is views, that slightest departure from the practices and observances which his faith enjoyed, was, in his opinion, unwarranted and deserving or lacked sympathy with his fellow-creatures at large: he had a large share of both;

but, when anybody crossed him in anything or criticised his doctrine, he had, for the time being, and perhaps for many days to come, nothing but contempt and hatred for the offender, and thought that he had no title whatever to his love and his good offices.

Dayanand's mother, on the other hand, was, like the mother of Nanak, nothing but a personification of patience, gentleness and sweetness. While her love for her child was unbounded, she had a genuine kindly feeling for all around her, ready to share their sorrows and to participate in their joys on all occasion. She was an ideal Hindu woman, unlettered no doubt, but the soul of simplicity, purity and goodness, a veritable Queen of the home. From such parents had Dayanand descended, and it was therefore but natural that while he had, on the one hand, the immutable resolves of his father, on the other, he possessed a heart embracing the whole world in its circle of sympathy.

Education

Dayanand was five years old when his education commenced and this is the age at which, according to the Shastras, a child should be put to his letters, by his own parents if possible. He proved and extraordinary apt pupil, passing from one elementary book to another in rapid succession. In his eighth year his *Yajnopavita Sanskara* was performed, and the investiture with thread of the "twiceborn" was forthwith followed by his initiation into the *sandhya* and *upasna*. Karsanji though a Samavedi Brahman, was a follower of Shiva, and as such he taught his son, Rudri, following it by the Samhita. No pains were spared to impress Dayanand with the sacredness and superiority of the Shiva faith, and the importance of keeping of the fasts peculiar to the creed was continually made clear to him.

The worship of Shiva, as the supreme, unapproachable deity, was specially insisted upon, and, in order that the deity might be always close by, it was hinted that a clay image of him could serve the purpose just as well as one made of stone or metal: the father's intention being that Dayanand could have a fresh idol as often as he pleased and should worship it daily without fail.

When Dayanand had reached his tenth year, he was fairly regular in his adoration of Shiva, but beyond paying this homage at stated hours, he did not concern himself much with Shivaism. The father, however, was not to be satisfied with this much. He was always for his observing the more rigorous fasts his elders kept, for his hearing the *katha* and for keeping long and trying vigils at night. The mother might protest that the boy was unequal to the hardship sought to be imposed upon him, that it was physically impossible for him to bear so much strain; yet the father was not to be easily dissuaded from his purpose.

With all the allowance he made for his tender years, as result of the loving mother's pleadings no doubt, he would take him frequently into Shiva temples to see what was going on there, and he would never visit a brother in faith but Dayanand was with him, to listen to what the men had to say about the excellence of the Shivaism. Whatever disappointment the father might have experienced on seeing Dayanand not up to the mark in austerity, he must have felt more than compensated for the disagreeable feeling by the progress which Dayanand was making in learning. By the time Dayanand was fourteen years of age, he knew the whole of the Yajur Veda Samhita by heart, some portions of the remaining three Vedas and some minor works on Sanskrit grammar. He understood but little (as also his father) of what he could repeat, but even is oral knowledge was worth much: it was to prove of service later on.

The fast of Shivaratri approached, and now that Dayanand was his fourteenth year, there was absolutely no reason, said his father, why he should not keep it. Dayanand was at first reluctant to comply with his father's wishes, but when the *katha*, setting forth the meritoriousness of the fast, was recited to him, he consented.

The mother strongly protested against her son being subjected to such a trial, saying that if he went without his usual morning breakfast and remained without food for the rest of the day and the night following, he would fall ill; but her expostulations were of no avail. Karsanji was bent upon having his way, and so the fast had to be kept. As the evening set in, the father and son went to large Shiva temple outside the village, where the rules in connection with the worship of the presiding deity of the sacred shrine were duly explained to him. One of the injunctions was that the devotee who kept the fast of Shivratri, must remain awake the whole night, as otherwise the fast would bear no fruit. Dayanand found the temple fairly crowded with worshippers and priests, some in a state of excitement, while others sober, silent and thoughtful. Presently, the worship began with the chanting of hymns, to which many of the laymen present cheerfully joined in singing.

The first quarter of the night passed off very well, the entire congregation remaining awake and displaying all the fervour and enthusiasm which could be expected of them. In the second quarter the proceedings became less animating, but the majority continued to keep awake and go one with the rites. As soon, however, as the third quarter came, the devotees seemed to have well nigh exhausted and were unable any further to resist sleep. Nodding of heads was visible all around, and one man after vainly endeavouring to battle with drowsiness and after fruitlessly exhorting his neighbour not to give in so easily, stretched himself, at full length, on the floor and commenced snoring heavily.

Dayanand's father was one of the batch which was the first to fall asleep, nor were the priests long in following his example. Finding that the dread Jamada was "safe," they stole out of the temple and lying down were soon ranging free in the land of dreams, though and lying down were soon ranging free in the land of dreams, though more nervous of them, no doubt, now and then found themselves suddenly deprived of their newly-acquired freedom by the sight of the apparition of their stern village official.

Dayanand was surprised at the scant respect which these worshippers of Shiva seemed to have for the fast by practically going against their professions, but he was determined that nothing should induce him to lose the reward which his leaders had deliberately forfeited. To prevent himself, therefore, from dropping into a slumber, he took to vigorously sprinkling water over his eyes, and to thinking. While thus employed, he saw something that drew him out of his abstraction and riveted his attention on itself.

A mouse creeping out of its hole began to take liberties with the image of Shiva, and make free with the offerings which had come to it from the worshippers. For many moments the boy watched the doings of the little creature, possibly amused a little, but serious thoughts followed, and he mused: "Is this the Mahadeva whom the *katha* represented as deity with human shape, with a trident in his hand and playing upon the drum - the God who bestows a boon upon one and pronounces a curse upon another, and who is the Lord of the Kailash mountain? This image has not the power to drive away even an insignificant mouse from its presence!"

Dayanand thought long and hard and intently, and this thinking laid the foundation of that great, all-embracing religious revolution which he subsequently wrought in the land of his birth. Thousands upon thousands of men and women remain awake the whole night of the 13th of Magh, but who ever sees the deity which is the object of his or her adoration or receives the reward which he or she aspires? Shiva, the real, all-pervading and all-powerful beneficent Being who rules the Universe, did, however, answer the prayers of a child, saying, "The boon sought after shall be thine, but here is work for thee to do, and that must be done before thou can reach thy goal.

Study the primeval Veda and enrich thyself with knowledge and wisdom, and, by means of these, bring thy brethren back to the adoration of one and the only true Lord of the creation, tearing them away from the worship of the created inanimate thing." Dayanand's soul heard the words and took in the inspiration in a vague, dreamy, half-conscious fashion, to be realised and worked out in the gradually increasing light and enlightenment of coming years.

Sir Sayyad Ahmad Khan, referring to Dayanand's reflections, skeptical in a sense no doubt, but like the intensely dark moments heralding the approach of happy dawn of light and life, turn his face from idolatry and seek out the study those portions of the Vedas which are concerned with the unity of the formless, self-effulgent God and with His other attributes?"

The question, " Is this shapeless stone the Mahadeva?" again and again pressed it self upon Dayanand's mind, but no satisfactory answer was forthcoming. At last, finding himself baffled, he awakened his father and requested him to resolve his doubts for him. That gentleman, unceremoniously aroused from a refreshing, half-finished sleep, demanded in a tone of surprise and anger: "Why do you ask such a question?" Dayanand replied: "The mice are running over this image of stone, and taking unwarranted liberties with it". The Mahadeva, of whom the katha spoke, is an animate being, how he can permit mice to run over his body? This idol cannot so much as move its head, much less protect itself from others. It appears to me that it is utterly impossible to reach the living omnipotent Deity through the agency of or through medium of this image.

Dayanand's father, perceiving his son's earnestness, found himself compelled to answer his question. He said: "The Mahadeva, who lives on the Kailash mountain, is represented by and invoked through this image, for he cannot be seen face to face in this age of *Kaliyug*. By being imagined as inhabiting an image of stone, metal or wood, etc., and by being worshipped through it, he is as much pleased as though he were actually present in the idol and were himself adored." The parent added, "Your habit of raising objections is anything but praiseworthy. Why, this idol is nothing more that an image of the God?". Dayanand had to remain content with the answer, but reasoning like this could never set his doubts at rest. The only effect which it produced upon his mind was to shake his faith in idol-worship, to make him look upon the institution as false. And his resolution was made then and there, that he would never in future worship Mahadeva till he had seen him face to face.

Shortly after the termination of the conversation between father and son, Dayanand craved permission to go home, for he felt tired and hungry. The permission was give (as it could not but be given under the circumstances), and a sepoy was ordered to escort him home. Karsanji, however, thought it his duty to warn Dayanand at parting not to eat anything during the night. But the moment Dayanand reached home, he told his mother that he was hungry and would have something to appease the his hunger. The good woman at once brought him some sweets, and while handing them over to him, said: "Did I not tell you that you would not be able to bear the hardships attendant on keeping a fast? But you would have your own way, and you see the consequences. Eat these sweets and don't return to your father now."

Dayanand ate the sweets and went to bed at about I am sleeping soundly for over seven hours. When Karsanji came home and hear how Dayanand had disregarded the parting warning, he was greatly annoyed and took his son to task for disobedience. Dyananand replied that the image in the temple was not identical with the Mahadeva spoken of in the katha, and consequently he did not feel bound to recognised its sanctity. At this the father could only utter a growl of displeasure, and then kept quiet, hoping to win over his son to his views on some subsequent occasion favourable for the purpose.

But this was not to be. Dayanand has an uncle greatly attached to him. He complained to him of the pressure that his parent was bringing to bear upon him and pleaded his intercession, backing up his appeal by declaring that keeping fasts and attending to the worship of the God interfered adversely with his studies. The uncle interceded, supported by the boy's mother, and the result was that Dayanand ceased to suffer from the galling restraint. Being now, in a manner, his own master, Dayanand threw himself wholeheartedly into his studies, reading, with a Pandit, Nighantu, Nirukta, Purva Mimansa and works on karmkand (ritual). His leisure was now devoted to his books.

An Attempt on the Swami's Life

The shastrarth at Anupshahar had been far-reaching in its effects. Thakur Mukand Singh, of Chhalesar, a Chauhan Kshatrya by caste, had been, throughout, present at the discussion, and was one of those who, at the termination of the discussion, had been compelled to come to the conclusion, in spite of their long-cherished belief to the contrary, that the worship of idols was degrading and sinful in the extreme.

As soon as he returned to his village he informed his kinsmen that it was his intention to have all the family-temples-some thirty in number and scattered in different hamlets - thoroughly "overhauled" and relieved of the presence of idols for good. And in pursuance of this resolve he had all the images lying in the temples in question removed form their strongholds and thrown into the Kali Nadi.

This action was deeply displeasing to his caste-men, as many as sixty villages in the neighbourhood actually went to the length of indulging in the threat that the perpetrator of such a sacrilege should be out-casted without delay. The threat somehow or other was not carried out, the Thakur's caste-men being wise in their generation, as persecution, in the majority of cases, will only add fuel to the fire and strengthen and invigorate where it seeks to crush. Verily the preacher of truth is a mightier and more irresistible iconoclast than Kings and Princes with unlimited brute force to accomplish their purposes with! While Swami Dayanand was yet staying at Karnvas, the report went round that a remover of the "forehead-mark" has made his appearance in the vicinity, and it was nothing surprising that a conservative man like Rao Karn Singh, a Raees of Baroli, a disciple of the Chaivite Rangacharya, who had come to bathe in the Ganges, should, on learning the nature of the doctrines which the Swami preached, become his mortal foe. One day the Rao was condescending enough to pay a visit to the Swami, accompanied by twelve armed men.

The Swami received him with great courtesy, though he could not help smiling as soon as the mark on the Rao's forehead caught his eye, and asking him further, in Sanskrit, why he, a Kshatrya, had put the beggar's sign on his person. This made the already angry Rao still more angry, and he enquired in a gruff voice, "Where shall I sit?" "Wherever you like," was the reply. As he and come with the sole object of venting his rage, he declared that he should sit just where the Swami sat. The Swami answered that he was welcome to please himself, and he made room for him at the same time, on his own seat.

As soon as the 'big' man was squatted down, he turned his blood-shot eyes towards the swami and exclaimed in wrathful tones: "Mendicant! You are not doing right things in disbelieving in the Ganges and the Tiraths. If you say anything against them in my presence, I shall deal with you severely." The fearful words failed to move the Swami, and, after the fashion of true Sanyasis, he calmly replied: "If you want to fight, you had better go to the Rajas of Jaipur and Dhaulpur; but if, on the other hand, you want to hear truth sifted and differentiated from falsehood, then invite your guru Rangacharya here, and we shall be ready for him." Having said this, the Swami entered upon a vigorous exposure of the Chakrankit Faith, of which the Rao was a follower.

At this the Rao was beside himself with passion, and laid his hand on the hilt of his sword. Before, however, he could use the weapon, a follower of his, one Baldev Parshad, a wrestler by profession, stopped him, saying, "don't' trouble yourself, Sir; I shall finish with the audacious Sadhu in the twinkling of an eye."

The wrestler raised his hand to strike, but Swami Dayanand was too quick for him. Seizing his arm, he gave him a push which sent him several paces back, reeling! The men around the Swami (there were some fifty of them) were astonished at this sudden attack on an inoffensive person, and that too a Sadhu, and one of them Rao Karn Singh and his band meaningfully in these words: "If you molest this Sanyasi, you will only carry from here a broken skull!" Crest-fallen and gnashing his teeth in impotent rage, Karn singh rose and beat a hasty retreat, vowing to be even with his enemy at some other time.

After he had gone, many of the assembly stood up and gave it as their opinion that such conduct should not be left unreported to the Police. The Swami, while thanking them for their regard for him, observed that if Karn Singh had failed to acquit himself as a true Kshatriya should, it did not follow that he too should prove himself false to his Brahminism. "I have, moreover," added he, 'received no hurt. The same of the thing is enough for the Rao. If he is wise, he won't repeat his feat again."

This was the first attack on the Swami's life, but, as we might suspect, it was not the last, even on the part of Karn Singh. Soon after this, he tried to incite some Bairagis to assault the Swami, promising that if they brought him his head, they should be liberally rewarded. "You are, each of you," said he, to make his persuasion the more effective, "single and alone in the world. If you do what I tell you to, you will have dharma from being defiled." The Bairagis, however, refused to commit such a horrible deed, telling him to keep his money to himself.

A Shastrarth

Swami Dayanand was well aware of the value of winning young men over to the Truth, and consequently whenever he came across these, he made a point of addressing them a few weighty words which never failed to lead, sooner or later, to results of a most gratifying character. One day, while, during his wanderings, he sat on the banks of the Ganges, thinking and enjoying the bracing breeze, two young men, approaching him from behind, commenced rubbing ashes over his naked body.

Turning round, the Swami fixed his piercing gaze on their faces and, pleased with the results of his survey, asked them how they passed their time. They replied that they were students, studying the Bhagvat and the Kaumidi. The Swami, while commending their studious habits, informed them that the books they were reading were utterly worthless productions, and advised them to go on with the Ashtadhayai, the Manu Smriti, and the Upanishads instead. At the same time he spoke to them on the true Vedic religion, showing, in the course of his remarks, how mischievous and false the Chakrankit Faith was.

The students were greatly impressed with the Sanyasi's words, and going into their village, repeated to their elders what had been said to them. They also succeeded in inducing a Pandit of the Chakrankit Faith to accompany them, with a view to hold a discussion the Sanyasi, but the moment the Pandit set his eyes on the Sanyasi, he turned upon his heel, and entering a temple, hid himself there. Evidently, it was not the first time the Pandit had seen the Swami, he was well aware how he should fare in a discussion with such a man.

The people were displeased at his precipitate retreat, and the majority were convinced that the Chakrankit Faith, which many of them were going to embrace, was not worth their acceptance. The Swami was unwearied in pointing out the excellence of the Vedic Sanskars to the "twice-born" and, as we have seen, he invested many a member of his community with the "triple sacred thread." Of those who received the Yajnopavit from the hands of the great man, the largest number belonged to the Kshatriya castes, inhabiting the villages situated in the neighbourhood of Karnvas.

The priestly class was in despair, and exasperated beyond measure, at finding their tricks exposed and their influence undermined, and they again and again asked themselves the question: "Are we really powerless to get this man out of the way, once for all?" Perhaps not as a Brahman of Anupshahar undertook proves very nearly succeeded in proving.

The unsuspecting Swami lectures on "Idol-worship" becoming intolerable, a priest, with his hear filled with hatred but yet suppression his real feelings with a powerful effort, came up to him with a smile and presented him with a betel-leaf. The unsuspecting Swami took the leaf, but before he had eaten it many minutes, the poison swallowed with it began to show its effects. Realising his danger, he sought the bank of the Ganges without delay, and descending into the water set about doing the Neoli-karm, or swallowing large quantities of water and passing out the same, according to a prescribed method, from the intestines, so as to carry away gradually all hurtful matter from the stomach.

The process was successful, and the Swami's life was saved. But according to the fashion of great men, and in keeping with the traditions of the order to which he belonged, the Swami did not so much as administer a reproof to the murderous Brahman. Others, however, were not so forgiving. When Sayyad Mohammad the Tehsildar of Anupshahar, heard of the Brahman's doing, he was very angry, and had the scoundrel sent to prison in a case pending in his Court against him, though lighter punishment could have fairly satisfied against him, though lighter punishment could have fairly satisfied the ends of justice. The Swami had great regard for the Tehsildar, but when the later came to see him, after the Brahman had been incarcerated, and told him how the fellow had been dealt with, the Swami felt annoyed and would not talk to the official. On the Tehsildar's enquiring what had done to displease the Swami, the answer was given in these words: " I have come into the world to release people from captivity and not to see them sent to prison. If the Brahman would be base, why then let him have his way; why should I be false to my own self?" It is said that Brahman was shortly acquitted in an appeal.

At Anupshahar, the Swami had also a discussion with Sadhu Krishnanand Saraswati, on "Idolatry." The Sadhu finding himself unable to make good his position on the authority of the Scripture and the ancient Shastras, became irrelevant and sought shelter in Nyaya. But the Swami was a greater and truer logician than the Sadhu, had here also he found himself driven to the wall. However learned our Pandits may be, they set the slightest possible value on 'relevancy.' The fact is, that they are seldom conversant with the works of the sages. No wonder then that the Swami always spoke of the authors of Chandrika, Kaumidi, and other books, in terms of absolute contempt.

Austere in life, seeking, even during intensely cold nights, no better bed than a heap of rice-husks, defying sickness of all sorts or taking in sickness, if he ever did take, his only sovereign medicine, the tulsi leaves ground with pepper, remaining days and nights wrapped contemplation on the bank of the Ganges, giving good counsel to all who came to him, and constantly distributing the Gayatri Mantra, written with his own hands, among high and low, Swami Dayanand lived out the five years from Samvat 1920 to 1925, he did little in the way of teaching during this period, sending those who seemed really desirous of study to his guru at Mathura, with letters of recommedation. While at Shahbazpur, he received the news of Swami Virjanand's death, and, in tones of deep grief, exclaimed, "The highest authority on Vyakarna is not more." It was after the demise of his revered preceptor that Dayanand set regularly to work, and of this we shall know in the following pages.

Leaving Home

The desire to give up family ties grew in Moolashankar. What is life? What is death? He wanted to learn the answers to these questions from a perfect sage. With this end in view, Mopolashankar was determined to leave home in search of a worthy guru (a teacher) His parents noticed his growing detachment and were afraid that he might run away from home to become a monk. They decided he should soon be married. Even a bride was selected. The preparations for the marriage began in right earnest. Moolashankar did not show any opposition, That gave his parents the impression that their son was willing to marry and they were happy. But Moolashankar's mind was firmly set upon renunciation of family life.

One day, as it was getting dark, Moolashankar came out of his room. He stood in the spacious courtyard and gazed for a moment at his wealthy house. In his mind he bowed for the last time to his parents and other elders from where he stood. His heart grew heavy. The eyes were full of tears. I shall never again set foot in this house,' he told himself and walked away.

At this time, Moolashankar was only twenty-one years old. All the efforts of Karshanji to bring his son back home were of no avail.

Wandering in Search of a Guru

After leaving home Moolashankar travelled to places like Ahmedabad, Baroda, Haridwar, Kanpur and Kashi in search of a guru. He wandered among hills and in forests but nowhere could he find an able guru. At this juncture, Moolashankar came across Swami Poornananda, a profound scholar and sanyasi. The Swamiji initiated the young man into the holy orders. Moolashankar became Swami Dayananda Saraswathi.

As Swami Dayananda wandered from place to place in search of yogis on the heights of the Himalayan regions, his life was in danger again and again. He had to wander day and night in forests where wild beasts roamed. And in the midst of his wanderings his devotion to his goal was tested, too. While he was staying at Okhi Mutt, the Mahant, who was in charge of that mutt, was impressed by his radiance, and said, "Stay here as the future master of this mutt. All the wealth of this mutt will be yours." But Dayananda, who had given up all desire, very politely declined the offer and said, "Sir, if I had desired wealth I would never have left my wealthy father's house. What I want is not earthly wealth, but the treasure of spiritual knowledge." So saying- he walked away from the place.

Even though Swami Dayananda wandered for ten years, he could not find an able guru. This filled him with despair. He climbed to the top of a mountain to kill himself. As he was about to jump down, a part of his mind said, 'Did you leave your house to die like a coward? You left to conquer death and again enlightenment This gave Dayananda fresh strength. He came down from the mountain, his mind firmly made up to find an able guru.

Then he came to know that perfect yogis lived in the dense forest near the source of the river Narmada. Dayananda walked hundreds of miles towards the south, without caring for the distance.

As he was approaching the river Narmada, Dayananda had the darshan of a monk, Poornashrama Swami by name, in a garden. He was happy to hear the story of Dayananda's wanderings. After hearing his story he said, "Dayanandaji, there is only one man on this earth who can fulfil your desire, and that man is Virajananda Dandeesha. He lives in Mathura." This was a ray of hope to Dayananda. Without any delay he set out for Mathura. He reached there on the 14th November 1860.

In Quest of Truth

The next two decades were spent in search of reality and truth. As a homeless wanderer, Mulashankara moved from place to place. He roamed about for some time in the Gujarat regions. He walked along the banks of the Ganga, the Narbada and the Alaknanda. He descended to the valleys and caves. He scaled the Himalayan peaks. He visited the religious festivals at Haridwar and Garh Mukteshwar. He crossed ice-cold mountain streams and trod barefoot on sharp stones With blistered feet, starving, ill-clad, unaccosted, the young pilgrim pushed on. He was in search of truth. He was on the look out for a preceptor.

What did he find ? He found sadhus without wisdom and godliness. He met monks steeped in greed and pretensions. He saw yogis drowned in the smoke of *charas* and *sulfa*. He came across *mahants* who had no means of earned income yet who had houses, elephants and riches. There were mendicants with lakhs of rupees.

There was a scramble among them to prey on the innocent multitude He saw the Vaisnavas, the Shaivas, the Bairagis, the commoners—all groping, all hobbling, all in a process of drift, sick with the symptoms of inner hollowness and mental blankness Inside the temples, Mulashankara found countless gods and goddesses whose stone and bronze images were supposed to be endowed with imaginary powers. The priests around them employed all skill and guile to ensnare the followers. The laymen were ignorant Certain day-today rituals engrossed their whole time and interest. The young pilgrim, tall and strong, with a handsome face, bold eyes, ample forehead and broad chest did not fail to attract the attention of many.

A *mahant* invited him to become his disciple, informing him of the wealth of the *Math.* But the pilgrim, who had by now assumed the name of Dayanand, said: "My father had more wealth than your *Math.* Yet I left my home. I gave up worldly pleasures to attain yogic knowledge and salvation. You have neither of these, and I cannot stay with you."

The Times of the Swami

The nation was in difficulty. The weak and worthless princes were everywhere getting routed. The British Empire in India was taking shape rapidly. The society as a whole was suffering from certain inherent weaknesses. The greedy priest was powerful and ready to exploit. The simple folk had lost the way. Ceremony and ritual had replaced reason and conduct. Superstition and blind faith was mistaken as religion. There was no questioning; no spirit of enquiry. The old values were decaying; the new ones had yet to get established. Ignorance and illiteracy stalked the land. Political leadership had fumbled at every step. Cultural direction was not available. Morally and religiously there was a complete void.

The woman of India lived in oppressive darkness. Since birth, she remained bent under pressing conditions of inequality. She was at times liable to be killed by her own parents. She could be married away in tender childhood. She was expected to burn herself at the pyre of her husband. If she did not become a *sati,* she was condemned to life-long widowhood.

Her's was a long, endless, tearful' life of unrelieved sorrow; detested by all, pitied by none. Yet she must not remarry. Was it in obedience to the scriptures? Was it for happiness in the next life? Was it for the purity of values in society? Was it to satisfy the claims of a holy religion? There was none to ask these questions and none to reply. There was hardly anyone to revolt. It was an age of abject surrender for the woman. It was an age of silent submission.

Naturally, the Hindu society seemed to Reek under the sins of its custodians. Its inner decay evoked challenges from outsiders. The Protestant missionaries from Holland and other parts of Europe and America had already begun their work. It was in fact a peaceful infiltration by the Christian missionaries. They mastered local languages and published Christian literature. They established printing presses and brought out books, tracts, newspapers and periodicals. They founded missionary centres, medical outposts and schools. They educated the converts, treated and tended the sick, and also offered employment to the needy. By the time of William Bentinck, a missionary was a familiar sight in the towns of India.

The Charter Act of 1833 gave to the missionaries, the facility of unrestricted entry into India, and their progress was remarkable. By the year 1850, there were in India 260 Christian centres, 360 foreign missionaries, 500 native preachers of Christianity, 266 churches and 91,265 Protestant Christians. In 1854, the number of students attending the missionary schools was four times the number in the government schools. The missionaries were acting as pioneers in female education, vocational education and training institutes. They had brought out texts in Bengali, Hindi, Tamil, Oriya, Assamese, Malayalam, Marathi, Gujarati, Kashmiri and Bhutanese. They were the principal relief workers in famines and epidemics.

The missionaries stood for emancipated womanhood, equality of status for all sections, triumph of reason, education for all and reforms based on fairness and humanism. There was no untouchability in their ranks, nor the evil of slavery.

Their resources were rich. They collected funds from all over Europe and America. The Government of the East India Company gave them all encouragement. Churches were built and funds provided to them out of the taxes paid by the Indians. Guns were fired in honour of the arriving 'Lal Padri'. They were allowed to move along with the troops from one military area or cantonement to the other. They entered the jails to convert the convicts. They were helped to convert even members of the royal houses. Promotions were offered to secure converts for the church. With all this help, its own usefulness, its progressiveness, the spread of western education and the expansion of railways, Christianity captured a vast field in India.

Hinduism was in no position to meet the challenge posed by Christianity. The missionaries mounted one offensive after the other. They ridiculed idol worship, attacked caste system and occasionally used abusive terms to deride Hindu customs, practices, gods and institutions.

May be, the converts to Christianity were not many. But the outlook changed. The Indian youth turned his back to even the best traditions of his religion and history. He became a colourless copy of the west. A craving admiration for western knowledge and speech took hold of his mind.

He began to feel uneasy, if not ashamed, about his own civilization or the ancient personality of India. English for him became the language of culture and advance. Macaulay was not wrong in asserting that English books were in great demand whereas the Sanskrit and Arabic books had practically no purchasers. The passion and fervour for western knowledge and methods may be judged from one incident.

In 1823, when a Sanskrit College was established at Calcutta, Raja Rammohun Roy lodged a protest with Lord Amherst' against it. In 1829, *a* meeting was held in the Calcutta Town Hall. Dwarakanath Tagore proposed that more and more Europeans should be enabled to settle down in India by removing all restrictions. The resolution was supported by Rammohun Roy and passed. There also came a time when some Hindu students in Calcutta were found bringing beef into their hostels in order to prove that they were fully westernised.

Similarly, the consumption of opium and liquor registered a great increase among the people. It seemed, the whole inner richness, the entire self-confidence that can be the reward of a people with a rich past and a great civilization, was withering. It was in such times that Hinduism needed and found its greatest defender and protestant reformer in the person of Swami Dayanand Saraswati.

Promotion of Education

It was about the close of the Samvat 1925, that Swami Dayanand, now resolved to have more system and regularity in his work, arrive at Farrukhabad. He had, as the result of prolonged reflection, come to the conclusion that schools and seminaries of a superior type were badly wanted in the country, and that preaching and shastrarth — holding, though extremely valuable in their way and indispensable for the success of his propaganda, could not alone achieve all and everything.

One great object, therefore, which his lectures at Farrukhabad were intended to serve, was to make clear to the people of means and influence, who could be brought to sympathise with his mission, the necessity of providing increased facilities for the acquisition, by promising vidyarthis, of sound and thorough education in Sanskrit.

The words of such a Sanyasi could not wholly fall on deaf ears. Lala Panni Lal Seth, a Vaishya, who had from some time past been building a Shivalaya for the location therein of Shivalinga, was so impressed by the Swami's speeches that, bidding eternal farewell to idol-worship, had a Pathsahla opened in the newly constructed building, undertaking further to pay Rs. 30 a month to the Pandit who was put in charge of the institution.

As to the expenses of food of students, some fifty in number, another generous man, Lala Durga Parshad, made himself responsible, for defraying these. The swami himself assisted in teaching the vidyarthis as well as the outsiders, and to many he gave the Yajnopavit. This Pathshala, in the interests of discipline and good management, was eventually removed to some other building. It remained in existence for about seven years.

The second Pathshala, which the Swami established, was one founded at Kasganj in Samvat 1927, Lala Girdhari Lal, Shopkeeper, undertaking to pay Rs. 1,700 towards its expenses from his charity fund (dharma-khata). A Pandit on Rs. 15 a month was engaged to do the teaching work. This Pathshala remained in existence from about four years, being partially supported by the people in general who sent it donations from time to time on occasion of joy in their families.

The third Pathshala was established in Mirzapur, in the same year as the second. Thanks to the large-heartedness of the people, it had an income of one hundred rupees a month to defray its expenses. The Pathshala ceased to exist after three years.

The fourth Pathshala was established at Chhalesar, at the request of Thakur Mukand Singh, who had gone to Banaras to bring the Swami, so that the opening ceremony might be performed in his presence. After a feast given to the Brahmans, on a grand scale, the Pathshala was opened. It drew vidyarthis from distant places, and remained in existence for six years.

The fifth Pathshala was opened Banaras, in Samvat 1930, and put in charge of a Pandit, engaged on a salary of Rs. 25 a month. It was soon discovered that the Pandit, afraid of his brethren and influenced by selfishness, was unwilling to work conscientiously and on the lines suggested by the Swami, and he was consequently replace by a better man. The Pathshala died out after three years.

The rules in force in these Pathshalas were generally these:

- No vidyarthi shall be admitted till he has first thoroughly learnt his sandhya.
- All Viyarthis shall be instructed in the Vedic Granths only - Ashtadhyai, Mahabhashya, and so on.
- Every vidyarthi shall rise early in the morning and do his sandhya... the vidyarthi (teacher) who fails to observe this rule shall forfeit his day-meal, care being taken that he does not go into the village (or city), to get from there anything to appease his hunger with. He will get his supper only after he had one his evening sandhya.
- No vidyarthi (from mofassil) shall be permitted to visit the village (or city) except for the purpose of having his meals in response to a causal or permanent invitation.
- The vidyarthis from the mofassil alone shall have food at the expense of the Pathshala Funds, the local ones providing for themselves.
- The intelligent and hard-working vidyarthis shall receive special consideration at the hands of the managers, as regards the quality of food supplies to them.

- The students who acquit themselves well in the examinations shall be allowed an extra quantity of ghee (clarified butter).
- All vidyarthis shall make a point of joining daily in the Agnihotra.

The above are excellent rules, and the Swami took care that the teachers working in the different Pathshalas did not connive at the infringement, by the students, of any rule having for its object the maintenance of discipline; he further did his best to have the right kind of instruction imparted to the students, and to make them eschew entirely the misleading writings of the latter-day Pandits: but for all that he found that the Pathshalas did not show any desirable results.

The vidyarthis sent out by the seminaries, after their course of education had been finished, for updesh-work, relapsed, with a few exceptions, into orthodoxy, and commenced the pope-lila of their forefathers. This was most disappointing, and under these circumstances, the Swami had no alternative but to close these schools, one after another. Whatever funds were yet in hand, to the credit of these schools, were merged into the fund raised for the publication of the "Veda-Bhashya."

Study at Mathura

Dayanand reached Mathura in the year 1916, V.E (1859), and put up in the temple of Lakshmi Narayan, the accounts he had heard of Virjanand's learning proved only too correct, and he immediately sallied forth in quest of his dwelling, which he was not long in finding. For there was scarcely anyone in Mathura who was unacquainted with the name of the Dandi Swami, who had not heard of his vast learning, and who did not know that the stern old Sanyasi always lived with his doors shut. Dayanand knocked at the door, and the question came in sharp tones from within, "Who is there?"

"A Sanyasi, Dayanand by name," was the reply.

"Do you know anything of Sanskrit grammar?"

Yes, I have studied Saraswata, etc."

At this reply the door opened, and Dayanand went in. Virjanand examined Dayanand, and, on the termination, told him that there was a vast difference between the true Aryan Literature and the books composed by common mortals, and as for himself, he had absolutely no respect for the latter and never taught them. Dayanand could not disabuse his mind of the idea he had clung to for years, in a moment, but the arguments of the Swami prevailed, and he eventually consented to have nothing to do with the works which had the stamp of true science and true wisdom on them. He even went so far as to throw in the Yamuna his old stock, so that Vrijanand might be pleased, and admit him as his pupil. But, though all this was satisfactory enough, the fact could not be lost sight of that Dayanand was a Sanyasi, and Virjanand could not see how a Sanyasi could afford to carry on his studies with him. "I am not in the habit of teaching Sanyasis," said he; "but if I take you in as a pupil, how will you manage to live?"

Swami Dayanand replied that he would find himself food somehow or other, no matter if it was the coarsest possible: all that he cared for was knowledge, and hoped, Virjanand would not refuse him. Finding him persistent in his entreaties, Virjanand at last granted Dayanand's prayer, and having raised a subscription of thirty-one rupees got him a copy of the Mahabhashya to commence his studies with.

Shortly after Swami Dayanand had come and taken up his abode at Mathura, a severe famine spread in the land, and even the well-to-do become sparing of their gifts to the suppliants. The hospitality extended to the vidyarthis began to be more or less withheld, and they were often hard to put to it for a meal. Dayanand behaved manfully in this period of trial, living on roasted gram, or on dry bread made of the same article, from day-to-day. These came to him from the house of Durga khatri, Dakawala.

Nothing less can be expected of a true Sanyasi, or of a true Brahmachari. In whatever character Dayanand may be regarded, he proved himself fully worthy of it. An austere life is an essential condition of true brahmacharya, and a Sanyasi that is not perfectly contended with whatever the householder gives him in the shape of victuals, belies the traditions of he order to which he belongs.

In course of time, a certain Pandit Amar Lal, a man of philanthropic mind and of unbounded charities, struck with the virtues of Dayanand, took upon himself to supply him with food and with books. He made a point of taking him daily home and of seeing him take his meals in his presence.

If ever he had invitation to dine at a friend's house: he would never obey the call till he had first fed his guest at his own house. Dayanand was deeply beholden to this generous man, and his gratitude lasted till death. It is said that the Pandit feasted no-less than one hundred twenty-five Brahmans daily at his dwelling! Another person, to whom Dayanand was indebted fro pecuniary help, was one Hardev, who used to give him two rupees monthly for "milk." A money-changer, named Govardhan Das, also assisted him according to his means, defraying his expenses on oil, which came up to four annas a month.

Swami Dayanand's life at Mathura was a life of incessant toil. He read day and night, spending hours in thought and contemplation, and frequently holding discussion with his fellow-students on various subjects of importance. In his moments of leisure, he would speak to those around him on the value of Brahmacharya, and exhort them, the Brahmans to particular, to be regular in the performance of their sandhya and their agnihotra. His extreme thirst for knowledge, his quick and clear perception of the nature of things, his lucid and convincing expositions of Shastric teaching, and, above all, his righteous ways made him a favourite with the vidyarthi community, and his company was sought after by them, one and all.

Swami Dayanand's reverence for Virjanand increased daily. He loved and served him with his whole heart, performing most cheerfully the humblest offices to please him and to make him more comfortable. He would sweep the floor, and bring pitcher after pitcher of water from the Yamuna, so that the dirt might be effectually washed out of the house, and his preceptor have his daily bath liberally.

Swami Virjanand was often cross with his foremost pupil, and, in his anger, would order him to be driven out of the house; but Dayanand would not mind his roughness and would regain his favour by his humility and his attentions. Whenever he found that his own entreaties were of not avail, he would get some influential man to intercede fro him with his teacher, and the desired forgiveness was eventually obtained. Swami Virjanand, it is said, would frequently inflict corporal punishment upon Dayanand.

One day he dealt him such a blow with his stick as to seriously injure his hand. The only reply which Dayanand made to his guru was to address him as follows: "Most holy Sir, you should not give yourself so much trouble on my account. My body is hard as iron and cannot be hurt much with your stick. Your own delicate hands might suffer by the exertion, and that would give me real pain."

The mark of the blow remained on Dayanand's hand as long he lived, and whenever he looked at it, the remembrance of the debt of immense and endless gratitude, which he was under to his guru, would make his whole being thrill with emotion.

Swami Dayanand stayed with Swami Virjanand for two years and-a-half, and during this period he had mastered Ashtadhyayi, Mahabhashya, the Vedanta Sturas, and many other works. And when his course of education was finished, and he thought it was time for him to leave, he, in conformity with the usages of olden times, approached his guru and, laying half a seer of cloves before him, asked permission to depart.

Swami Virjanand gave him his blessings and called upon him to produce, after the fashion of the students of yore, suitable dakshina (present) marking the termination of his course of education. Dayanand made answer that he had nothing that he could venture to offer to his most revered guru. "Do you think I would ask you for anything you have not got?" was the rejoinder. Being silenced by the loving rebuke. Dayanand said: "Most holy Sir, I am ready to lay at your feet whatever you think I have really got in my possession."

> "Dear son, you have got it, and that is true knowledge. If you would pay me my dakshina, give this knowledge to thy motherland. The Vedas have long ceased to be taught in Bhraartavarsha (India), go and teach them; teach the true Shastras, and dispel, by their light, the darkness which the false creeds have

> spread. Remember that while works by common men are utterly misleading as to the nature and attributes of the one true God, and slander the great Rishis and Munis, those by the ancient teachers are free from such a blemish. This is the test which will enable you to differentiate the true, ancient teaching from the writings of ordinary men."

Swami Dayanand bowed his head in acquiescence, assuring his guru that he would do his best to accomplish the task assigned to him, upon which the guru once more gave him his blessing and permitted him to depart. How far Dayanand kept his word and how far he succeeded in redeeming that word, is known to the world. Few men have laboured as Dayanand did. His self-sacrifice and his patriotism were of the highest possible type, almost who can but say that they might once more prove the making of India? Verily, they will!

Review of Studies

Swami Dayanand's life, as we are well aware, had, for years been the life of a Brahamchari and a Sanyasi combined, and anything but lacking in the vanaparastha stage. He had from his childhood onwards been passionately found of study, profoundly meditative and wholly indifferent to the comforts and attractions of the world. We may, in the contemplation of his personality, before, in obedience to a welcome summons from a great teacher, he appeared on the arena of great reforms, recognise in him almost exclusively the Brahmachari, but what of that? His was an ideal brahmacharya of the ancient type, identical with and embracing both the Vanaprastha and the sanyasa.

He devoted long periods to reflection and self-subjugation, and he was formally initiated into the sanyasa, and was thus Vanaprastha and the in one. But we maintain that even if he had not gone through the forms, even if he had not put on ochre-coloured garments and sought the forest and the cave, he would still be a true Vanaprasthi and a true Sanyasi, for it is the spirit which imparts life and reality to all distinctions, titles and appellations. Henceforward, we shall know him as Swami Dayanand Saraswati.

Swami Virjanand's great pupil entered upon the work which he might take in hand as of right; but it was not much that he accomplished during the first five years (Samvat 1920 -25), AD 1863 - 68 the greater part of this period being applied to a revision and review of his past acquisitions. The strongest man when preparing for a leap would go back several steps to be able to put the success his entire energy into the exertion awaiting him, and so it is with the preacher and the teacher.

However able and gifted these may be, they must take stock of all their resources before they burst upon the public, to brave and to bend it to their will and to thus accomplish the great mission of their life. Whatever little we know of the work of Swami Dayanand during the five years specified, may be described in the compass of a few chapters.

Soon after parting with his teacher, the Swami visited Agra. Here he put up in Lala Gulla Mal Aggarwal's garden, giving himself up to his books and preferring retirement. One day, a wealthy Sanyasi, named Kailas Parvat, came and halted in this very garden and commenced a katha. The Gita is no easy book, and it were no surprise if an average Sadhu, acquainted but imperfectly with the Shastras, should break down when expounding a particularly difficult verse.

Kailas Parvat, in due course coming to one of the difficult couplets, failed to explain it to the satisfaction of his audience. Some one among the gathering humbly requested Swami Dayanand, who happened to stay there at the time, to interpret the verse. The Swami complied, and his exposition was so learned and beautiful that the listeners were charmed. Kailas Parvat joined in the applause, praising the Swami's superior learning and advising those desirous of study to come to him for their lesson. The counsel was gladly followed by the individuals to whom it was given, and several of them commenced coming to Swami Dayanand for instruction.

At the request of the people, the Swami began a katha of the Panchdashi. But he had not gone through many pages when he came across a passage which said that God himself is subject to the power of maya (delusion!) Hastily throwing down the book the

Swami informed the congregation that he should no longer have anything to do with such mischievous and misleading stuff.

It was the composition of a common man, and he could not, in defiance of the express orders of his guru, teach a book prejudicial to the works of the Rishi's. The Swami got the Sandhay (the Arya Prayer-book) first published at Agra, and the publication pleased his admirers so much that a gentleman named Rup Lal had thirty thousand copies of it distributed.

During his residence at this place Dayanand was in constant correspondence with Swami Virjanand, who remove the doubts that arose in his mind from time to time. He sometimes waited upon him in person, to have answers in full.

In Samvat 1921 (1864 AD), after about two years residence at Agra, Dayanand set off towards Dhaulpur in search of the Vedas, and from here he repaired to Lashkar Gwalior. Early in 1865 AD the Maharaja had the saptah or seven-days katha of the Bhagwat set up. No less than four hundred Pandits were to take part in and conduct the rites connected with katha. Hearing of this, the Swami, who was then on the Abu Hills, came down with four or five vidyarthis, and began to fearlessly expose the absurdities and the immoral teaching of the book.

The Maharaja was not long in being informed of the Swami's arrival. He once ordered some of his men to wait upon him and ascertain his opinion as regards the desirability or otherwise of the katha which the state Pandits had commenced.

The Swami's reply was that such a thing, as the result would show, could be productive of nothing but pain and suffering. "If His Highness is sincerely desirous of doing something meritorious," added the Swami, "he should have the Bhagwat discontinued in favour of "Gayatri-recitation." When the reply was communicated to the Maharaja, he burst out laughing, remarking playfully that it was not for him to contradict a Sanyasi like the Swami; but as for himself, he could not revoke his order, as the preparations in connection with the katha were complete.

The katha came to an end, but, strange to relate, the very night the reading terminated and the royal drums beat to announce the joyful event, the Maharani was prematurely confined to give birth to a stillborn child. And only a month or two after cholera of a virulent type broke out in the city, carrying away thousands, including the Maharaja's son, Of course, the Swami was no believer in miracles. When he spoke unfavourably of the Bhagwat, he did so because the book is really an execrable production and an outrage upon the glory of the Supreme, who alone should be worshipped and adored. Honouring and reading such books can do not good to any one either in this world or for the next.

If a series of misfortunes befell the Maharaja, they were not effects of the Swami's prophecy. The Swami must have spoken of the veil of reading the Bhagwat, in like terms, in many other places, and it may be presumed that the announcement did not lead to anything like the disastrous consequences which followed his declaration in the Gwalior State. Enlightened men will always be careful how they connect as cause and effect events not linked together by any such relation, events which are mere accidents and nothing else.

The Swami repeatedly sent challenges to Ramacharya, Gopalcharya and others for a shastrarth, but no one came forward for a discussion. Leaving Lashkar Gwalior, Swami Dayanand proceeded to Karoli, and thence having passed onto the capital of the Jaipur State, in company with three Brahmans, put up in a garden. There or four shastrarths were held here, on a minor scale, and in each of these his deep learning and acute reasoning exported admiration from all present. In one of the discussions, held in the presence of Vyas Bakshi Ram, in a State Mandir, the Raj Pandits went so far as to deny that the Mahabhashya was an authoritative Vyakarna! When the Swami called upon them to put the same in writing, they looked foolish and said nothing.

At the request of Thakur Ranjit Singh of Achrol, conveyed through Thakur Hamir Singh of Bikaner, the Swami visited the former and the two conversed on dharmic subjects. The Swami's words produced the desired effect on the Thakur's mind. He gave up idolatry, and going daily to the residence-place of the Swami, would hear him explain the Manu Smriti and the Upanishads. The katha was attended by many other people besides.

The expositions of the Swami were so clear and so conviction carrying that his listeners could not fail to be influenced for the better. Witness are not wanting, even so late as now, are not wanting, even so late as now, whose sense of gratitude compels them to depose that they were real gainers by the Swami's presence in their midst. If they were addicted to drinking, it was that noble individual whose comments on the words of the Rishis weaned them from their evil habit. If they were loose in morals and were wont to set the dictates of virtue at defiance, it was he who taught them to behave better. And so on. Every man who had occasion to come in contact with the Swami, felt all the better for having been in his company.

The Swami, though a believer in one God and worshipping Him alone, had still the symbols of Shaivism on his person. He converted thousands of people to his own purer form of Shaivism, distributing rudraksas (necklaces or rosaries) to all his admirers. It was he who initiated the Maharaja Ram Singh into the creed. In Samvat 1922 (March, 1866 AD) Swami Dayanand left Jaipur for Pushkar, where a great fair was going to be shortly held. Having reached this place, he put in the Brahma Mandir, and, inviting discussions, commenced a vigorous refutation of idol-worship. Many Brahmans took up the challenge, but were invariably worsted in the struggle.

Seeing how utterly unable they were to cope with the Sanyasi, they, in their despair, waited upon a learned man named Baikunth Shastri, and solicited his help. The Shastri promised to hold a Shastrarth with the Swami at his own quarters, but failing, for some reason or other, to keep his appointment, the Swami himself repaired to his abode, and the contemplated discussion came off in the presence of four hundred Brahmans.

The Shastri spoke in favour of the Bhagwat, and the Swami against the teaching of that book. So scathing was the Swami's criticism on what the Shastri had not alternative but to take shelter, like average Pandits, in mere "word-controversy." But here also he found in his antagonist more than his match.

As a last resource, the Shastri conducted the Swami to his guru, who, on hearing the arguments of both parties, gave his verdict in the Swami's favour. Baikunth Shastri bowed to his master's superior judgement, and had the frankness to acknowledge in public that Dayanand was in the right.

It would appear that during his continuance at Pushkar, the Swami had ceased to be even a nominal adherent of Shaivism. He advised the people to cast off the great symbol of Shaivism - the necklace, and to have nothing to do with the creed. As a result of this, Baikunth Shastri was deluged with complaints against the Swami, but that good man replied that he failed to see why he should meddle with the Sanyasi's doing. "But, said he in conclusion, "whatever" the worth of Dayanand's teaching, he will never succeed in his mission till he has gained some prince as his disciple."

Preaching the Faith

Now Dayanand had the light that could illuminate the path of humanity. Now he had the sincerity and power to save the suppressed. He had the confidence to wrest the initiative from the pretenders.

The task was, however, difficult. Dayanand had no material resources whatsoever. There were hundreds of sects among the Hindus who would oppose him to defend their religious empires. The mass of the people believed that there was Vedic sanction behind idol worship, child marriage, practice of *sati,* blood sacrifice, and many such rituals. Then, there were two highly developed religions to contend with. Christianity was progressing due to the fact of British rule. Islam, a highly practical religion, was devoted to the principles of one God and human equality. It had a pull for the 'untouchables' of the Hindu society. The Swami was conscious of all these factors. He was out for the adventure. He was willing to pay the price.

Swami Dayanand Saraswati undertook extensive tours, published literature and threw open challenges for religious discussion. He debated with Pandits, Muslim Maulvis and Christian missionaries. He lectured to the masses. He talked to the princes. He condemned idol worship and meaningless sacrifices.

The Swami began his work by writing a pamphlet against the popular religious book, the Bhagvata Purana. At Gwalior, he challenged the Vaishnava Pandits for debate. They left the field. At Jaipur, there was a debate with the Brahmans in the presence of the Maharaja. The Brahmans were effectively silenced. At Ajmer, Swami Dayanand held another debate with Christian priests led by Robinson. Robinson and others acknowledged the matchless debating talent and Vedic study of the Swami. They wrote of their opponent: "We have not come across in life a single such learned man of Sanskrit. Such people are few in this world."

The Swami reached Haridwar one month ahead of the *Kumbh*. The *Kumbh* provided a complete picture of Hindu unity as well as Hindu thoughtlessness. The Swami saw at Haridwar "the mountain ranges, one behind the other, the snow-clad peaks, the pure sparkling waters the rishi caves, the endless line of religious centres and *Maths*." He also saw there "a vast multitude, steeped in darkness and ignorance, drowned in blind faith and rituals, chased by suspense and clouded thinking." He saw there "the nature's 'beauty and man's crookedness."

The Swami pitched his camp at an open space and started lecturing to the people. He debated with the Pandits from Kashi and exposed them. He criticised the eighteen Puranas, idol worship, *Tantric* scriptures, drugs and intoxicants, adultery, stealing, lies and pride. Regarding the Ganga water, the Swami- said, "It is only a drinking water. It cannot get you *Moksha*. Only good actions can get you' salvation."

At Anupshahr (U.P.), the Swami debated with such success that the idol of Saligram was floated down the Ganga. At this place, a Brahman poisoned him but the Swami threw out the poison through a yogic exercise and saved himself. The Muslim Tehsildar Syed Mohammed who was a devotee of the Swami arrested the culprit and presented him before the Swami. But he had to be set free. The Swami remarked: "I have not come to this world to get people imprisoned. I have come to get them released."

At Farrukhabad (U.P.), there was a debate with a well-known Pandit, Angad Shastri, on idol worship. The Shastri accepted defeat. He became Dayanand's disciple along with many others.

Idols were thrown into the river. At Kanpur, the local English magistrate was in the chair when the debate with Pandit Haldar Ojha took place. The magistrate declared Ojha routed.

Kashi was the citadel of Brahmans. It was known for its scholars and debaters. Swami Dayanand Saraswati sent a message to the Kashi ruler asking for debate with the Brahmans of Kashi. The priests demanded time for preparation and Vedic studies. Fifteen days were granted to them. After that a debate was fixed at a place called Madho Bagh.

The brave disciple of the blind faqir of Mathura was alone. He had only courage and truth as companions. The *mandap* and the assembly were under the control of the city kotwal. The Brahmans had already inflamed the feelings of people by telling them that a *nastik* (non-believer) has entered the holy city who criticises god Vishwanath. The Pandits arrived in royal Palkis, under royal umbrellas, shouting slogans and accompanied by vast processions of citizens. The lone *Sanyasi* soon found himself encircled by a hostile mob of 50,000 idol worshippers. The Kashi ruler took his seat.

The numerous Pandits shot forth their questions: "What is *Dharma*? What is, *Adharma*? Do the Vedas permit idol worship ?" The *Sanyasi* had ready answers. In return, he closely questioned them, tested them, countered them, silenced and routed them. They failed to defeat the *Sanyasi.* Soon the mob brought there for the purpose took hold of the situation. The hostile people had run short of arguments; they threw stones and shoes on the *Sanyasi.* Dayanand could save himself through sheer courage and presence of mind.

The Pandits marched back to the city proclaiming their victory although the Rishi had remained unbeaten. The facts could hardly be reversed. The newspapers reported the debate and declared him triumphant. The Kashi affair brought Rishi Dayanand some fame and glory. Even the ruler of Kashi apologised to him.

In the year 1872, the Rishi reached Calcutta and met the leaders of the Brahmo Samaj. Keshab Chandra Sen had a talk with him. Sen said it was a pity that such a scholar of the Vedas did not know English language. He could otherwise be a very desirable companion for the trip to England. The Rishi replied, it was a pity that the leader of the Brahmo Samaj preached to the people in a language which they did not understand. So far the Swami had lectured in Sanskrit with the help of interpreters. But on the advice of Keshab Chandra Sen, the Swami started lecturing in Hindi. The idea of organising the Arya Sarnaj originated after the Calcutta visit. Dayanand also met Ishwarchandra Vidyasagar, Barrister Chandra Shekhar Sen, Barrister Umeshchandra Bandhopadhya and Pt. Satyavrat Samshrami. He gave a number of talks at the house of Keshab Chandra Sen. In the year 1874, Dayanand visited Bombay where the Arya Samaj was founded on 20th April 1875. His famous work, *Satyarth Prakash,* was published. The idea of Arya educational institutions was also mooted here.

In July 1875, the Swami visited Poona at the invitation of Justice Ranade. Poona was the stronghold of Snatana Dharma. A huge procession of the Vedas, placed in a Palki, followed by Dayanand on the back of an elephant was taken out. He delivered fifteen talks there which have since been published.

In the year 1877, the Swami reached Delhi where the royal Durbar was being held. He arranged a meeting where Keshab Chandra Sen, Sir Syed Ahmed, Baba Navinchandra, Baba Harishchandra Chintamani, Munshi Indramani and the Swami himself were present. This was perhaps to evolve some kind of religious unity. But no agreement could be reached.

In the Punjab, the Christian missionaries had been having a free hand. Conversions were numerous. The Swami reached Ludhiana in April 1877 and stayed in the cottage of Dr. Rahim Khan, after being expelled from the garden of a Hindu. The tide of Christianity was soon rolled back. The Arya Samaj was founded at Lahore on 24th June 1877. The Punjab soon became a stronghold of the Arya Samaj movement.

While in the Punjab, the Swami received an invitation from the ruler of Kashmir, The Swami declined to go there saying: "In Kashmir there are many temples built by the ruler. I shall condemn idol worship. It will give pain to the ruler." It was suggested that if Dayanand stopped condemning idol worship, the Kashmir ruler would welcome him Dayanand asked: "Should I please the ruler or obey the divine will?"

The Maharana of Udaipur was the disciple of Dayanand. One day, he said: "Maharaj, if you stop condemning idol worship it will be most helpful. This state is under god Mahadeva. You can, if you wish, become the high priest of the temple whose estate could bring you lakhs of rupees." Dayanand was angry: "You have tried to tempt me to violate divine principles. What is this temple and what is the worth of your small state I can leave behind its frontiers in one race "

Till the end of his life, Dayanand remained uncompromising in his principles. He refused to abstain from speaking the truth under any threat. After receiving an indirect warning from the Commissioner of Bareilly, the Swami said: 'People say do not reveal the truth The Collector or the Commissioner would be angry. Let the *Chakravarty Raja* be angry. This body is perishable. To try to preserve it by withholding the truth is a sin. Let anyone destroy my body. But show me that brave person who can claim to destroy my soul.'

In, the year 1883, people asked Dayanand not to go to Jodhpur: "Do not condemn prostitution there, as the prostitutes there are very powerful. The people are by temperament upstarts". But these warnings had no effect He said: "Even if they burn my fingers like so many candles, I will go there to speak the truth." He did speak the truth in its purest form and frank style. Even the ruler of Jodhpur heard the truth and decided to reform himself. But, the price had to be paid. On 29th September 1883, Dayanand was poisoned at Jodhpur. He was taken to Mount Abu and finally to Ajmer. On 30th October 1883, at 7 p.m. Swami Dayanand Saraswati expired.

Devotion to His Guru

By his extraordinary devotion and sense of service Dayananda soon became the most beloved disciple. Every morning, whether it was hot cold or raining, Dayananda fetched water for his teacher's bath and for other purposes from the river Yamuna. It was also his duty to sweep the floor and keep the premises clean and tidy. And Dayananda did every kind of work without the slightest hesitation. Several incidents show his extraordinary devotion to his master.

On one occasion, as Virajananda was teaching, something made angry with Dayananda. Then with Skinny hand he hit Dayananda on the back so hard that the teacher's he began to ache. After a while Dayananda slowly approached his guru and said in all humility, "Gurudeva, my body is hard like stone and beating like this cannot hurt it. Only your hands will ache. Hereafter, when you punish me kindly make use of a cane instead of your hand."

Swami Dayananda's request was not in vain. At another time when Virajananda was displeased with Dayananda for some reason he struck him with a stick. Seeing this, Nayansukha, his schoolmate, said, "Gurudeva, it is not proper to treat such a great sanyasi in this way. He should be treated with respect." When the lessons were over, Dayananda took objection to his friend's disrespectful behaviour and said, "Do you think that our Gurudeva beat me out of hatred? Just as a potter shapes the lump of clay by pounding and beating it, the guru shapes the personality of his disciple by beating him and correcting him. You should not have spoken like that Later on, when Dayananda attained the status of a 'maharshi' and became the teacher of the people, he used show the marks on his shoulders made by Virajananda and say: 'These marks always remind me of all that I owe to my master.'

Triumph at Kashi

After his education, as ordained by his master, Swami Dayananda undertook to travel to preach Vedic Knowledge among people. He went places like Agra, Ajmer, Jaipur, Gwalior Meerut, Haridwar and Kanpur. There he discussed the scriptures and the meaning with the pundits and scored resounding victory over their Wherever he went, he told the people "Idol worship is not mentioned in the Vedas.

The rational mind cannot accept idol worship. God is everywhere God has no shape or form." Without Supporting or opposing any particular religion he pointed out the shortcomings of every one of them. He bitterly criticised the harmful and wicked customs that have come down through the centuries. He explained the greatness of the religion preached in the Vedas and gave a clarion call to all People to unite under its banner.

So Swami Dayananda sought to awaken people to their heritage. In the course " of his travels he came to Kashi (Banaras) on 22nd October 1869. He took part in debates with the greatest scholars in Kashi. The meeting was attended by fifty to sixty thousand people. At the appointed hour, the president of the gathering, Maharaja Eshwari Prasad Narayan Singh of Kashi, took the chair. On one side was Swami Dayananda all alone; on the other side were twentyseven distinguished scholars Of Kashi.

The debate on the interpretation of the scriptures began. The question was whether the Vedas approved image worship. The scholars had to admit defeat in the face of Swami Dayananda's arguments. Just then, a scholar Madhawacharya by name came up with two sheets of paper and asked a question. Dayananda picked up the sheets and began to read. A few minutes must have passed. Suddenly the Maharaja of Kashi declared, "Swami Dayananda has not been able to answer the questions posed by the pundits." So saying he clapped his hands. The scholars of Kashi shouted, "Dayananda has no answer. Great victory to the Kashi pundits! Defeat to Dayananda!"

Rowdies began to throw stones, slippers, cowdung and such things at Dayananda. Some of them hit Dayananda and he was wounded. Blood dropped from some of the wounds. Dayanandaji, who had attained a state of perfect serenity, endured everything and remained as if nothing had happened. But the chief pundits of Kashi Taracharan Tarkaratna, Bala Shastri and others said, "Really what Swami Dayananda says is perfectly true. But we do not have the moral courage to go against the prevailing customs and traditions. So we have chosen to oppose him." So they said honestly in public.

The Maharaja of Kashi deeply regretted having taken sides in the debate on the scriptures. With great respect he invited Swami Dayananda to his palace and begged him to excuse him (the Maharaja) for his improper behaviour. So, from the point of view of both scholarship and morality, it was Swami Dayananda who won a great victory in a true sense, in the debates about the correct explanation of scriptural texts. It was Swami Dayananda's keen desire to unite all people under the banner of a single religion. And he always worked hard for this end.

Religious Services

Arya Sanmarg Darshini Sabha

While Swami Dayanand was a Agra, a Sabha, called the Arya Sanmarg Darshini Sabha, was established at Calcutta, with the object of having it decided and settled, once for all, by the most distinguished representatives of orthodoxy in the land (that could be got hold of for the purpose, of course), that Dayanand's views on *Shradhs, Tiraths, Idol-worship, etc.*, were entirely unorthodox and unjustifiable. Sanskrit Scholars and rises to the number of three hundred responded to the call of the Sabha, and a grand meeting, composed of the local men and of he outsiders, came off in the Senate Hall on 22nd. January, 1881.

It is significant that not one of the numerous distinguished Pandits present thought of suggesting or moving that the man upon whom the Sabha was going to sit in judgement, should also, in fairness, be summoned before the august tribunal, to be condemned or acquitted after he had been fully heard. It may be urged that the Sabha was not in a humour to acquit Dayanand under any circumstances, but still he should have been permitted to have his say before he was condemned. Surely, one man could be dealt with very well by assemblage so illustrious and so erudite. But the Pandits and their admirers were wise in their generation.

Swami Dayanand, though one, had proved too many for a still more learned and august gathering at Banaras. His powerful intellect and the still more powerful truth, which he was called upon to defend and advocate, had carried everything before them, and left the formidable and unique multitude opposed to him no other alternative than to resort to a mean trick if they would extricate themselves, from their most embarrassing position and make the ignorant mass believe that the victory had been theirs.

It was, thus, wholly inadvisable that Swami Dayanand should be present. "Lord! Who could miss the man when we are present?" must the great Pandits have said to themselves. Among the great ones in evidence and gracing the occasion, were: Pandit Mahesh Chandra Nyyaratna, Pandit Tara Nath Vachaspati, Pandit Banke Bihari Lal of Cawnpore, Pandit Jamna Narayan Tiwari, Pandit

Vrindavan Sudarsdnachari, Shastri Ram Subramania of Jaunpur, Maharaja Jotindrao Nath Tagore, C.S.I., Maharaja Kanwal Krishna Bahadur Mukhopadhya, Junwar Debindrao Mulluck, Hon'ble Babu Krishna Lal Paul, Babu Charu Chandra Mulluck, Lal Narain Das of Mathura, Rai Badri Das Lakhim Bahadur, Seth Jugal Kishore, Seth Nahar Mal, etc., etc.

Proceedings of the Meeting Opened by Pandit Mahesh

Chandra Nyyaratna explaining the object of the Sabha and laying before his brother Pandits the following questions for consideration:

- Are or are not the Brahmanas entitled to be as much believed in as the Samhita portion – the Vedas, and are or are not the other Smritis as much worthy of being accepted as the Manu Smriti is?
- Are or are not we allowed, according to the Shastras, to worship Shiva, Vishnu, Durga, and other gods and goddesses; to perform the Shradhs, in honour of the departed ancestors; to reside at and bathe in Tiraths like the Ganges, living and bathing at Kurukshetra, and other Tiraths and Kshetras?
- Does not the word 'Agni' occurring in mantras like *Agni mile prohitam,* etc., mean God or Fire?
- Are Agnihotra and other Yajnas performed for the purification of oar and water, or for obtaining heaven (swarga), etc.?
- Is or is it not a sin to belittle the 'Brahmana portion of the Veda?'

Pandit Ram Subramania Shashtri replied to the questions, seriatim, and we give the substance of what he said:

- 'In the Veda Samhita it is written that whatever Manu said, is worthy of acceptance; hence the Manu Smriti is worthy of acceptance then the Veda, which enjoins the acceptance thereof, will also become unworthy of acceptance. Dayanand Saraswati has accepted the Manu Smriti (as authoritative), and he has declared as such in his Satyarth Prakash also. And similarly, there are many arguments which prove that the Brahmana portion is fully as worthy of being believed in (i.e. is authoritative) as Samhita, and that the Vishnu, Yajanavalk and other Smritis are, in every way, on a level with the Manu Smriti.

- 'all these (worship of Shiva, etc.), are allowed in the Shastras. The worship, the establishing, etc., of the Shivalinga, according to the well-known shloka of the Purana, bear all the fruit attendant on worship (pujan). There are many other *shlokas* (the speaker cited these too) which say that the worship of Shiva, Vishnu, and Durga is allowed in the Shastras, and that whoever neglects the worship, commits a sin for which *prayaschit*has to be performed. The worship of idols also is supported by a passage in the Brahmanas. Dayanand is wrong in interpreting the passage as meaning that it speaks of the dwellings of the sages and of Brahmaloka, etc. As to Shradhs, the word *pitriman* occurs in the Vedas and it proves that *Shradhs* in honour of the departed are allowable.

  The Smritis say that whoever say does not perform *Shradhs* in honour of the departed is born in the race of *Chandals* for thousands of generations. This shows that *Shradhs* and *Tarpans* are allowed both by Shruti and Smriti. And the *Tiraths* are mentioned in the Rigveda. It is said there that bathing in the Ganges etc., gets one heaven (swarga) and destroys one's sins in the Manu Smriti it is said that bathing in the Ganges and living at Kurukshetra is an expiation for lying.'
- 'The word Agni in such mantra means Fire.
- 'The object of the Yajnas is to secure Swarga to the Soul, and the performance of the same does obtain one Swarga.
- 'The Brahmanas being part and parcel of the Vedas to belittle them is to belittle the Vedas: in other words, it is a sin to speak disparagingly of the Brahamanas.'

Arya Samaj Founded

Swami Dayananda wished that his work of social reform should continue even after his death. So he founded an institution called 'Arya Samaj' at Bombay on the 10th of April 1875. Gradually it grew into a huge institution and spread even beyond the shores of India. Millions of Hindus were influenced by the Arya Samaj. Arya Samaj has rendered boundless and unequalled service to society through its religious centres, its gurukulas, schools and colleges, educational institutions for women, orphanages and asylums for widows.

Mercy to the Man, who Poisoned Him

Swami Dayananda argued that God has no shape, and therefore, idols should not be worshipped. This was not acceptable to the majority of Hindus. But none of them could answer his arguments. So some of them began secretly to plan his murder. Thousands of Hindu converts were taken back into Hindu fold by purification rites conducted by Dayananda. This made the followers of these religions angry. So Dayananda was in danger both from the followers of his own religion and from the followers of other religions. And he had to walk along this path full of dangers.

An Anupashahar, a certain Hindu deceived the Swamiji and gave him pan-supari (betel leaf and nuts) Containing poison. Afterwards Dayananda realised that he had been poisoned. He went to the river and with the help of Yoga, he removed the poison by vomiting all the food he had swallowed and saved himself. Even then he did not utter a single word to the man who poisoned him. But he felt sad that the Hindus could not understand their true well-wisher. Syed Saheb was the tahsildar of the place and a devotee of Dayananda; he came to know what had happened and arrested the poisoner. When he learnt this, Dayananda was angry and said, "Sir, I have come here to free people from bondage and not to put them in bondage." On hearing this Syed Saheb was moved to tears. He felt that the Swamiji was in every way worthy of his name 'Dayananda' (one who delights in mercy).

At last the killers gained the upper hand. Once Swami Dayananda went to Jodhpur. Maharaja Jaswant Singh, the Prince of the state, was a man of bad character. He was in love with a girl called Nanhi Jan. Many a time the Maharaja had brought shame upon himself by his conduct. Dayananda told him clearly that his action was morally wrong and shameful. So Nanhi Jan came to hate the Swamiji bitterly.

It was the night of 20th September 1883. As usual the Swamiji drank some milk and went to bed. At about midnight he felt a severe pain in the stomach. When he woke up Dayananda realised that poison had entered his stomach. Immediately he vomited a couple of times, but it was of no avail. The poison had already entered the blood and spread throughout his body. It caused a burning sensation in his stomach and chest. On the next day, a doctor, Dr. Alimardan Khan, was called in. But his medicine only made Dayananda's condition worse. His body was full of sores. And blood was oozing out. This hellish torture lasted several days. The Maharaja, too, was very sad; but he could do nothing. However, he arranged to send Dayananda to a different place for treatment. And he himself was one of the bearers of the palanquin for a short distance.

One day, when there was no one near by, Swami Dayananda called his cook Dhaul Mishra. Seeing the blood oozing out of Dayananda's body, the cook could not control his grief. He said, "I listened to traitors and mixed powdered glass with your milk. My God, I have committed a heinous sin! Please forgive me." So saying he broke down. Dayananda consoled him with the words, "it was my fate. How are you to blame?" He then placed two hundred rupees in his hands and said, "If the Maharaja comes to know this, you will be in trouble. So go away to distant Nepal and hide yourself. Let this money be with you for your journey." So saying he sent away the Cook to a place of safety.

Afterwards Swami Dayananda was removed to Mount Abu for further treatment, and from there to Ajmer. But no effort could save him. The 30th of October 1883 was Deepavali day. He had a shave and bath, and lay down on his bed in a white loin cloth. Afterwards he called his disciples to his bedside and took a last look at them all with a benevolent smile. He then recited the Gayathri manthra and closed his eyes in Samadhi. It was six in the evening. The word 'Om' came from his mouth; and then his breathing stopped.

Dayananda was a great philosopher, a mighty logician, a magnificent speaker, a great man of letters, social reformer, patriot, philonthropist and sage, and a precursor of armed revolution; he was the embodiment of pure and noble conduct. He taught people to think independently and fearlessly.

Dayananda was a great Rishi (a sage). He sacrificed the great joy that would have been his by observing yoga practices. He chose a very difficult life for the well-being of mankind. But what did he get in return for all this? Beatings, insults, abuses and poison. He accepted all this with a smile. And he always wished the well-being of all mankind.

Effect of the Sad Events on Dayanand's Mind

While Dayanand was busy with his books, often revolving in his mind, in the midst of his lessons, the question which the affair in the temple had been instrumental in confronting his mind with, and accident happened which made the seriousness of the problem still more apparent to him. He was at the close of his sixteenth year when the event in question occurred and no one need doubt that he was wholly unprepared for the said occurrence.

Swami Dayanand had two brothers and two sisters, all younger than himself, and for whom he had great affection. One night, while his father, in company with himself and other male members of the family, was attending a nautch-meeting at the house of a friend, a servant came with the news that his eldest daughter, now fourteen years of age, was suddenly taken ill with cholera. Everyone hastened home, the physicians were summoned, and nothing was left undone that promised to afford relief, but all in vain. The condition of the patient grew worse every moment and she expired after four hours of great agony.

Weeping and lamentation commenced, the bereaved mother rending the air with her cries. It was terrible shock to Dayanand. He felt like one utterly unnerved and stupefied. "Ah!" Said he to himself when he was able to reflect, "who can defy death? Not one of the beings, that ever lived who could escape the cold hand of death. I, too, may be snatched away any time and die. How, then, shall I be able to fulfil my resolve of alleviating human misery, and where shall I find the assurance and means of attaining Mukti, the final beatitude?" It was then that he made a resolve of seeking the way to release himself from the bonds of life and death and go out in search of Truth.

He know that man's happiness and sufferings are the results of his actions in his previous birth. Those who had led a noble life in accordance with the scriptural injunctions are born in noble families, while others, whose previous life had been spent in perpetrating evil and falsehood, take birth as lower creatures. The saints and virtuous people, perched, as the result of karma, on the highest plane of existence, will think in this fashion, and average man is apt to misconstrue their words and actions. The fact is, that they do not look upon the world as something discardable: no, the very reverse of it, but the world is not an end to them, but a means of gaining what is higher than the world, what is infinitely more valuable and more glorious. They think, as Dayanand thought, in the strain of the Divine verse:

> Sambhootincha Vinaasham Cha Yastadde Dobhayam Saha.
>
> Vinaashena Mrityu Teertva Sambhootyaa Mritamash Nute - Yajur 40: 14.
>
> *"Whoever thoroughly understands the nature of the visible creation and of the imperishable atom from which the visible creation springs at one and some time, the same shall, by virtue of his knowledge of the primal atom, triumph over death, and shall obtain beatitude by virtue of his knowledge of the visible creation and by reason of his virtuous activity in that creation."*

These thoughts which filled Dayanand's mind, he did not express to his parents, but confided to his friends.

The nature of the aspirations which now filled Dyananda's chest was not long in being known to his father and mother. They were alarmed, particularly the latter, and began to devise means for preventing their son from carrying out his purpose. They were not to blame, they were actuated by love - not the enlightened love of the saint but the intense blind love of the world's children. A plan suggested itself for frustrating the boy. It was resolved that he should be married as early as possible. " Once he is secure in the toils of grihasthashrama (married-life), " said they, "he can never give us the slip." They soon disclosed their intentions to Dayanand, who was so frightened at the idea of marriage that he flew to the friends of the family with an earnest appeal to prevail upon his parents to delay the function. They listened to his prayer, and succeeded in inducing Karsanji to postpone the marriage for a year.

Science of Yoga

Parting company with the mahatamas of Joshimath, Dayanand set off towards Badarinarayan, and on arriving there visited the great temple. It afforded him great pleasure to discover, in the person of Rawalje, the Mahant of the temple, a man deeply reads in the Shastras, and he conversed with him for several days on the subject of the "Vedas and the Darshanas."

Swami Dayanand was informed by the Mahant that learned Yogis, adept in the science of yoga, were not to be met in the neighbourhood of Badarinarayan. The information was extremely disappointing, but as such men now and then came to visit the temple (so his host assured him), he determined to look out for these, and in the meantime to explore the neighbouring hills, to make certain if these were wholly destitute of the presence of Sadhus and Sanyasis of the right type. Early one morning he left Badarinaryan, and, proceeding along the foot of the hills, arrived at the margin of a stream called Alakananda, and following the direction of its current struck in to a wood.

At this time, the entire mountain was wrapped in a covering of snow, and it was with the greatest difficulty that he reached the source of the stream. He place appeared to walled in by lofty hills on every side, and no path was visible which might be followed. Dayanand was in great distress. He was very lightly clad, and the cold was so intense that he could hardly stand it. He had nothing with him so subsist upon, and his exertions had so sharpened his appetite that, as a last resource, he began to eat ice.

But such food was anything but satisfying and Dayanand had to give up on with his repast. "Let me see, if I can cross the stream," said he; "I might find a way out of the difficulty on reaching the other side." In pursuance of this resolve he descended into the stream, but it was not joke to cross it. The water was shallow in some places, but very deep in others, and pieces of ice with sharp, piercing edges were whirled down the current in hundreds every minute. And the bed of the stream was strewn with stones, some lying fault, with surfaces extremely slippery, and others planted upright with points that would penetrate the flesh like a sharp piece of iron. The attempt was made and when Dayanand reached the other side, his feet were wounded and bleeding and utterly benumbed with cold, and he felt like one in a state of stupefaction.

For many moments he sat all but forgetful O himself and of what was going on around him, but there was danger in continuing as he was, and with a vigorous effort he roused himself from his torpor. Finding that his legs and feet refuse to work, he tightly wrapped both in his torn garments and essayed to move forward, but the attempt was unsuccessful. "Oh! That some fellow creature would come to help me." He exclaimed; "if I stay longer where I am, I should certainly perish without realising the dream of life accomplishment of the object for which I left home."

While he was looking wistfully in every direction to see if he could espy some one who might be of service to him in his trouble, his eye lighted on two-hill-men advancing towards him. They made their obeisance to him and offered to take him to their huts. Dayanand, while begging to be excused form accepting their kind offer, told them what had brought him in that dreary region. Upon this, the hill-men offered to lead him to a place named Sadpat Tirath, which offer he thankfully accepted.

The next instant he had to refuse it. "I am perfectly exhausted," said he, " and at this moment can't move a step. You have better leave me to my fate." The two hill-men sadly bade him farewell and ere long were lost to sight. In time, Dayanand, by the grace of God, came to feel better and resumed his wandering, and passing through Vasudhara, a Tirath, and skirting Managram, he reached Badarinarayan at about 8 pm. His prolonged absence had made the good and learned Mahant very uneasy, and as soon as the latter saw him, he felt that load had been taken off his heart. At supper Dayanand ate sparingly, and then retired to rest. With the appearance of morning, he tool leave of his hose, and proceeded towards Rampur. On the way, he stopped with a Yogi and passed the night at his cottage. This man, according to Dayanand, was deeply learned in Sanskrit literature, and his words had a most encouraging effect upon him. As soon as the day broke, Dayanand set forward, and travelling through jungles and over hills, he arrived at Rampur, putting up at the house of Ramgiri.

This Sadhu commanded great respect in Rampur by virtue of his pure character - a commodity which one's worst enemies will seldom fail to appreciate. He was an eccentric man, passing sleepless nights, and often talking to himself in loud and lusty tones. One not in the secret would think that he was talking with somebody in his room, for he always seemed to address a second person. Often he would commence screaming and if anyone rushed to his rescue on such occasions, he would, on entering the Sadhu's room, find that there was nobody there but himself.

Swami Dayanand sought an explanation of this singular conduct, but his disciples could give him none except that such was their preceptor's habit. Dayanand sought a private interview with the Sadhu himself, and learnt that he was engage in accomplishing the siddhis of Yoga-vidya. His conversation, however, led Dayanand to the conclusion that his knowledge of the science and practice of yoga was imperfect. Leaving Rampur, Dayanand turned his face towards Kashipur, and from there went to Daronasagar, where he passed the entire winter during his residence here, it, one day, came into his mind that seeking the heights of the Himalayas he should destroy himself; but with reflection better counsels prevailed. It was a cowardly act, he confessed to himself, a true manly soul ought to fight to the end, acquire all he can of knowledge and wisdom and then resignedly wait for the call.

The most vigorous and elevated natures are not wholly above the weakness of giving away to despair, but, unlike average humanity, they will not surrender themselves to it body and soul; they will get over the fit and will re-enter upon their wonted energy and with a renewal of their determination either to reach the goal, or to perish nobly in the attempt. Dayanand felt, in the light of Shastric teaching and in the glow of the light within, the heritage of past karma, that his was to try, in faith, and not to be impatient for the fruit: God would grant the fruit in His own good time, if he was true to himself and to his mission.

From Daronasagar, Dayanand pressed on to Moradabad, and visiting Sambhal and Garhmukstestar reached the banks of the Ganges. One day, as he sat near the water's edge, thinking he espied, all of a sudden, a corpse being carried down by the rapid current. Dayanand had with him, along with other books some works on physiology and anatomy, and he had often given time to the study of these. But his knowledge was mere book-knowledge, untested and unverified by actual observation and experiment.

The sight of the corpse reminded him that here was his opportunity, and he forthwith plunged into the river and dragged the body to shore. Taking out a sharp knife from his pocket, he cut open the body near the heart which he tore, and began to examine it closely. He found that the description of the heart, as given in his books, was totally wrong. After that he cut open the head and the neck, and, as formerly, discovered that his books did not describe their anatomy correctly. He was disgusted with the spurious composition, tore them to pieces and flung them into the river along with the corpse. The incident shows Dayanand's love of knowledge and research. To the Sanyasi the touch of even some living men is pollution, and they will on no account bring any part of their body into contact with a corpse. Dayanand deliberately and of his own accord handled a corpse, proving thereby that true knowledge is worth more the mere sentiment and that true men of science will have it in spite of sentiment.

Source of Nerbuda and his Encounter with a Bear

Swami Dayanand stayed for a short time on the bank of the Ganges, and then left for Furukhabad. Before the nest year (V.E. 1913 or AD 1856) had quite run its course, Dayanand had visited many places lying between Allahabad and Kanpur. Subsequently proceeding to a place in the vicinity of Banaras, he put up, on reaching his destination in the temple of Vindhyachaleshvarji, where he spent one whole month. Then going to Banaras proper, he stayed there for twelve days in a cave. Here he came across many individuals profoundly versed in Sanskrit literature. Chandalgarh was the next place he visited. Here he put up in the temple of Durgakouhar, and applied himself whole-heartedly to the study of Yoga-vidya and to the practice of its teaching.

In the Chaitra of 1856, Dayanand set off in search of the source of the Nerbada, having heard that the tract around was the abode of learned Sanyasis and Yogis. Proceeding along the bank of the stream, he found himself in a great jungle, not wholly destitute of huts at irregular intervals. Stopping in one of those he drank some milk and then resumed his journey. He had advanced about a mile and-a-half when he found himself in a wood still more drearier, abounding in plum trees and prickly shrubs, and choked with tall grass which completely hid the path from view. While making his way through these, he suddenly found himself confronted by a huge big black bear.

The ferocious animal reared it self on its hind legs, and with a terrible roar advanced towards him. For one instant Dayanand stood rooted to the spot, but the next he was calm as ever, and taking up a stick bit the bear on the nose. The blow was dealt with a tremendous force, and proved effective. The animal ran away shrieking with pain. The men in the huts, hearing the noise, hurried out with clubs and hunting dogs, an finding a Sanyansi in trouble (as they thought), offered him help and service, adding that the jungle was the abode of numerous, bears tigers, elephants, etc., and advising him to cut short his journey.

Swami Dayanand declined their assistance with thanks and informed them that he was bent upon proceeding forward and taking his chance. The villagers at parting presented him with a stout club, saying that it would be of great use to him in his dangerous trip. Dayanand accepted it, but the next moment he threw it away and fearlessly advanced on his track. For hours he travelled on. At last the sun went down and everything was enveloped in gloom. At last the sun went down and everything was enveloped in gloom. No light indicating habitation could be seen anywhere. Now and then he stumbled against trees rooted out by elephants. To add to his distress, he soon found his passage blocked by a still more awful and almost penetrable jungle. Nothing but thorny hedges and prickly pears were visible on all sides. To turn back was out of the question.

Swami Dayanand crept into it on his knees, and, following a zig-zag track, at last emerged into open space. He felt utterly exhausted with the effort. His clothes were torn to threads, and his body was wounded in twenty places and bleeding profusely. It was, however, no time and no place to make a halt. The darkness was gathering apace overhead, and it was no longer easy to distinguished objects even at short distances. Dayanand moved forward as best he could, and having steered clear of many dangers through continuous masses of rank vegetation, lighted on some straggling huts girt round with heaps of cattle-dung. A stream of clear, transparent water flowed not far from the huts, and the sheep and goats were still grazing on its bank.

Swami Dayanand saw a neat cottage standing under a tree and wished very much to go into it and rest, but then it would inconvenience its inmates, and to inconvenience them he did not like. So he climbed up the tree and passed the night on it. As soon as it was dawn, he alighted from the tree and, going to the margin of the stream, washed his wounded feet and other parts of the body, and then prepared to engage in upaasana. Before, however, he could sufficiently compose his mind for his devotions, he heard a noise resembling that of the roar of wild beast, but it was nothing but the sound of a tom-tom. A party of villagers, composed of men and women, was advancing towards him with a large number of cows and sheep, on its way, no doubt to some temple to celebrate a religious festival.

When the procession was sufficiently near to where Dayanand sat, it came to a halt at the sight of a stranger in such an isolated locality, and an old man detaching himself from the rest came forward and asked Dayanand where he had come from.

Dayanand replied that he had come from Banaras and that he was proceeding towards the source of the Nerbada river. On hearing this answer the party departed, and Dayanand became absorbed in contemplation.

About half an hour after this, a man, who appeared to be a person of consequence, followed by two servants, came and sat down near Dayanand. He invited Dayanand to go home with him, but Dayanand begged to be excused, saying that he was all right where he was. When, in answer to his enquires, he made known to the chief what he was after, the old man was pleased and ordered his servants to stay with him and show him every attention.

Learning that he Sanyasi abstained (at present) from the use of solid food), he had a large bowl filled with milk brought to him. Dayanand partook of the refreshing drink, and with the setting of the night retired to rest. To guard against the attacks of the wild beasts, the chief had a fire lit around the stranger, and Dayanand slept soundly till morning, under the watchful eye of the assiduous chief's servitors.

On getting up, he performed his ablutions and then did his sandhya, after which he proceeded on his way, eventually reaching his destination. For three whole years he wandered along the banks of the Nerbada, and it was during these wanderings that he came to hear of the great Sanyasi Virjanand at Mathura. Something whispered into his ear that this was the man he had been looking for in vain for so many years, and towards Mathura, accordingly, did Dayanand bend his steps.

Brahmacharya

A year's respite was great thing. The present danger was warded off, and who could say but affairs might take a favourable turn at the expiration of the period? But after all, if Dayanand found that his parents were inexorably resolved upon giving him a wife, he could use his legs and put a distance between himself and the place of his birth. In the absence of immediate danger he must go on acquiring knowledge, to fit himself for the life which he must come to leas sooner or later. He read on therefore, with all the passionate ardour of a true student, enlarging his acquaintance with the Sanskrit language and giving in keeping to a most retentive memory a mass of facts which, though calculated to help him to recognise and appreciate, by contrast, all the better the real truths in the fullness of time, even as darkness helps one to recognise and appreciate the worth of life all the better.

The twelve months slipped by quickly enough, the suspicious parents must renew their importunities as regards an early time to approach on him on the subject, Dayanand commenced importuning them for increased facilities for the acquisition of knowledge. He said that it was absolutely necessary that he should go to Kashi to prosecute his studies further with advantage. It was the great seat of Sanskrit learning, and experts in different subjects could nowhere be found in larger numbers.

The request took the parents' breath away, and they told him shortly that they would not accede to it. To weaken their opposition and to ultimately bring them to comply with his wishes, Dayanand spoke to them of the value and excellence of brahmacharya, drawing upon the Shastras and ancient history for quotations and examples to illustrate his meaning. But it would not do. They would not listen to his representations, and informed him that he must be a householder before many days were over!

Swami Dayanand's parents acted after the fashion of other parents in India when they insisted upon his marrying. Indeed, they showed themselves vastly more prudent than the majority of parents in their country do. This majority, as we are well aware, is only too fond of seeing their children married before they are ten or twelve years of age, and some, overpowered by their love for their offspring, will go so far as to get them bound in the holy bonds of wedlock in their eight year. Dayanand was now fully twenty years old, and, to judge from what he was when he appeared before the public, he must have been a healthy and powerful youth at this time, or even a year or two earlier. But for all this, it cannot be denied that Dayanand's parents were also short-sighted like many more others in their situation. They could not rise to the height of realising the greatness of perfect brahmacharya, of conceiving the vast possibilities of the vow. Dayanand looked to the ideals of ages gone by.

If not one married in those days till he had completed his twenty-fifth year, and if large numbers never married till they had reached their thirty-sixth or forty-fourth year, he could not understand why the descendants of these men should be hurried into marriage before they had reached even the minimum marriageable age. And, further, why should not an individual be permitted to forego entrance into the grihasthaashrama when, swayed by a natural, intense, over-powering impulse, he would rather be wedded to a life of study and contemplation? The Shastras allowed such a concession in rare cases, and were not wholly unacquainted with Brahmacharis and Brahmacharinis of the type in question. It was, however, clear that the young men's parents were fully determined to disregard the rules of brahmacharya in their son's case.

One of the greatest causes of India's greatness, in times of yours, was its adherence to the law of brahmacharya. It secured each individual a perfectly developed body and a well-disciplined mind, cultured in various degrees. The result of this was that every individual was a man, even something of a hero, physically and morally, and serviceable to himself and others, intellectually. India was certainly low in the days of Magesthenese, but even then the land was very loyal to the requirements of brahmacharya and every town and city and village abounded in the right sort of men and women. The present national degradation will never cease till the nation is once more affluent in true Brahmacharis and Brahmacharinis. Where the body and mind are weak, there must be cowardice, physical and moral, and all the innumerable evils which are born of these. Mark what the Upanishad takings its inspirations from the Word Divine says of brahmacharya.

> "There are three kinds of brahmacharya, the ordinary brahmacharya, the middling brahmacharya, and the highest brahmacharya. The ordinary brahmacharya is the living of a life of perfect celibacy, devoted to study, up to one's twenty-fourth year. The student must bear in mind that keeping this brahmacharya secures one an exemption from physical and mental ailments and a life of peace and tranquillity ranging over seventy or eighty years. The middling brahmacharya

> is living a life of perfect celibacy up to one's forty-fourth year. This brahmacharya conduces to the fullest development of the physical powers, gives the mind a thorough control over the body and the senses, and makes one a terror to the wicked and the sinful, physically, morally and intellectually. The teacher should impress the value of the forty-four years' brahmacharya upon the student's mind by pointing out its advantages. The highest kind of brahmacharya is the living a life of perfect celibacy, devoted to study up to one's forty-eighth year. Even as the perfection of the alphabet lies in forty-eight letters, even so does the perfection of brahmacharya consist in forty-eight years. This brahmacharya conduces to the fullest and harmonious development of all the powers of man."

Finding that nothing that he could say would move his parents, and that his mother in particular was dead against his leaving home, Dayanand, in despair, asked to be permitted to reside at a village a few miles from his own, and where the landed property of the family principally lay. The father thought that Dayanand would not object to taking care of the property, and he proposed that he should take upon himself the work and the responsibility of a superintendent.

But Swami Dayanand was disposed to do such thing. He wanted to reside in the other village because a learned man resided there, and if he was not to be allowed to God to Kashi, he might as well study for some time with this learned man. This request was granted, and Dayananda was thankful that it had not been refused, for, apart from the fact that his removal to the neighbouring village would enable him to continue his studies for some time, it would be a distinct relief to him to be away from his parents. They were continually talking of his coming marriage, which was annoying to him, and he knew that if he ever ventured to intimate that he preferred remaining as he was, he was bound to be severely taken to task for harbouring such a foolish (!) idea.

Swami Dayanand commenced his studies with the new Pandit, and the latter was delighted with his progress. One day, in the course of conversation, Dayanand openly confessed to his teacher that he had no intention whatever of marrying, and that he positively disliked being a "householder." The teacher reported Dayanand's words to his father, who had him immediately recalled to his native village, and ordered that preparations for his marriage should be made without delay. Dayanand was at a loss what to do. He consulted his friends, but they, like his parents, being unable to sympathise with his lofty aspirations, advised him to marry.

After much reflection, he was convinced that his only means of escape from marriage lay in flight. He had already counted upon the possibility of such a contingency, and now it must become a fact. Any hesitation, when affairs had come to such a pass, would be fatal. He must bid farewell to home and friends once and forever - in that lay his salvation. Just as the preparations, which had been pushed on with startling vigour during a whole month, were complete, and when a week or so more would find him married, Dayanand braced himself for a final effort, and so soon as the shades of the evening came on, he stole out of the house, with his mind fully made up never to see foot in it again, if he could help it!

Renunciation of the World

His Pursuit and Capture

Swami Dayanand left his father's home in the Jyeshtha of Vikrama Samvat 1903 (1846 AD), and he was at this time over twenty-one years of age, a lively youth with intellect stamped on his forehead, but, withal, simple and artless in the extreme. The first night he passed at a village some eight miles from his own, and long before it was dawn, he was speeding along by-ways and unfrequented paths again. When the evening se in, he had done about twenty-five miles, and being too tired to proceed farther, he put up in a temple of Hanuman, in a certain hamlet. He did well to have avoided the highway, for his father, interpreting his absence only too correctly, had dispatched servants in pursuit, and they were searching for him. Even before he had time to leave the temple, and this he did on the third day after quitting home, he heard from a petty official that a party of horsemen and footsepoys had visited the village to which the temple was attached, looking for a lad named Mool Shanker.

Swami Dayanand thanked Heaven for the narrow escape and resumed his journey. He had not gone far when he fell with a party of begging mendicants, who engaged him in conversation. So wrought upon his simplicity as to prevail upon him to surrender all his ornaments and various other things to their idol. "As long as you don't give up everything of value, you possess, to the image," said they, "so long you need not expect to rise above worldly attachments." Swami Dayanand believed the imposters and parted from them considerably lightened of his valuables.

While pursuing his flight, Swami Dayanand heard here and there from people about Lala Bhagat at Sayle, a town some six miles from Mooli, a well-known station on the Wadhwan-Morvi line. Dayanand turned his steps towards this town, which he duly reached, finding the house of Lala Bhagat, a distinguished saint, crowded with wearers of ochre-coloured clothes. Here a Brahmachari conferred upon him the privileges of the order to which he himself belonged, and named him Shuddhachaitanya (pure-minded), making him put on ochre-coloured garments and keep a Kamandal (the beggar's gourd) as his constant companion. Following in the footsteps of the Sadhus of the place, Dayanand began to practice austerities. He held idol-worship in abhorrence, but he was still under the influence of superstition in various ways. As an instance of this, he was one night sitting under a tree and practising under a tree and practising yoga, when, all of a sudden, a curious noise, made by some birds roosting on the tree, broke upon his ears. He was alarmed, thinking that the tree was haunted by evil spirits, and getting up in haste joined his group! Leaving Sayle, Dayanand arrived, in his new habiliments, at a town called Koutha Gangada, in small principality, near Ahmedabad (Gujarat).

The town was alive with the presence of numerous Bairagis, who had managed to entangle a princess in their toils. The worthies, seeing Dayanand habited in reddish-yellow garments, had a derisive laugh, their secret object being to win the newcomer over to their order, Dayanand would not be caught this time, though he suffered himself to be persuaded so far as to part with his stock of silk-dhotis to them and to buy three rupees worth cotton ones instead. Here Dayanand stayed for three months, known to all his neighbours as a Brahmachari.

Ere turning his back upon Koutha Gangada, Dayanand learnt that the annual fair at Siddhapur, a Railway station on the bank of the Saraswati, would take place in a few days. Thinking that he might come across some yogi there who could point out to him the way to salvation, Dayanand set off towards the locality. In the way he encountered a Bairagi whom, on nearer approach, he recognised to be one perfectly acquainted with his family. When the eyes of the two met, tears rolled their cheeks. On the Bairagi's asking why he saw him dressed in ochre-coloured garments, Dayanand told him all.

The Bairagi was at first moved to laughter, but soon assuming a stern and serious tone he told him that he had made a great mistake in taking the step he had. After this the pair separated, each pursuing his different way. On reaching Siddhapur, Dayanand put up in the temple of Nilakanth Mahadeva, already crowded with Dandi Swamis and Brahmacharis (students). The fair came off. Wherever Dayanand hear was a learned and pious man, there he would go and converse with the worthy soul in his ecstasy he little dreamed, that something unpleasant was in store for him and that he must soon face it.

The Bairagi, whom Dayanand had met on his way to Siddhapur, had communicated with his parents, telling them, in his letter, where Dayanand could be found. We won't say it was treachery on his par: on the contrary, it may be that he was actuated by the best motives. Perhaps, like many others he could not understand Dayanand (it was apparent from his parting rebuke to Dayanand that he did not), and he thought he was doing the youth good in informing his parents of his whereabouts. But whatever the real facts, certain it is that it was his communication that once more set the father on the son's trail.

Karsanji came accompanied by several sepoys and went through every part of the fair making enquiries about his missing son. His efforts were at last crowned with success. Entering one morning the temple of Mahadeva, he found himself suddenly face to face with Dayanand. Seeing him dressed in ochre-coloured clothes he flew into a passion and, in a voice of thunder, asked: "What means this?" So terror-inspiring was his visage that Dayanand dared not meet his gaze. He raved and stormed at the youth, calling him the disgrace of his family, the cause of eternal shame to his race, and so on. Dayanand was in a mortal fright, and moving from his place, fell at his sire's feet, saying that he had done what he had by evil counsel of others, and that he fully intended to return home from Siddhapur.

He humbly craved forgiveness for any offence he might have given, and said he was thankful to his father that he had taken so much trouble on his account. This show of contrition and humility failed to appease the anger of Karsanji. Taking hold of his garments, he tore them to pieces, and dashing his bowl on the ground smashed it to fragments. Then having dressed him in new suit of clothes he took him to where he had put up, and said, "Will you kill you mother by running away from home?"

In spite of all that Dayanand had said to set his father's mind at rest, the old man had no faith in his words. He stationed the sepoys upon him, giving them strict orders not to let him go anywhere. Night came and still Dayanand found himself watched as closely as ever. He was helpless, not knowing what to do, and bitterly thinking of turn which affairs had taken. For he had, as his father rightly suspected, no mind to go home. It was fright that made him tell an untruth: in his heart of hearts he resolved to regain his freedom as soon as he saw a chance of doing the same.

While he lay in his bed, despondent and musing over his fate, what did he find on stealing a look at the guard but that he had fallen a sleep? "Now or never," said Dayanand, and creeping out of the room he ran with all his might. He had gone about half a mile, when he saw a temple with a lofty papal tree growing near it, and shading the building on all sides by its huge branches. He could not but see that the guard would soon awake, and, missing him in his bed, would give an alarm, upon which his father and his attendants would be again after him. Under the inspiration of the moment, Dayanand climbed up the huge tree and hid himself on a lofty branch just near the top of the building. He had not been settled many minutes in his "retreat" when several horsemen came dashing in the direction of the tree but, though they looked closely in every nook and corner of the temple, they failed to find any trace of their master's son.

The priests of the temple were interrogated, but they could give no information. At last disappointed with their fruitless search, the pursuers turned up back and were soon lost to view. During the time the search lasted, Dayanand had sat closely "packed up" and did not so much as breathe, for fear that his presence might be detected by anyone. The sun at last rose, but Dayanand would not leave his hiding-place yet. He was in fear of the priests, of his father and his men and even of a causal way-fearer whom he might meet in the event of his leaving his retreat before nightfall. He had nothing to eat but he had a lota full of water, and this water he partook when the wanted to refresh himself. When the livelong day had at last ended he slipped down the tree, halting at a village some four miles from the temple. Early in the morning he started off afresh, and passing through Ahmedabad, arrived at Baroda. Here associating with the Sannyasis and Brahmacharis of the Non-dualistic school he himself became a Vedanti, believe in the identity of God and soul.

During his residence here he heard that a meeting of learned Sadhus was shortly going to be held on the bank of the Nerbada, and no sooner did he hear this than he set off towards the place specified, to be present at the conference. Reaching there, he had a talk on the Shastras with Sachchidanand Paramahansa. At this place hearing that large number of learned Brahmacharis and Sanyasis lived along the bank of the river, Dayanand proceeded in search of the same and met several. With one of these - Paramahansa Parmanand - he resumed his studies, and, in the course of a few months, had gone through Vedantasara, Arya Harimede, Totaka, Arya Harihara, Totaka, Vedantaparibhasha, and similar other works.

Wanderings and Initiation into Sanyasa

As Brahmachari, Swami Dayanand, in conformity with the usual practice, had to cook his meals himself. This greatly interfered with his studies. To be rid of this trouble, he made up his mind to enter the Sanyasa Ashrama. The initiation would be, moreover, useful to him in another way: it would give him a name which would completely hid his identity and would minimise the chances of his being reclaimed by the members of his family. They knew him as Shuddhachaitanya, but when the name had been dropped in favour of a sanyasa name, a great clue to his whereabouts would be lost, and he could then count upon the enjoyment of greater freedom in his movements. With this idea in his mind, he requested a Sanyasi named Chidashrama to initiate him into sanyasa. His request was refused on the ground of his extreme youth. The refusal, however, had no discouraging effect upon Dayanand.

He was firmly resolved upon being initiated, and he stayed a year and a half on the bank of the Nerbada, studying and waiting his chance. In the meantime, a Dandi Swami and a Brahmachari came and halted in a forest near the town of Chanod. The name of the Dandi Swami was Purnanand. A Dakshini Pandit, a friend of Dayanand paid a visit to this learned Sanyasi, along with Dayanand and introduced him to the Sanyasi, and a conversation on Brahmavidya ensued.

Swami Dayanand could not but perceive that the Sanyasi was a man of profound learning, and he moved the Dakshini Pandit to request him to initiate him into the Sanyasa. The Pandit conveyed his wishes to the learned Sanyasi, making a powerful recommendation on his behalf.

The young man, he said, was passionately devoted to the study of Brahmavidya and valued it above all things, but, as at present circumstanced, he could not fully satisfy the craving of his soul for, as a Brahmachari, he has to prepare his food with his own hands and to attend to other similar sundry things, which took away a large portion of his time. In order that his entire time and leisure be at his disposal, to be exclusively devoted to study and reflection, it was necessary that he should enter the sanyasa and might it not be hoped that the erudite Swami would grant his application? Swami Purnanand's first answer was much the same as that of the Chidashrama Swami.

He declared that he could not see his way to initiate one so young, and he added: "I belong to the Maharastra. The young man ought to wait upon some Gujarati Sanyasi and get initiated by him." To this the Dakshini Pandit replied that when the Sanyasis belonging to the Deccan went so far as to initiate into the sanyasa even men of inferior castes, Swami Purnanand should have no objection whatever in bestowing the privileges of the order upon one who came of a prominent Brahmin family. After much discussion the Swami prevailed upon to entertain the young man's petition, and on the expiration of the third day after the meeting, the important function took place, and Shuddhachaitanya came to be named what we have called him from the very beginning of our sketch - Dayanand (Saraswati).

Swami Dayanand was sanyasi in twenty-fourth year, but his initiation did not mark, as in most cases if does and ought to, the completion of his education. To all intents and purposes, he was still a Brahmachary, and he himself felt that he was such. His initiation had, however given him one thing - made him absolutely his own master, and this was a privilege, for which, as we are aware, he intensely longed with the one, sole object that he might drink his fill at the fountain of knowledge.

In the course of the new trip which Swami Dayanand had undertaken, he came to hear of one Swami Yoganand, and adept in Yogavidya. He went to him, and commenced with him the study of the highest branch of metaphysics. When he had gone through some elementary works on the subject, he proceeded to Cinor, where he came across a Brahman named Krishna Shastri, who was well-versed in Sanskrit grammar. With this Shastri he was for some time, and then left for another town, where he studied the Vedas with a certain Pandit.

Here after some time, he met two Yogis, named Jwalanand Puri and Shivanand Giri. Associating with them he resumed the practice of yoga, and he would often hold discussions with them on the science of yoga. Eventually, the two Yogis left for Ahmedabad, telling Dayanand that if he would learn something more of their science, he should follow them shortly to the place they were bound for. After the expiration of a month, Dayanand left for Ahmedabad and rejoined the Yogis. They were true to the great mysteries of Yogavidya. Dayanand fully availed himself of their instructions, and he always thought of the two Yogis with a feeling of profound gratitude.

At Ahmedabad, Swami Dayanand hear that the Koh Abu was the abode of many distinguished Yogis, and he set off thither. On reaching the top of the mountain he found that the report was not unfounded. Many Rajyogis dwelt there, and he waited upon them. These Yogis, Swami Dayanand declares, had deeper insight into their science than even the first two Yogis, from whom he parted at Ahmedabad. He stayed with them, and learnt many more valuable secrets. Thus wandering about, Dayanand met many more Yogis and Pandits, deriving considerable benefit from their company and improving himself physically, intellectually, and morally. He made a point of staying wherever a truly learned man was found, and of studying with him in the capacity of a humble student. He was thirty years old when he visited the Kumbha Fair of Haridwar. (1912 V.E.). As long as the fair lasted, Dayanand remained in the wood surrounding the Chandi Hill, practising yoga, and on the termination of the fair he went to Rishikesh, where he had interviews with many Yogis and mahatmas and learnt more of practical yoga from them.

Tantras and Animal Food

Dayanand withdrew from the society of his teachers at Rishikesh, and passed some days in solitude, dividing his time between study and contemplation. One day, in a solitary ramble, he came across a Brahmachari and two Sadhus natives of the hills, and joining them, the party left for Tehri a famous seat for learning. While staying here one of his new acquaintances sent him an invitation to dine at his house. At the appointed hour a servant waited upon Dayanand, who, accompanied by a Brahmachari, repaired to the house of his would be host. On arriving there, he saw a Pandit was cutting up meat, and that a few steps farther on, several Brahmans were engaged in cooking the same article. Heaps of bones lay beside them, and head of several animals already cooked. The sight greatly disgusted Dayanand, and thought the master of the house extended to him a cordial welcome and pressed him to enter the best room in the house, he found himself compelled to return to his dwelling at once. "Don't let me disturb you," said he, "but go on with your work," and uttering these few words he came back to his cottage and felt at case.

Before many minutes, however, had gone by, a fresh man waited upon him, and informed him that everything was ready and that his presence alone was wanting. "Every variety of meat-dish," explained the messenger, "will be served to your holiness, it has been prepared expressly for yourself, and the master hopes it will please you." Dayanand replied that the very sight of meat made him sick, to eat the same was out of the question, and hat if the man's master must have him share his hospitality, he could send him some flour and vegetables, and his own Brahmachari would do the cooking. The disappointed host had to comply.

Shortly after this, Dayanand asked the two Pandits for a loan of the books whose praises they so warmly sang, and the Pandits willingly agreed to lend him the entire lot. Dayanand, however, chose those only which go under the name of the "Tantras". No sooner had he opened one of these than he was astounded at the nature of its contents. They were so obscene, so utterly subversive of the moral and social relations which have ever existed and ought to exist between one member and another of a family and between one member and another of society at large, that no one, not absolutely and hopelessly depraved and debased, could help recoiling at the bare contemplation of what they taught.

And one book was as bad as the others, teaching little else than what will vitiate and degrade, what will demoralise. Things, many and various, have brought about the fall off India, but nothing has perhaps contributed more to prostrate the Indian community morally and intellectually than the Tantras. Alas! That such a literature should have ever come to exist in the land of the saints and sages. Dayanand's soul sickened as he turned over the leaves, and at last he threw them away with a loathing. During the rest of his life he never thought or spoke of these but his heart was filled with indignation at the villainy of those who had brought them into existence.

From there Swami Dayanand set off towards Sri Nagar, and, on reaching there, put in a temple on the Kedarghat. Here had occasional discussions with the Pandits, and whenever he found one of these too warm an admirer of orthodoxy, he would quote from the Tantras and so completely seal his lips. Of the Sadhus whom Dayanand met at this place, Ganga Giri pleased him the most. Dayanand came to have great esteem and regard for him and stayed with him for two months. As soon as the autumn set in, he, in company with the two hill-sadhus and his Brahmachari, left for some other locality, and visiting Prayag (Allahabad) and other places arrived at the tomb of Agastya Muni, thence proceeding to a hill named Shivpuri.

This is the place where some people (the Jains) believe salvation is attainable while one is yet living. Dayanand passed the four months of winter here, and then separating himself from his companions, bent his steps towards Kedarghat alone. Passing through the Guptakashi, Gourikund and Bhim ganga, he reached the temple of Triyugunarayana. He did not seem to like the place at all, and consequently returned to Kedarghat without delay.

When he had seen sufficient of the inhabitants of this place, he thought he would visit the neighbouring hills. These hills are covered with perpetual snow, but the fact did not daunt Dayanand. He had heard that these were the abode of mahatamas, and he must seek them but in defiance of every inconvenience and danger. He went and commenced making his enquires. But not useful information was forthcoming. The people interrogated would ether deny all knowledge of the existence of men Dayanand was after, or would tell such stories regarding them as no man with a grain of common sense would believe. Dayanand did not know what to do. After fruitlessly wandering for twenty days exposed to the piercing, intense cold of the mountains, he retraced his steps to Kedarghat.

His recent excursion in the hills, though attended with much suffering, had created in Dayanand a great liking for the free and bracing mountain air, and one day he ascended the Tunganath Hill. The temple on the summit he found crowded with priests and crammed with idols, and not much pleased with sight, he prepared to descend the same day. He saw before him two paths, one leading to the west, and the other to the south. He took the one leading to a jungle, and before he and gone far, he found himself in the midst of a thick wood. Sharp stones and huge boulders lay strewn everywhere, and the streams and rivulets were wholly destitute of water. Laying hold of the grass and of the dried-up bushes, Dayanand made a shift to reach the bank of a stream, and mounting the ridge of a hill ran his eye in every direction. Nothing but inaccessible steeps and jungle were to be seen.

The sun was near setting, and Dayanand could not see how he would manage to pass the night in such a dreary place without food and water. At last he resolved to seek some habitation. His progress was slow, and the thorny bushes through which he had to pass tore his garments to shreds and drew blood from his body. He, however, went on limping along with wounded legs and lace-rated feet, and, after undergoing many hardships, lighted on the highway.

He had to grope his way in the darkness, and in time, the signs of habitation appeared. It was an insignificant, uninviting hamlet, and Dayanand set off towards Okhimath to which it led. Here he passed the night, and as soon as it was morning, proceeded to Guptakashi. Desirous of exploring Okhimath at leisure, he returned to it again, and found that almost all the caves were inhabited by imposters. Here a great Mahant wanted to make Dayanand his disciple, offering him wealth and assuring him that he should succeed him to the gaddi.

He rejected his offer, saying that if he wanted wealth he should not have left home and separated himself from his parents and friends. At the same time he told him hat even the event of his settling down with him, he could not gain the object for accomplishment of which he had severed his connection with the world. The Mahant urged Dayanand to stay with him for some time, he refused, returning to Joshimath the very next day. Eventually, he met many learned Sanyasis and Yogis here, and he took further lessons from them in connection with practical yoga.

Last Days

Swami Dayanand contemplated leaving Jodhpur at, or towards, the close of September, but, as we have already informed the reader, he was unable to do so before the next months had half expired, and we have further informed the reader that when he bade farewell to the Rathore sovereign and his people, he was in the very reverse of the best of health. Only five days after the letter, reproduced in English in the proceeding chapter, had been sent to Maharaja Pratap Singh, the Swami caught a bad cold, but it was, after all, nothing very serious, especially in the case of a person of the Swami's build and physique, and the 28th and 29th September passed off without giving any indications of the fact that great, almost frightful sufferings were in store for the Swami, finally terminating in death.

He did not at all appear to be in any danger whatsoever, when, after his usual draught of milk, he retired to rest on the night of the 29th. He had not, however, slept much when he felt a violent pain in the region of the stomach, and a dull, heavy sensation in the chest, as if it was choked up with something which struggled to get out. To relive the pain he left his bed several times. And threw up matter thrice; but though he suffered much, he waked no one. The violence of the pain abating at last, he thoroughly rinsed his violence of the pain abating at last, he thoroughly rinsed his violence of the pain abating at last, he thoroughly rinsed his mouth with water and went to sleep. The morning was far advanced when he rose on the following day (a very unusual thing for him), and as soon as he rose, he threw up again. He felt suspicious, and, as the painful heaviness was still present in the chest, and a feeling of utter uneasiness pervaded the whole frame, he thought he would repeat the practice which he had formerly resorted to with success.

Drinking a good deal of water, he thrust his two fingers into his throat, and brought on vomiting again, being under the impression that if poison had got into the body, no matter how, it would be cast out, more or less, in this way. But there was little relief still. The Swami caused fragrant drugs to be thrown into the *havan-kund*, and drank a decoction of *ajwain*, (lighusticum ajwain) etc., but with no beneficial results. On the contrary, he became worse, the colic pains having commenced to add to his sufferings. Dr. Suraj Mal was at last called in, who administered some medicine that would stop vomiting, and also allay the patient's thirst. The medicine failed to do any good. The colic was as bad as ever, the breathing became rapid and painful, and there was coughing besides. Maharaja Pratap Singh, who heard of the illness late on the 30th, sent Dr. Ali Mardhan Khan to attend the Swami. The Doctor had the region of the abdomen tightly bandaged, and had the patient cupped on 1st October.

This relieved the cough a little, but failed to produce any desirable effect as far as the colic was concerned. On 2nd October, he administered some pills, and on the 3rd gave a purgative, but till 2 O'clock in the night there was not motion. At ten the motions commenced, and continued the whole night. By morning the Swami had thirty, nor did they cease during the day, and he was now so weak that with every motion he fainted. The case did not improve on the 5th, indeed he had now a hiccough in addition to be tormented with. Day after day of intense suffering passed. There was a constant looseness of the bowels, an unbearable pain in the pit of the stomach, frequent vomiting, and a continued hiccough and over and above all this, his face, throat, tongue, palate, forehead, etc., become covered with blisters.

On the 15th of October, Doctor Adam came to see the Swami by desire of His Highness. The Doctor evidently saw that the case was hopeless, and he advised the Swami's removal to Abu, observing that change of climate might do him good. The Swami, already disposed to leave Jodhpur, approved of the advice, and communicated his intention to the Maharaja. His Highness, on hearing the nature of the Swami's resolve, came in person to the great teacher's lodgings and besought him to postpone his departure, urging that he was not fit to move in such a condition, and that if he went away as he was, it would give the State and its Ruler a bad name. The Swami, however, was not be turned from his purpose, and the Maharaja had to ultimately agree. A sum of Rs. 2,500 was presented, and the 16th of October was fixed as the day of departure.

As the hour of departure drew near, the Maharaja with his brother, Maharaja Pratap Singh and other dignitaries of the State, made his appearance, to pay his respects to the Swami, and to see him off. Some royal tents, six camels, three chariots, one phaeton ere to accompany the Swami, who himself was to travel in a Palanquin, attended by a number of courtiers, on of these being Doctor Suraj Bhan. The parting moment came, and it was clear to all present that His Highness, as also his brother, was in real distress.

Who could say how the disease would terminate and if His Highness's worst fears were realised and the illness had a fatal ending, neither he or his descendants could, for generations, hold up their heads when the sad event was mentioned in their presence. His Highness felt after the noble race from which he came. What has not the true Rajput done and dared to prevent a slur being cast upon his fair name. His Highness with his own hands tied his own special belt round the Swami's waist, and mark his appreciation of the invaluable lessons he had received from the Swami and of the profound respects in which he held him by reason of his lofty virtues and his unique attainments, he walked some two hundred paces by the side of the palanquin before he eventually tool leave of its occupant.

The shades of the evening had already fallen, but in spite of the breeze, in spite of the fact that a pankha-coolee was incessantly fanning the Swami, in spite of his having a dripping cloth, in several folds, on his head, he felt as if he were on fire. After a whole night's travelling, the party reached, Ropat, where the next twenty hours were passed. On the 18th the Pali station was reached, and the tents were pitched near a Mandir, which turned out to be the dwelling of some Sanyasis. On hearing who had arrived all these came out, and touching the feet of the Swami retired. The Swami discovering that he was in the immediate vicinity of Sadhus and Sanyasis, caused his tent to be removed to a distance, to prevent his proving source of inconvenience to the individuals in question in any way.

A man was sent from this place to Ajmer to consult the local physicians, and to bring from there any medicine that the best native skill could suggest and prescribe for a case like the Swami's. The Ajmer Samaj consulted the well-known Yunani Hakim Pirji, and the medicine which he prescribed was got prepared without delay and handed over to the messenger, who rejoined the Swami at the station, hours before he had time to resume his journey, along the Abu Road, for the Mount Abu, which he did on the morning of the 21st October. The medicine was taken. It did bring some relief, but it was not much.

While the party was on its way to its destination, it fell in with Doctor Lachhman Das, Assistant Surgeon, who was proceeding on duty to Ajmer. Seeing the Swami in the State he was in, he at once turned back and followed him to the Abu, which was reached on the evening of the 21st, and where the Doctor treated the patient for two days. The treatment appeared to be doing good from the very first, stopping the hiccough and removing the looseness of the bowels within forty eight hours, but it was not to be continued longer. His officer coming to know what the doctor had done, was extremely put out, and after reprimanding him severely for having returned to Abu in defiance of his orders, to the contrary, directed him to be off at once. The brave Mohyal, indignant that his deepest feelings should have been so slighted and disliking the pre-emptory nature of the order now issued, tendered his resignation on the spot, but the officer refused to accept it at such a short notice. The Doctor had no option but to set off to Ajmer, his faced bathed in tears. Before taking his leave of the Swami, he entreated him in most earnest tones, to come to Ajmer, where he himself should be constantly by to see him and to direct everything.

The Swami thanked him, but said that he could not follow his suggestion. The doctor, however, actuated by the best and most patriotic of motives, was resolved to do all he could to have the Swami near him. On the way the encountered several gentlemen, from the Punjab and elsewhere, hurrying to their beloved teacher, and he besought them, one and all, to exert themselves to the utmost to induce the Swami to leave for Ajmer.

The Swami was going down, those by his bed-side. – Munshi Lakshman Saroop, Pandit Lakshman Datta, Lala Shiv Dayal, Seth Sevak Lal Krishn Dass, and numerous other gentlemen, professional as well as laymen could not clearly but perceive. His condition on the 23rd was that of man in the utmost state of exhaustion. He could speak with effort, and could not turn in his bed without efficient assistance. The blisters were still present, and as bad and ugly as ever. Though retaining complete possession of his sense, his hands and feet were always cold. During the next three days, at the desire of His Highness, Maharaja Jaswant Singh, Dr. Adam and Assistant Surgeon Lala Gurcharan Das came to see the Swami several times, but neither could do nay good. Maharaja Pratap Singh came on the 26th, but his influence and wealth, though he was willing they should be fully pressed into service for the Swami, were as powerless to bring about any good result as those of lesser men. His brother was willing to make a present of two thousand rupees (and of more if need be) to anyone who should restore the Swami to health! Finding how matter stood, and to try as were, a last chance, the attendants of the Swami, big and small, came to the determination of removing him to Ajmer. Dr. Lachhman Das had given them hope, and who could say but he might, after all, be able to save the Swami?

The Swami was unwilling to go, but the united representation of his well-wishers present, had, at last, its way, and to Ajmer he suffered himself to be taken, reaching that station on the morning of the 27th. It may be mentioned that while being conveyed to Ajmer, the Swami felt a strong desire to eat *dahi* (tar or curds). The article was supplied, and it is affirmed that it would have been better if he had not eaten it, being injurious for a person suffering from dysentery (sangrahni).

As contemplated, the Swami was again placed under the treatment of Dr. Lachhman Das, but it would not do. The disease began to assume a still more alarming aspect, foreshadowing, in an unmistakable manner, the end that was near. On the 29th the entire body became covered with blisters, and the restlessness became considerably greater.

But for all that the Swami, with the help of two or three gentlemen, sat up in bed, and unsupported by anyone, remained in a sitting posture for some time, deep in *Samadhi*. On the 30th Hakim Pir Imam Ali (popularly known as Pirji) came and saw the Swami after having thoroughly examined the Swami, he gave it as his opinion, that he had been poisoned (the arsenic having been administered to him, he could not say how), and he said that if the Swami, instead of going to Abu, had come direct to Ajmer, the fatal substance would, very probably, have been got out of the system.

This, in other words, meant that the poison had, by this time, been fully absorbed into the system, and that it was now beyond the reach, of human skill. After the departure of this celebrated physician, Dr. Newton was called in. The cough at this time being most troublesome, he had three or four seers of poultice (linseed, boiled in milk), prepared and applied to the chest of the sufferer. But no good came of it. The Doctor declared that he had seldom come across any man who under such suffering was so calm and resigned, and so self contained.

As the Swami threw the poultice away, he remarked: "This is worse than useless now."

It was a just remark, considering the change that was coming over him. The colour of the urine, at this time, was black as coal. At 11 am the Swami was seated on a chair to answer the calls of nature for the last time. When he was clean, he took the water with his own hands, and performed his ablutions, thoroughly cleansing his mouth with a *datan*. After this he lay down on the bed. The regulation of the in-going breath, the result of no little effort at such a moment, clearly showed that the Rishi was in communion with his Maker.

At 4 pm the teacher desired the Swami Atamanand and Gopal Giri to be brought before him, and as soon as they made their appearance, he asked them to sit down, and then said: "What do you want?" the answer was, that all they desired was that he should be restored to health. The Swami replied: 'What is left of this body now to get well? And extending his hand he placed it on the head of each in turn, and said "Live in peace." A few minutes after this, he directed that one hundred rupees, in cash and a shawl be given to Swami Atmanand and a similar present to Padnit Bhim Sen, but both the gentlemen humbly begged to be excused from accepting the gift, and they had their wish.

At about 5 pm, the Swami, who had, now and then, give his loveful glance to the arrivals from various parts of Upper India and Rajputana, now beckoned them, one and all, to come and stand before him. They came, and stood contemplating the noble figure lying prostrate before them, but not for long. At a signal from him they retired behind him, and set down silence. The doors of the room and the skylights, in deference to his wishes, were thrown open and looking at the ceiling he asked: "What *paksha* is it now? What is the *tithi*" and what day?" the reply was that it was the end of the *Krishna-paksha* and the beginning of the *Shukla-paksha* and that the day was the Tuesday.

Upon this he composed himself for contemplation, and began to chant Veda-mantras, following the same with *Ishwara-stuti* in Sanskrit and in Bhasha. When repeating the *Gayatri-mantra* he remained wrapt in trance for some minutes, after which opening his eyes, he exclaimed:

> "Merciful and almighty Lord, such is Your will, yea, such is Your will, and let this Thine will be fulfilled!"

The Demise

And simultaneously with closing the prayer, he turned in his bed and controlling the outgoing breath after the manner of Yogis, cast it out utterly with one vigorous effort! It was at 6. pm the 31st of October, 1883, the Dipawali Day, that India's greatest saviour of modern times expired. Were the preparations for a universal illumination in Aryavarta at this moment in honour of the departed soul? And was the universal illumination that came off almost synchronously with the exit of the departing soul, a representative of the inconceivably bright and glorious light of which the latter part of the following mantra speaks, and in which the spirit of the Rishi was to range and to dwell:

> "Etaavaanasya Mahimaato Jyaayaamashcha Purushah Paado Aasya Vishvaa Bhootaa Ni Tripaadasyaamri-tam Divi"

Swami Dayanand was 59 years of age at the time of his death.

As soon as it was known that Swami Dayanand was no more, two Sanyasis made their appearance, claiming the body and declaring that they should, in accordance with the usages of their Order, inter it. The claim was refused. Maharaja Sajjan Singh, longing to have last look at his departed guru, suggested, through this representative, that the cremation of the body might be postponed for a couple of days, but His Highness was informed that, this could not be done, since it was the unanimous opinion of the gentlemen in attendance that the sanskar should be performed without delay.

In pursuance of this resolve, the body was washed and bathed early on the morning and having been wrapped in a shawl of the *geru* colour, placed on a *baikunthi* (a kind of bier) and borne towards the place where it was to be cremated, soon after it had struck ten. The procession, perhaps the grandest and most representative of its kind ever witnessed at Ajmer, moved on with bowed heads and with hearts weighed down with grief. This preceded the hearse, chanting hymns from the Vedas.

On arriving at the spot Rai Bahadur Pandit Bhag Ram, pointing to the body deposited in from of him, spoke of the undying achievements and singular virtues of the soul which had tenanted it, and of the irreparable loss which the country had suffered by the early departure of that soul. After this the body was placed on the Vedi, and burnt with two maunds of Sandal-wood, ten maunds of pipalwood, four maunds of ghee, five seers of camphor, one seer of saffron. In less than an hour the frame that had been instrumental in doing so much for the world, was a handful of ashes!

2

Personality and Character

A lion surveying the inferior herd defying his power could not look sublimer than he, when face to face with, and roused against, the daring and blasphemous skeptic of little knowledge and puny intellect. And yet his withering look of scorn or of contempt was not meant for the persons themselves, for malice was utterly foreign to his nature.; it was only meant for the views, so false and mischievous in their character, which, in their ignorance and conceit, the unblushingly put forward and advocated.

The Profile

Swami Dayanand was a man of gigantic built. He was over six feet in height, and had a compact, well-knit body, which later, instead of giving him a stoutish look, only contributed to make the symmetry of his person singularly perfect. He had a broad and expansive forehead, considerably protruding forward, which unmistakably indicated his possession of an intellect of the highest order; while his unusually raised crown pointed as unmistakably to his kinship with the sage and saint whom the Word Divine, as the Upanishad, differentiates from ordinary mortals by, conferring upon him the epithet of *dhir*.

The expression of the face, when in repose, was pre-eminently contemplative and dreamy, grand in its smoothness; for deep minds are like deep waters, seldom unruffled, powerful in their wealth and abundance of *depth,* and carrying on their mighty operations in silence in their own all-sufficient and capacious retreats. When, however, the great Teacher was excited (and it was but rarely that he was excited), the glory of his face was the glory of a thunder and lightning.

He was for chastising faults as the Word Divine taught him, and as he admitted do often in his interpretation of passages from that Word, and not for chastising the individuals who had faults. His memory was marvelously capacious and retentive, the mass of facts stored in it and ever ready for sue being tremendous. What the learned Pandits hopelessly essayed to hunt up in books, he could draw forth from this mental storage-house in a minute.

His voice, in the words of the founders of the Theosophical Society, "was clear and loud, well calculated to give expression toe very shade of deep feeling ranging from a sweet childish caressing whisper to thundering wrath against the evildoings of the priests.

He was the most self-possessed of men (speaking as men go in debate), giving the most patient hearing to his adversaries and never interrupting while they were speaking, and his replies were almost invariably given in a tone and in a language calm and gentlemanly in the highest degree. No man could gasp sooner or better than he; he saw into the soul of things without any apparent effort, and interpreted the others' utterances with a faithfulness which left nothing to be desired. He was never irrelevant and never diffuse, and he insisted upon others' keeping to the point. Humorous and often sarcastic remarks fell upon his lips, but these were wholly free from anything offensive or gross, and were never out of character with the dignified gravity and seriousness which generally characterised his demeanour.

Though acknowledged to be one of the greatest men of his age, even by those who differed with him on many points, he was simple and unostentatious in his habits and tastes. When alone, his entire apparel consisted of a wrapper and an under-cloth (dhoti), and in public too he generally appeared in as unassuming a dress as he could get hold of. He could command thousands and lakhs if he had liked, but though he valued wealth as a means to an end, though he regarded it as a great factor in the moral, intellectual and spiritual evolution of man, he regarded it as something absolutely worthless and positively injurious when valued for its own sake or interests of the flesh. His will showed his large-heartedness and his moral elevation.

A Strong Man

Swami Dayananda had a wonderful physique. When he was at Kasganj an incident happened which showed his exceptional strength. It so happened that two strong bulls were fighting in a street. Hundreds of people watched the fight from a distance, shivering with fear. The fight went on for quite some time but showed no signs of coming to an end. Swami Dayananda pushed through the crowd and walked up to the bulls. The people watching him ware terrified and shouted, "Swamiji, if you go near them, you won't return alive. Come back!" But the Swamiji did not pay attention to them. He went towards the bulls. Suddenly he took both the huge bulls by their horns and pushed them away with a tremendous force. Without looking back the bulls went away in different directions. The people near by were amazed at the superhuman strength of the obstinate sanyasi. It was because of this superhuman physical strength that Dayananda could live for a month even after drinking deadly poison.

Great Patriot

A greater patriot, a sincerer and more earnest advocate of education and enlightenment, a truer and stronger friend of virtue in its all forms, a nobler philanthropist, Aryavarta has not produced for centuries past and will not see for ages to come. In purity of character, in utter fearlessness, in the acuteness and comprehensiveness of intellect, in devotion to his Divine Word and its truthful Teachings he as exact prototype of his equally great predecessor, Shankracharya. Like the Rishis and Maharishis of old times death had no terrors for him: it was a passage which, when traverse, let to the portals of house of immortality and everlasting bliss. Men of the type of Swami Dayanand are the making of thousands in their life and after their death, and the day will come (may it please God, that it comes soon!) when India will again shine all the glory of its pristine splendour.

Love for Motherland

Even though Maharshi Dayananda aimed at the welfare of all humanity, he had great love for his motherland, India. Once an English officer was greatly impressed with Dayananda's speech and said to him, "Swamiji, please go to England and teach the way of dharma (righteousness). I shall bear all the expenses." Thereupon Swamiji said, "In the few years of life left to me I shall try to spread the knowledge of the vedas among my countrymen. Once the lamp of wisdom is lighted here, its light is bound to spread towards the west too."

He did not give a thought to the fame he could attain in foreign lands. He chose to stay in his own country and strive to improve the lot of his countrymen. This shows his boundless love for his country.

Once, addressing a huge gathering, Dayananda thundered: "Your ancestors were not uncivilized men living in forests. They were great men who enlightened this world. Your history is not a bundle of defeats. It is the eulogy of the conquerors of the world. Your Vedic Scriptures are not the songs of cowherds. They are the immortal truths which shaped mighty souls like Sri Rama and Sri Krishna. Awake! Arise! Be proud of your glorious history. Take inspiration from it to mould the present. Shame upon the modern education which fills you with contempt for your ancestors!"

Pioneer of the Cause of One National Language

Swami Dayananda was convinced that a common language is a good means of unifying the members of a society. He, therefore, was of the opinion that Hindi should be given the place of the national language. Swami Dayananda was born in Gujarat and had a fine command over Gujarati language. Still, even in Gujarat, he chose to make speeches in Hindi instead of in Gujarati. He wrote all his looks in Hindi.

Reformer of Society

Although a sanyasi, Dayananda had a sensitive and compassionate heart that melted at the sufferings of the poor. 'To love the creation of God is to love God Himself' - so he taught people. To awaken people from lethargy, the Swamiji travelled all over India Wherever he went, he roundly condemned the caste system, idol worship, child marriage and other harmful customs and traditions. He preached that women should have equal rights with men and laid stress on pure conduct in life. This created a stir among the people. Over the centuries, with the passing of time some wicked customs had crept into Hinduism. These customs stood out prominently and therefore the real power and greatness of Hinduism were dimmed. With the teachings of Swami Dayananda true Hinduism came to shine forth.

Thousands of young people who had been influenced by Western Culture and were about to accept Christianity turned back and became the staunch followers of Vedic religion. Some time Hindus who had gone over to other religions wished to come back. But the Hindus would not permit this. Swami Dayananda took the Christian and Muslim converts back into the Hindu fold by performing purification rites for them. So it may be said that Dayananda brought about a revolution in the social life of Indians. He laid particular emphasis on the equality of women. He used to say that India had fallen to such a miserable condition precisely because women were not given education but were kept in ignorance. As long as women were prisoners of foolish customs like the purdah, progress was beyond reach like the reflection of a bundle of jewels in a mirror. They should throw away their purdahs. Seetha and Savithri are remembered not because they were behind the purdah, but because of their chastity and virtue. So he went on preaching.

Swami Dayananda was bitterly opposed to Untouchability. "Untouchability is a dreadful curse of our society. Every living being has a soul which deserves affection; in every human being there is a soul worthy of respect. Any one who does not know this basic principle cannot understand the true meaning of the Vedic religion." So he preached.

Swami Dayananda was fully convinced that the nation cannot prosper unless education spreads. But our education system should not be a mere carbon copy of the western type of education. There should be a law to compel the parents to send every boy or girl who is eight years old to school. Every boy and every girl should be sent to Gurukulas where they stay with their gurus. There should be separate Gurukulas for boys and girls.

The King's son and the farmer's son should be equals in a Gurukula. They should all be made to work alike. The Gurukula should be situated far from the town and the city, and should enjoy calm and serenity. Our culture and our great books like the Vedas should be introduced to our students.

Side by side, mathematics, geology, astronomy and other sciences which are important in modern life should also be taught. Swami Dayananda founded gurukulas at various places to fulfil these objects. Among them Kangadi is famous even to this day.

Sanyasi, who Knew no Fear

Swami Dayananda was a fearless sanyasi Whatever he believed to be the truth he spoke out without fear. Once a priest Shulbred by name, threatened him saying, "It you criticise Christianity, you will have to go to jail.' Dayananda, replied at once, "My friend, was not Jesus Christ crucified for speaking the truth? But I fear no one to speak the truth."

Swami Dayananda used to point out flaws in other religions as he pointed out the flaws in Hinduism. Because of this, he had to incur the wrath of the followers of other religions several times. While he was giving a discourse at a Jodhpur meeting, the relative of a Diwan there placed his hand on the sword and said,

> "Be careful, don't criticise our religion." The Diwan even said, "You should be cut to pieces."

Swami Daya anda said, "I shall point out defects wherever I find them. I am not a rabbit to be frightened by the cries of jackals like you;" and he pin-pointed the flaws in his religion, too.

Personality and Impact

Swami Dayanand possessed a radiant personality and exceptional physical strength. He was born of stout parents. He had observed unbroken celibacy. He remained free from domestic worries and worldly emotions. He had toughened his body in the extreme cold of the Himalayas and on the burning sands of the river banks. He passed through these rigours in the scantiest of clothes. He disciplined his body and mind by leading a life of hard toil and pure thinking. He learnt yoga and practised it.

His physical strength and moral courage were astounding for all the above reasons. He would often cover a distance of 39 miles between Agra and Mathura in three hours. Strong wrestlers would sometimes request 'permission to massage his body to test his strength. They always went back dazed and honoured from the experience. The Swami once said: "'Lift my leg before you try to shampoo it". They exerted to the extreme but failed. In the open assembly at Roorkee in August 1875, while discoursing on the benefits of *Brahmacharya,* the Swarm stretched his arm and thundered: "I am over fifty; I challenge anyone to bend my arm". None responded to the call. At Wazirabad, in the same year, he likewise challenged the wrestlers present in a meeting. None came forth. Unmindful of the wild beasts and difficult terrain, he passed through dense forests and hills all alone to explore the sources of rivers, Narbada and Alaknanda. He wandered unarmed in snowy regions and untrod areas in search of yogis.

Truth was the very breath of his life. No temptation could turn him away from truth. There were dozens of attempts on his life. Hired ruffians were set upon him. Powerful chieftains drew their swords. Stones and bricks were hurled. His hut was set on fire. A snake was thrown over him. He was poisoned a number of times. He held aloft the ensign of truth.

The *Mahant* of Okhimath promised him rich dividends if the young seeker of truth became his disciple. The Raja of Banaras offered him money if Dayanand stopped the criticism of idol worship. The Raja of Venkitgiri offered to finance entirely the publication of one of his works, *Veda Bhashya,* on the same condition. The Maharana of Udaipur threw a very rich temptation for the same purpose. The ruler of Kashmir invited him. But the Rishi rejected all these offers with supreme contempt. He clung to the ideal of truth. In his sojourns and lectures he faced excited mobs, angry goondas, religious bigots and murderers He remained unshaken and tranquil. He glowed with confidence and inner peace in the face of perils.

His meetings were often attended by Europeans and English officials of high status. High churchmen, commanding officers, Inspectors General of Police, Magistrates and Collectors were, at times, attending his lectures. The Swami never fashioned his words to suit their pleasure. He always spoke the truth on Vedic authority. His comparative study and exposition of different religions was not conditioned by anyone's presence. Truth remained the only consideration. The English churchmen and officials, the Puranic Brahmans, the Muslim Ulemas were occasionally provoked by such a forthright criticism of some of their religious beliefs. But, many times, they also realised and acknowledged that they were in the presence of a man of great intellect and unbeatable moral courage. They felt in the burning words of this lone Sanyasi an inexpressible love of truth. Maulvi Murad Ali, Editor of the *Rajputana Gazette* (Urdu) of Ajmer met Dayanand five times. He had close discussions and felt "thoroughly satisfied". He acted as a strong supporter of cow-protection, and the Rishi was pleased to give him a copy of his photograph.

His passion for truth is best illustrated by an incident. In 1877, at Chandpur, a religious conference had been called. The most distinguished scholars and divines of Islam and Christianity arrived. Dayanand represented Vedic thought. Someone confided to him that the Muslims and the Hindus should unite to refute Christianity. But the Rishi refused, saying "rather all should meet together in love to find out the truth without attacking anyone."

Man of Heroic Action

The patriotism of Swami Dayananda was not merely an effusion of words. He was also a man of heroic action. The War of Independence in 1857 was a failure. The Indian National Congress was born in 1885. Swami Dayananda was one of the heroes who, after the 1857 failure, kept the love of freedom alive in the hearts of Indians till the Congress was founded. For this purpose he travelled throughout India. He tried to bring the princes of different states together and so he founded several branches of the Arya Samaj in places like Jodhpur, Udaipur and Shahpur, and many princes became his disciples. Swami Dayananda was fully convinced that only an armed revolution could drive the British out of India. Therefore he sent a noted revolutionary, Shyamji Krishna Varma, to France, so that he might receive inspiration as well as training for his mission.

Arya Samaj and the gurukulas (homes of gurus where disciples stayed and received instruction) shaped patriots and gave them training and inspiration for armed revolution. Swami Shraddhananda, Bhai Paramananda, Lala Lajpat Ray and Lala Hardayal were Arya Samajists who openly fought to drive the British out of India. Famous young revolutionaries like Gendalal Dixit, Roshanlal and Ramprasad Bismil were proud to call themselves Arya Samajists. From the very beginning the British were suspicious of Swami Dayananda. Therefore, a team of spies followed the Swamiji everywhere. It has been found that the British had a hand in the poisoning of the Swamiji at Jodhpur.

3

Religious Debates

Shastrarth at Kashi

For ages, the centuries untold has Kashi (Banaras) been the seat of learning in India, and the centre of religious influences. No European city, ancient or modern, not even Rome, has ever been or is so powerful with the student or with the religious enquirer as Kashi in this continental country. It has all along been a conglomeration of teaching and examining universities, without system and without method, no doubt, according to the present-day conception of a teaching or an examining university, and its theology, pure and ennobling, or adulterated and debasing, has made itself felt among millions and millions from an antiquity dating back thousands of years.

There is reason to believe that the earlier periods of its existence Kashi was an educational locality of the highest scientific value, and the inculcator of the purest religious sentiment. Its observatory and the fact that the Puranic literature, the necessary consequence of the ascendancy of Jainism (the child of Buddhism) had absolutely no existence in those days, lead to no other conclusion. As time went on, and the genuine thinker and teacher became every day a scarcer commodity, the great city degenerated into a "sham" of its former self, and the reign of imposture set everywhere.

It may be grand even in these days, but its grandeur is the grandeur of the fabled "tree of knowledge," offering an inviting and delicious fruit no doubt, but leading to the eater's banishment from Paradise once and for ever! Or its grandeur may be likened to that of a certain temple mentioned in the history of Nanak's life, attractive from without but within presided over by a hypocrite, whose only business was to plunder and fleece the traveller who happened to take shelter within its walls.

Kashi gives knowledge, but a knowledge that fills the mind with superstition and leads the soul astray. It extends a hearty welcome to every wayfarer that would travel Heavenward, but instead of showing him the way, it strips him of all his store and compels him to tread the path of destruction, which can only lead to darkness (in the life to come!)

Ever since the birth-hour of Jainism Kashi has been the stronghold of Puranism, and greater and more learned champions of idolatry and kindred institutions will be found nowhere. Swami Dayanand felt that if he was to deal Puranism a blow from which it would find it hard to recover, if he was to bring home to the orthodox world the truth (though it might never acknowledge it) that the worship of stocks and stones was absolutely false and degrading and opposed to the teaching of the Scripture and the ancient Shastras, he must assault the "citadel of myth and marvel itself." With this conviction in his mind, he quietly left Kanpur in the Kartak of Samvat 1926 (22nd or 23rd October, 1869), and reaching Kashi took up his quarters in Anandbag, right on the road leading to Durgakund. His shastrarths at Farrukhabad and Kanpur had already made him widely known in the leading orthodox circle at Banaras, and he news of his arrival spread like wildfire in the city. Pandits and vidyarthis flocked to him from all sides, displaying their learning and their powers of argument, but invariably returned discomfited and crestfallen.

The public at large heard the Sanyasi's arguments with wonder and astonishment, tried to say a word in favour of idolatry, but finding themselves compelled to be silent, returned home in doubt and despair. And as the Swami was, from the very first, bent upon being the aggressor, to bring matters to a crisis in this great city of idol-worshippers, he, one day, wrote down a question connected with in the Mahabhashya on a piece of paper, and sent the slip to the famous Pandit Raja Ram for an answer.

The Pandit sent back the reply: "Let a knife be placed between us before I answer your question. If I can satisfactorily answer the question, I will cut off your nose, but if I fail, you may cut off mine!" When the answer was conveyed to the Swami, he said: "By all means. Put two knives instead of one. If you are for a shastrarth (weapon-contest), instead of a shastrarth (Shastric contest), we might as well go in for it."

The place where the Swami had put up one of the most frequented ones. It was visited by thousands of vidyarthis daily, and Vairagis in huge crowds. A party of the latter one day waited upon the Swami, but perceiving that they were wholly unable to maintain their ground against their adversary, they took to abusing him. This was a species of argument which the Swami would not condescend to answer, and his opponents finding themselves baffled (how they wished they had a member of their own order to reply to!), retired, indulging in still more foul language.

Somebody carrying. The news of this most unbecoming behaviour to the Maharaja of Banaras, he administered a severe rebuke to the offenders, observing that every one was welcome to have a shastrarth with Dayanand, but that no one was to abuse him under any circumstances.

The Swami's fearless and thorough exposure of idolatry at last aroused the Maharaja of Kashi to a sense of the danger which menaces the dominance of orthodox belief under his very nose. He called together a meeting of his Pandits and emphasised the necessity of their holding a shastrarth with him without further delay.

After much deliberation the necessity of a discussion was admitted, but it was hinted that a discussion with Dayanand could not be held till it had been first ascertained what books he believed in. "He is in the habit of setting down this and that book as utter nonsense," complained the Pandits, " and who knows but hat he may try with us the same trick just when we are on the point of running him to earth!" Very modest this of the Pandits, but, for all that, the Maharaja could not but admit the justness of their contention, and authorised them to take the necessary steps towards finding out what constituted authoritative literature and Dayanand's opinion. Accordingly, five Pandits - Shaligram Shastri, Dhondi Raj Shastri, Damodar Shastri, Bhardwaj and Ram Krishn Shastri were deputed for the purposes. When these gentlemen put in an appearance, some one form among the numerous students, who surrounded the Swami at the time, gave out that vidyarthis from the opposite party were approaching, and the result was, that when the Pandits disclosed their errand, the Swami indifferently replied that the discussion should come off in few days, and under the supervision of the City Kotwal. As to what Shastras he believed in as authoritative, he would give a written answer to the question as soon as the Pandits from the opposite party saw him.

The five Pandits not quite clear as to what the reply meant, returned to their chiefs, but soon discovering the mistake that had been committed in ignorance, they once more waited upon the Swami, and informing him of their status, begged for an answer to their question. This time the Swami, gave them the needed answer, telling them to put down, in writing that he believe in, as authoritative the four Vedas, the four Upavedas, the six Angas, the six Upangas and the Manu Smriti. The Pandits asked on what authority the Swami believed these books to be authoritative. "I will answer this question at the time of the shastrarth," replied the Swami, "if you Pandits desire to have its answer." Again the Pandits asked to be informed as to what particular verses in the Manu Smriti the Swami regarded as meaningless interpolations, and false. The answer of the Swami was the same as before.

The leaders of orthodoxy could not reasonably take exception to their opponent's reply, and consequently they set about making preparations for a "tussle." Monday, November 16, 1869, was fixed as the date of the shastrarth, by mutual consent. Knowing how much depended upon the issue of the struggle, the Pandits resolved that the learning of the city should be completely represented on the occasion. The news of the discussion was received in the various parts of the city, and in the neighbourhood of Banaras, with mixed feelings, profoundly stirring whatever side arrayed, that a crisis was at hand.

The officials of the city, yielding to natural curiosity, sharpened by the intense prevailing excitement, suggested an alteration in the date fixed, but the Maharaja of Banaras, for reasons of his own, expressed his inability to adopt their suggestion, and desired that the shastrarth should come off on the day specified instead of on - Sunday.

The specified day came, and at the hour appointed Anandbag presented a spectacle superbly grand and imposing. Some affirm that no less that fifty thousand persons were present on the occasion, while others put the number at a considerably lower figure, asserting that the gathering did not exceed ten thousand souls. Whatever the actual number, there is reason to believe that it made up the biggest assembly of its kind ever witnessed in Banaras.

Besides many other famous Pandits there were many of the richest and most influential local men, many Thakurs from the villages around, and several ministers of the Gospel (Bible) who formed part of the surging mass of humanity assembled. The police arrangements were satisfactory, the Kotwal with fifty of his men being in attendance, but in spite of all that they could do, a large number of the rowdies of the town, notorious characters, out and out, found their way to the very spot where they were least wanted, - the spot reserved fro the controversialists and the pick of cream of the locality.

The well-wishers of the Swami, apprehending personal violence, made known their anxiety to him, adding that had the discussion taken place at Farrukhabad, there would have been not fear of a disturbance. At this the Swami burst out laughing, and replied. "It is always the firm conviction of genuine Yogis that the sun of truth is stronger than any forces which darkness can muster. He, who following the Will Divine, is above all partially and preaches the truth, what has he to fear? Men of truth hide not the truth through fear. They will risk their lives rather than be false to a Divine Commandment. I have nothing to be afraid of, for I live for the Ishwara (God) and the Dharma (duty). Let us wait and see what happens." After uttering these words the Swami desired a barber to summoned, and having got himself thoroughly shaved, he had a bath and spent some moments in contemplation and meditation, and then taking his meal repaired to the meeting.

The Maharaja of Kashi and his son soon followed. As soon as his highness entered the assembly, the orthodox Pandits rose and give him their blessing, and disregarding all discipline, followed at his heels and surrounded the Swami, thus largely usurping the place which, in all fairness, belonged to the Swami's supporters. They further had an order issued by the Maharaja that no more men should be allowed to come near the Swami or the Pandits, which meant nothing less than the exclusion of the Swami's admirers from where they had every right to be present! Of this move the Swami was duly informed, and he, in his turn informed the Kotwal of what had been done.

That good official perceived the justice of the complaint, and at once conducted Pandit Jyoti Saroop and other sympathisers and followers of the Swami to him. The latter received them with every mark of respect, and desired them to take a seats near himself. Nothing could be more distasteful to the orthodox Pandits, who made a significant sign to the Maharaja, as much as to say that the addition to Dayanand's ranks was wholly undesirable, as Dayanand alone was more than a match for them all!

The chief understood the sign, desired that the Pandits should take the front places, and the Jyoti Saroop should retire to a distant seat. Similar shameful treatment was meted out to the other supporters of the Swami, but it was no time to grumble, for a shastrarth must be had at any cost, and so he kept quiet and let the Maharaja and his Pandits please themselves.

Before the Shastrarth began, Swami Dayanand asked the Maharaja of Banaras if he had brought the Vedas with him. The reply was, that the Pandits present knew the Vedas by heart, and hence it had been deemed unnecessary that they or the Maharaja should come provided with the Books of question. Upon this the Swami observed that, in the absence of the Vedas, the import and drift of an authority could not be fully understood, as the passages preceding and following a quotation cited had often an important bearing on the quotation, and minimised the chances of its being twisted and distorted to suit a present purpose.

Presently after this remark from the Swami, the rule was laid down and proclaimed by the Kotwal, Pandit Raghu Nath Sahay, that only one Pandit Tara Charan Nayayak came forward to open the discussion. On his admission that all who were faithful to the requirements of *varna* and *ashrama* believed in the Vedas as the final authority, the Swami desired him to cite, from the Scripture, a passage which enjoined the worship of *Shaligram* and other images, and to declare, if no such passage existed, the truth.

To this the Pandit making no satisfactory reply - indeed, he did little more than seek to evade the question, Swami Vishuddhanand cried out: "Vyas says in a Sutra that the Creator of the world is a conscious, intelligent Being and not inanimate; where is the authority for this in the Vedas?" The Swami answered that the question wash wholly irrelevant, adding that nothing should be said by either party that hand not something to do with the subject under discussion.

Vishuddhanand, compelled to come to the point, rejoined that since the worship of Brahma was allowable in the mind in and the sun, there could be nothing objectionable in worshipping the *Shaligram* also. To this the Swami replied that, although such expressions as - *mano Brahm iti upasit and aditya Brahm iti upasit*, were to be met with in the Brahmans (which, in the opinion of the orthodox, were identical with the Vedas!), no such injunctions -*pashan Brahmiti upasit*, were to be found in these works, and under these circumstances, how could the worship of *Shaligram* be justifiable?

Swami Vishuddhanand made no answer to this, but another Pandit Madhvacharya came forward and, quoting a *mantra* asked what it dealt with. "With clouds, wells, tanks, etc." was the reply, and the Swami cited authorities from the Nirukta and Brahamanas in support of his reply. On being thus answered the Pandit turned his attention to the word *'Purana'*, asking of the words was to be found in the Vedas. The Swami replied in the affirmative, adding that although the world occurred in many places in the Vedas, yet nowhere had it any reference to the Bhagvat or any other so-called Purana.

Many minutes were spent in discussing this point, Swami Vishuddhanand, Pandit Bal Shastri and others, speaking one after another, and Swami Dayanand replying to each all alone. Once while the Swami was quoting a passage from the Upanishads, the orthodox Pandits in a body shouted out that the passage was nowhere to be found in the Upanishads, upon which their opponents observed that if what the Pandits asserted should be found to be true, he would acknowledge that he was defeated.

The Pandits readily signed the agreement, but it was on their part of a huge blunder, as they found out a minute later. The Swami opened the Upanishads and showed them the passage, covering them with shame and convincing those present that their knowledge of the Shastras was far from being perfect. Finding themselves checkmated everywhere and displaying lamentable ignorance of the Shastric teaching (the great Swami Vishuddhanand could not tell so much as what *dharma* and *adharma* consisted in), and discovering further that their adversary could quote whole chapters of the Vedas and other works by heart, and could furnish lucid and comprehensive expositions of the same, the Pandits made haste to sound the Swami's knowledge of Vyakarna, and, upon their arrogating superiority in that branch of Science, the Swami asked "What is the *Kalma Sangya (retained object?")* Vishuddhanand remained silent, but Bal Sahstri essayed to make an answer, only to fall back crestfallen. Baffled at every point exasperated beyond measure, the Pandits now hit upon a plan, which was nothing but a foul trick, to circumvent Swami Dayanand.

It was now 7 p.m. and rapidly growing dark. Madhvacharya, see in his opportunity, took out two leaves from a manuscript, and placing them before the Pandits said: "This is the Veda (Samhita), and here it is written that on the tenth day after the termination of yajna, the yajman should hear the Purana read. What the word 'Purana' means here?" Swami Dayanand desired him to read out the passage, but before he could do it, Vishuddhanand (in accordance, no doubt with a pre-concerted plan) took the leaves and handed them to the Swami.

The Swami desired him to read out the passage, but before he could do it, the famous man of Kashi excused himself from doing it, on the ground that had not his spectacles with him, and begged the Swami to take the duty upon himself. Suspecting no deceit, the Swami took up the leaves and silently began to go over them.

He had hardly been looking them two minutes, and was just going to reply, when Swami Vishuddhanand exclaiming that he was being unduly detained, the whole host of Pandits, with the Maharaja of Kashi at their head, stood up, and, clapping their hands, shouted out, at the top of their voice, that the dearly-earned victory might be celebrated in a becoming fashion, the notorious characters in attendance commenced raining down stones, old shoes and dung on the Swami. The life of the Swami was in jeopardy, but thanks to his own activity and the vigilance of the Police, the place was soon cleared of the scoundrels.

Thus ended the first shastrarth at Kashi. Swami Dayanand did not leave the town at once. On the contrary, he stayed for three months longer, proclaiming the falseness of idolatry with the beat of drums, and preaching to all the true doctrine. Perhaps the Maharaja of Kashi and the Pandits were not prepared for this they sought vengeance in sending forth the flat that henceforth no true follower of orthodoxy should visit the Swami under pain of incurring the penalty that attends the omission of a great crime. Foul-play was also had recourse to.

Once the Swami narrowly escaped being poisoned. A Brahman bringing victuals for him, the Swami declined accepting the offering inasmuch as he had already had his meal; but not to disappoint the Brahman entirely, he took the betel-leaf from him and put it into his mouth to chew it. The taste was curious, and the Swami knew at once that it was poisoned. He spat out the deadly leaf, and, in order that the fact of its being poisoned might be fully authenticated, his well-wishers had it sent to the hospital and analysed. The Swami's suspicions turned out to be well-founded.

Press on Kashi Shastrarth

The shastrarth at Kashi was an event of the greatest importance, and created a profound sensation through out the country. The utter incapacity of the most famous Banaras Pandits to cope with Swami Dayanand in learning and argument, and the unrighteous course which they had finally adopted to overcome him and to wipe out their disgrace, were duly noticed by the Press in every part of India and freely commented upon.

Hindu Commentator

We shall have to content ourselves with quoting the remarks of only a few of the papers. The *Hindu Commentator*, a Sanskrit journal of Calcutta, whose editor was present at the discussion and took notes, wrote, as follows, in this issue of December, 1869:

> "Swami Dayanand is a Sadhu, who has girded up his loins to destroy falsehood by the dissemination of truth.
>
> Swami Dayanand (S.D): Do Indra and other devatas (Gods) exist in heaven (swarga)?
>
> Swami Vishuddhanand (S.V.): *The very mantras of the Vedas are devtas.*
>
> (At this answer the Maharaja of Kashi frowned)
>
> S.D.: How is worship to be done, then?
>
> S.V.: *Through the image of Shaligram, etc.*
>
> S.D.: Where is this written in the Vedas?
>
> S.V.: *The Sama Veda alone has a thousand shakhas. Have your read them all?*
>
> S.D.: Listen! Listen! The thousand shakhas mean nothing more than that the Veda can be interpreted in a thousand ways. The Samhita is one and one only.
>
> S.V.: *Yes, even that or space is God.*
>
> S.D.: (With a smile) - That is the Ishwara! But of that which is irrelevant, it is utterly useless to talk here. The discussion here is on idol-worship. In support of that you must cite authorities.
>
> S.V.: *(Placing his hand on the Swami's back) - Mendicant, thou has not finished thy education yet; study yet a while.*
>
> S.D.: (Removing his hand) - Has thou read everything?
>
> S.V.: *(With a sarcastic laugh) - Yes, I have read everything.*
>
> S.D.: (Looking him full in the face) - Vyakarna also?

S.V.: *Yes, that also.*

S.D.: (Sternly) - What is the Kalma Sangya (retained object)? (In a voice of thunder) - Answer, answer!

"When Vishuddhanand could make no reply to this, Bal Shastri, who could not but see that the honour of Kashi was at stake, and that utter disgrace would be the portion of the orthodox Pandits (if the question remained unanswered), came forward to save his great Pandit Vishuddanand and said: 'I shall reply to this.' The Swami replied: 'Do you explain what the Kalma sangya is'? Bal Shastri replied that the definition hand not been given, but that the commentator had, in a certain sutra, treated it as uphas (jest or something too insignificant to taken notice of.). Upon this the Swami said: 'In the commentary upon what Sutra has the definition not been given, and the uphas only been indulged in? Illustrate your answer by examples.' Upon this Bal Shastri and the other Pandits also said nothing and preserved silence.

"The Maharaja of Kashi heard the shastrarth from beginning to end, and was not at all satisfied. And upon this he thus spoke "Although Dayanand is stubborn and ignorant, yet no one Pandit can defeat him in any way. He is like Karna, who six warriors, joining together, felled to the ground. When no strength remained in him, he fell. Hear more. This discussion does not end by merely defeating Dayanand. Let all the Pandits join together and discuss, and having prepared a book containing the arguments for and against idolatry, publish it."

"Shri Hari Krishan Vyas, Shri Jainarian Tarak Panchanan, Shri Krishan Vedant Saraswati, etc., who were present and were counted among the learned, observed that the shastrarth had not been satisfactory conducted, though it was true that Dayanand had been defeated!"

The *Tattva Bodhni* of Calcutta wrote in its issue for 1794 Shalvahan:

> "Thanks to the efforts of the Ruler of Kashi, the Pandits from different places held a shastrarth with the object of refuting the contention above specified, but from the perusal of the pamphlet (*Sattya Dharma Vichar*) it appears that no Pandit could defeat the Swami

> by proving idolatry justifiable. For this reason the Swami ought to be regarded as the greatest Pandits of the Vedas."

Again, in its issue for Aswaj, 1794, Shalvahan it wrote: "At this time Swami Dayanand Saraswati, a Veda-knowing Pandit, going into Kashi, etc., proclaimed that the Vedas did not enjoin idolatry. Upon this a grand meeting of the Kashi Pandits and of Pandits from other places was held under the auspices of the Ruler of Kashi, but not a single Pandit could produce authority in support of idol-worship from the Vedas."

The *Rohilkhand Akhbar* wrote in November, 1869:

> "Dayanand Saraswati Swami obtained a victory over the Banaras Pandits, and the Banaras Pandits falsely gave out that they had been victorious."

The *Gyan Pradinst Patrika* of Lahore wrote in April, 1870:

> "It is apparent from what both parties said that the shastrarth between the Kashi Pandits and the Sanyasi was mostly on subjects perfectly irrelevant, but there can be no doubt that, when discussing the subject of idolatry, the Pandits could not prove it on the authority of the Vedas."

Hindu Patriot

The *Hindu Patriot* of 17th January 1870, had the following in connection with the shastrarth:

> "The stronghold of Hindu idolatry and bigotry which, according to Hindu mythology, is not liable to the influence of earthquakes, has lately been shaken to its foundation by the appearance of a sage from Guzerat, the name of this great personage is Dayanand Saraswati. He has come with the vowed object of giving a deathblow to the system of Hindu worship.
> "He considers the Vedas to be the only religious books worthy of regard, and styles the Puranas as cunningly-devised fables - the inventions of some shrewd Brahmans in the later period for the subservience of their selfish motives.

"The Vedas, says he, entirely ignore idol-worship, and he challenges the Pandits and great men of Banaras to meet him in argument. A curious and protracted *logomachi* took place between Dayanand Saraswati and the Pandits, but the latter, notwithstanding their boasted learning and deep insight into the Sahastras, met with a signal discomfiture. Finding it impossible to overcome the great man by a regular discussion, the Pandits resorted to the adoption of a sinister course to sub-serve their purpose. They made over to the sage an extract from the Puranas that savoured of idolatry, and handed it over to the Saraswati, saying that it is a text from the Vedas. The latter was pondering over it, when the host of Pandits, headed by the Maharaja himself, clapped their hands, signifying the defeat of the great Pandit in the religious warfare. Though mortified greatly at the unmanly conduct and bad treatment of the Maharaja, Dayanand Swami has not lost courage. He is still waging the religious contest with more earnestness than ever. He has the shield of truth to protect him, and his banner of victory is waved in the air."

"The Pandit has lately published a pamphlet, entitled the *Sattya Dharma Vichar*, containing particulars of the religious contest above alluded to, had has issued a circular calling on the Pandits of Banaras to show the part of the Vedas which sanctions idol-worship. No one has ventured to make his appearance."

"Hearing the great fame of the sage, we made up our minds to pay him a visit, and accordingly went to Anandbag, near Durga Vati in Banaras, in which romantic garden he has taken up his temporary residence. The Rishi-like appearance of the venerable Pandit, his cheerful countenance and childlike simplicity, made on our minds an impression never to be effaced. When he began to speak, *manna* dropped from his lips, and the wise instructions he gave us forces us to the conviction that the golden age of India has not altogether disappeared."

"The great Pandit after 18 years of research into the Vedas has come to the conclusion that they do not savour of idolatry at all, and with the view of resuscitation the Vedic religion of the ancient sages of India, he has come out on his mission of religious reformation. He has bid adieu to all worldly enjoyments, he has assumed the austerities of an anchorite, and is buoyant with the hope of regenerating Hinduism and securing a lasting boon for his countrymen. With the view of promulgating correct theistic doctrines and dispelling h misunderstanding of the present Sanyasis and Pandits who hold pantheism to be the main doctrine of the Vedas, he is now appealing to his educated and enlightened brethren to establish a Vedic school, the teachership of which he will most gladly accept.

Christian Intelligencer, Banaras

"The fame of the reformer, who lately put the whole city of Banaras in commotion, seems to have gone abroad. Some account, therefore, of him and his views and the public disputation held with him, from one who was present oat the disputation, and met and conversed with the reformer several times before and after that event, will perhaps be not uninteresting to the reader of the *Intelligencer*.

"The name of the reformer is Dayanand Saraswati Swami. He is a native of some village in Guzerat. He is a fine-looking man, large and well-proportioned; his face, especially, expressive of much intelligence. His outward appearance is that of a Sanyasi or a religious beggar, almost entirely naked. He speaks Sanskrit fluently, never stopping wile speaking, though his Sanskrit is not of the polished kind and often not even correct. He is good reasoner, and pretty fair in a controversy, at least so far that he generally allows his opponent to state his case without interruption; but extremely authoritative in all his positions. His case and mind is made up, and believing his acquaintance with the Vedas to be superior to that of any of his adversaries, he will listen with a kind of contemptuous courtesy to anything that they may have to bring forward, and often, especially in the case of inferior Pandits, only answers, by authoritative assertions, to the contrary."

"He is well-versed in the Vedas. He is devoted himself entirely to the study of the Vedas from his eleventh year, and thus he is more practically conversant with them than most, if not all, of the great Pandits of Banaras, who only know them second hand or even less. At any rate, and this is the most remarkable feature distinguishing from other Pandits, he is an independent student of the Vedas, and free from the trammels of traditional interpretation. The standard commentary of the famous Sayanacharya is held of little account by him. It can be no wonder, therefore, that his Vedic studies conducted in that spirit led him to the conviction that almost the whole of the comparatively modern Hinduism is inactive and irreconcilable contradiction with the Vedas.

"Being an active character, he determined not to keep his conviction to himself but to impart it to his countrymen, and to try and effect an entire reform of the Hindu society. Briefly, his object is to place the Hindu society exactly in the state it was in two thousand years ago, that is, at the time when there existed none of the present Six schools of Philosophy, and not one of the eighteen Puranas, the source of modern Hinduism with its caste and idolatry, when the Vedas and the Vedic religion alone were in the ascendant, when one God only was adored, and the

Vedas only were studied, and the sacrifice of *homa* only was, with all the attendant rites, performed by the Brahmans - for themselves, the Kshatryas and Vaishyas. At least is the fond ambition of this reformer.

"But history is a stranger to such changes. No community or nation, especially on like the Hindu, will attempt, or desire to attempt, to step back into the state in which it was two thousand years back. It is, however, not improbable that his efforts may pave the way of another reform, an it's not impossible that he may succeed in convincing the Hindus that their existing religions is entirely at variance with the teachings of the Vedas.

"Of this fact, the generality of the Hindus are totally ignorant, and the few who are conscious of it, or who have come to suspect the reality, think it safest to preserve silence on the point. If they are once convinced of the fundamental error, there is not the slightest doubt that they will at once give up the Hindu Religion. For their faith in the prevailing Hindu Religion is the result of a conviction on their part that the religion has been so from ancient times - that it is the religion of their remote ancestors, who, it is believed, were directly inspired by God. The Vedic period cannot be brought back, it is dead and gone, it cannot be resuscitated.

"The conditions, which may now be brought about, must be different, more or less. We have hopes that the Christian Religion will now spread. At all events, the religion that will now spread will be identical with something superior to the present idolatry and the restrictions of caste. I must, however, declare that I am not sure whether this reformer's efforts in the interest of reform will be successful even so far. He travels up and down the banks of the Ganges, and stops here and there in the larger towns to disseminate his views; but, as far as I could ascertain, he seems to have met nowhere with much success except at Farrukhabad, near Kanpur, where, indeed, the report is to be trusted, his success has been complete.

"The Brahmans of that place in a body are said to have declared for him and to have cleared the temples of all idols. It is certain that a very rich Maharaja of that place had become a convert to his views, and has established a school where reformed Hinduism is taught. It is not unlikely that, perceiving the extent of his influence, all those poor Brahmans should have become his followers, who get their living from him. This seems to be the fact and anything more we are told is probably exaggeration.

"His arrival at Banaras was in reality a failure. The excitement which his arrival here produced at first was prodigious, but it has largely subsided, though it still prevails among many to a certain extent. If the people of our mission were to act wisely on the present occasion, and some secret help were given to the movement of this reformer, it is not improbable that what his previous attempts have been unable to achieve, may be accomplished now.

"The date of his arrival at Banaras, I do not know. It must have been in the beginning of October, I was then absent. I first saw him after my return in November. I went to see him after my return in November. I went to see in company with the Prince of Bharatpur and one or two Pandits. The excitement was then at its height. The whole of the Brahmanic and educated population of Banaras seemed to flock to him.

"In the verandah of small house at the end of a large garden near the monkey-tank, he was holding daily levees, for a continuous stream of people who came, eager to see and listen to, or dispute with, the novel reformer. It does not appear, however, that the heads of the orthodox party or the Pandits for the greatest repute ever visited him, unless they did it secretly. The intensity of the excitement at last induced the Raja of Banaras, in concert with his Court Pandits and other men of influence, to take some notice of the reformer, and to arrange a public disputation with him and the orthodox party, in order to allay the excitement by a defeat of the reformer. But I fear there was a determination from the beginning that they would win the day by any means, whether foul or fair.

"The disputation took place on the 17th of November, in the place where the reformer was putting up. It lasted from 3 to 7 pm The Raja himself was present and presided. The great Vedantist, the leader of the party of the Pandits, - I mean Vishuddhananda Gaur Swami, who is said never to have left his retreat before, came out from his place on the bank of the Ganges, to assist the Hindus with his erudition and to urge them on to victory. This shows how greatly the reformer was feared by these people. All the famous Pandits present, and other people, were on the spot in crowds. A posse of the Police was also in attendance, guarding the entrance and taking the necessary precautions against a rush inside. The Police I have a suspicion, were also keeping any eye on the powerful opponents surrounding the Sadhu, to prevent their dealing with him in a high-handed fashion. But there was no disturbance, and the proceedings terminated peacefully, except that at the last, when the meeting broke up, the Hindu party gave a should indicative of their unfairly acquired victory.

"This victory, gained by means, fair or foul, accomplished the object they had in view, the excitement subsided as rapidly as it had risen. The people who formerly flocked to Dayanand in crowds, now commenced to visit him in numbers which could easily be counted. The reformer came, as it were, to be outcasted, the orthodox Pandits threatening to excommunicate anyone who should dare to visit him henceforward. Shortly after the discussion in question, the reformer sent a written answer to his opponents, but nobody took any notice of it.

"A month after this he had a pamphlet, containing his teaching, published, and called upon his adversaries to furnish an immediate reply. The Hindus still declined to answer. Nevertheless, the reformer stayed where he was till the end of January, 1870, after that he left Banaras for Allahabad, to be present there at the approaching fair and to preach to the people who might attend it. When, after that, I last saw him, he had not yet decided whether, on the termination of the fair, he would go to Banaras or somewhere else. When the reformer had left the place, the Hindu party had an account of the discussion published, mentioning therein the points of dispute.

"The teachings of the reformer can be put under there heads: Those concerned with the Hindu Dharma Shastras;

- Those, with the origin of idolatry;
- Those, with the Puranas and the Caste-question.

Connected with these there are many other minor points. His views as to the teaching of the Shastras are at the bottom of his entire scheme of reform. The following books only he believes in as authoritative:

- The four Vedas
- The four Upavedas
- The six Vedangas
- The twelve Upanishads
- The Sharirak Sutras

- The Katyana Sutras
- The Yoga Bhashya (Vakavak)
- The Manu Smriti
- The Mahabharata

"Of these he believes in the Vedas because they are the word of God, and in the others because they are founded on the Vedas, or make a particular mention of the same. The remaining books, elevated to the position of "Shastras" by the Puran Hindus, as, for instance, the six Darshans and the eighteen Puranas, he regards as of minor importance, for their contents are either opposed to the teaching of the Vedas, or they are silent as regards their supreme authority. Taking his stand on this principle he refutes everything in the Hindu creed that is either clearly antagonistic to the Vedic teaching, or that does not find support in the Vedas.

"From this statement it will be evident that he does not differ with the Puranic Pandits as regards the dictum of the Shastras - that the Vedas are the supreme authority and that whatever is opposed to them is false. The point at issuer really is, what are the Vedas? Dayanand believes in the existing Vedas only, that is, in the Samhita or in whatever may be shown to be right on the authority of the same. The other Pandits, on the contrary, believe and maintain that originally there existed many other Vedic works, now no longer available, which supported every Hindu Shastra and everything Hindu not countenanced by the existing Vedas. But this very hard to prove, though certain English scholars of Sanskrit declare that the Pandits are in the right.

"Max Muller is one of these. What he says, stated briefly, is this: 'The lost Vedas were first mentioned in the discussions of the Buddhists, to prove some of the Brahmanas as parts of the Vedas. It is not easy to prove the theory. It may have been put forward (by the Brahmans) as something convenient to back up their contention with. It is dangerous argument, however, though it is though the Brahmans would never have advanced it, if they hand not regarded it as sound.'

"I am inclined to think, however, that Max Muller is not right in his argument. In as much as many things did not find support in the existing Vedas, the Brahmans (Pandits) had no alternative but either admit that such-and-such thing was not allowed by the Vedas, a suicidal admission on their part, or to assert that originally other Vedas existed, though the declaration may or may not have any foundation. The latter assertion might render their position still more critical, yet there could be no doubt as to which of the two alternatives they would prefer. Dayanand wholly denies that the Vedas were ever lost. What part may be there real fact, it will be evident to an import enquirer that if any other Vedas originally existed their general import would be the same as that of existing ones, and they could not be in any way favourable to the present Hindu Faith.

- "Idolatry and the Puranas: Dayanand utterly condemns idolatry not because it is the harmless error but because it is a positive sign. He is opposed to the worship of gods or polytheism. He believes in one only God, and in those attributes of His only which commonly begged in by theists. His God is primarily the creator of the Vedas and then of universe. Hence the Vedas, compared to the universe, are everlasting, though compared to God they are non-eternal. In the Vedas God is spoken as Atma, Agni, etc. according to the different Divine attributes, God, though distinct from the world for Dayanand does not believe in the Vedantic doctrine, that everything is God, yet pervades and permeates it as the principle of life. To illustrate Dayanand's position: God is believed in as Agni because Agni means life, and consequently He is worshipped through Agni (fire). To avoid misapprehension it must be distinctly understood that when he says that God in the universe is Agni, by Agni he does not mean fire, but that something which stands for Spirit and Life. Again he does not mean that this ordinary fire represents the Divine form or is a Divine representative, but only this, that it pre-eminently reveals His glory presence, and that, being such a manifester of Divine glory, God can be very well worshipped through it. The Agni it self should not be worshipped but should be sued only as a medium of His worship. The worship of God consists primarily in these there things:

- Studying the Vedas, for the acquisition of Divine Knowledge.
- Obeying Moral laws as the commandments of God.
- Adoring the divinity through the Agnihotra, etc.

"By doing these there things salvation may be attained. There never was an incarnation (of the Deity) for man's salvation, nor can there ever be one. Such a thing is opposed to the attributes of the Deity. Thus Dayanand condemns Hindu incarnations as thoroughly as he does the Christian incarnation. In other words, he has no faith whatever in Divine incarnation. And if there were ever any incarnations, these were those of the sages and saints (devtas) and not of God. Consequently, the reformer runs down nearly all the Puranic stories or legends, and especially the lila of Krishna.

"Caste, etc. - This reformer looks upon caste as a merely political (civil) institution, established by the rulers of the times for the convenience and comfort of their subjects, and not as a natural or religious mark. It is not a natural mark or symbol, inasmuch, as God did not create the four castes as four distinct kinds of men; on the contrary, all human beings are the same in their general and species, and it is not a religious mark inasmuch as the salvation and the destiny of men in the world to come do not depend on caste.

"The castes are merely different professions or privileges, and were organised by those in power to prevent confusion, and for the better discharge of the duties of different kinds. Certain persons, specially fitted for the purpose, were chosen by Royalty for conducting worship and for the cultivation of moral science and philosophy, and these were named *Brahmans*. Others were constituted *Kshatryas*, to guard the empire against external danger and to preserve internal order; the *Vaishya* class was organised for trade and commerce and for agriculture, while the people that yet remained were put into the *Shudra* order, to serve all.

"Every caste was granted privileges of a distinct nature, and they were made hereditary. But inasmuch as all these divisions were made and fixed by Royalty. Royalty alone can elevate, to the position of a Vaishya or Kshatrya or a Brahman, any Shudra that may be deemed worthy of the promotion. Similarly, one who deserves to be degraded may be degraded to the position of a Shudra by Royalty. To be brief, every Brahman, who is incompetent to perform the duties of a Brahman, falls at once to the level of Shudra, and every Shudra that acquires worth and excellence may rise to be a Brahman. The individual concerned, however, has no power to make the change in his status; the Royalty alone will do it for him. The last named condition renders the reformer's theory impracticable. Government, in these days, has nothing to do with the regulation of privileges of this nature. In other words it should be the concern of the *biradari* itself to degrade an immoral Brahman to the level of a Shudra, and to exalt a good and intelligent Shudra to the position of a Brahman.

"The discussion commenced by Dayanand, asking Pandit Tara Charan, the Raja's Court Pandit, who had been appointed to defend the cause of orthodoxy, whether he admitted the Vedas as authority. When this had been agreed to, he requested Tara Charan to produce passages from the Vedas sanctioning idolatry, *pashanadipujna* (worship of stones, etc.). Instead of doing this, Tara Charan, for some time, tried to substitute proofs from the Puranas.

"At last Dayanand happening to say that he only admitted Manu Smriti, Sharirak Sutras, etc. as authoritative, because founded on the Vedas. Vishuddhanand, the great Vedantist interfered, and quoting a Vedant Sutra from the Sharirak Sutras, asked Dayanand to show that it was founded on the Vedas. After some hesitation Dayanand replied that he could do this only after referring to the Vedas, as he did not remember the whole of them. Vishuddanand then tauntingly said that if he could not do that, he should not set himself up as a teacher in Banaras. Dayanand replied that none of the Pandits had the whole of the Vedas in his memory. Thereupon Vishuddhanand and several others asserted that they knew the whole of the Vedas by heart.

"Then followed several questions, wholly irrelevant to the subject under discussion, but put by Dayanand to show that his opponents has asserted more than they could justify. They could not answer none of his questions. At last some Pandits took up the thread of the discussion again by asking Dayanand, whether the terms *'pratima'* (likeness) and *'purti'* (fullness), occurring in the Vedas, did not sanction idolatry. He answered that rightly interpreted they did not do so. As none of the opponents objected to his interpretation, it is plain that they either perceived the correctness of it, or were too little acquainted with the Vedas to venture to contradict it.

"Then Madhvacharya, a Pandit of not repute, produced two leaves of a Vedic manuscript, and reading a passage containing the word 'Puranas' asked to what this term referred. Dayanand replied: it was there simply an adjective, meaning ancient, and not the proper name. Vishuddhanand challenging this interpretation, some discussion followed as to its grammatical correctness; but at last all seemed to acquiesce in it. Then Madhvacharya again produced two other leaves of a Vedic manuscript, and read a passage with this purport that upon the completion of a *yajna* (sacrifice) the reading of the Puranas should be heard on the tenth day, and asked how the term Puranas could be there an adjective. Dayanand took the manuscript in his hand and began to meditate what answer he should give. His opponents wanted but two minutes, and as still no answer was forthcoming, they rose, jeering and calling out, that he was unable and was defeated, and went away. The answer he afterwards published in his pamphlet.

"Unquestionably, Dayanand should have had more time. It is, however, apparent that there was some difficulty in replying, and Dayanand subsequently published his answer in the form of a pamphlet, declaring that word *'vidya'* ought to be affixed to the word 'Purana', the compound meaning the ancient knowledge of the Veda. This answer is not satisfactory. There cannot be much doubt in this, that the word 'Puranan' here stands for the eighteen Puranas. But as the passage is out of a Brahmana of the Samveda, which contains many modern additions, its value would not, after all, be much in the eyes of the non-Hindus, and, I suspect, even of Dayanand; for he once admitted to me that the Brahmanas did contain modern interpolated portions, and that any passage sanctioning idolatry, was to be considered as such as a spurious portion.

> "This reformer is not unacquainted with the Christian religion. He has read the Gospels, though, in my opinion, not very carefully. I had a talk with Dayanand on the subject. At present his own scheme of reform claims his special attention, and he cannot afford to devote much time to the investigation of a different faith".

A correspondent of the Pioneer, writing to the paper, said that Swami Dayanand had failed to make out his case against the Banaras Pandits, and in consequence had lost his prestige. To quote his own words, "the Swami hung down his head, and the Pandits clapped their hands in triumph. An attempt was made by some turbulent spirits to hoot the Swami, and to inflict a personal chastisement on him for his audacity in questioning the propriety of the national mode of worship, but the presence of the Maharaja quenched the thirst of their spirit." In answer to what the writer calls an "unvarnished account of the discussion." The following lines appeared in the leading Anglo-Indian paper of India:

> "I refrain from giving the details of the discussion, for they would hardly be intelligible to the majority of your readers. Those who take a special interest in the controversy may refer to a small pamphlet, entitle the Shastrarth, which can be had of Messrs. Brij Bhooshan Dass, of Banaras. Suffice it to say that the question at issue was whether idolatry is sanctioned by the Vedas which, according to the orthodox Hindu, are Divine Revelation. The Swami maintained that the Vedas do not inculcate idolatry, and the Pandits did not produce at the time, nor have they produced since, a single passage from the Vedas that could dislodge the Swami from his position. The answers of the Pandits were extremely evasive. The whole controversy was no better than a regular *tamasha*, for the Brahmans did not confine their arguments to the point at issue, but carried on altercations on various points of Hindu jurisprudence, logic, and Sanskrit grammar, which had not the least bearing on the main question. How can your correspondent, in the face of the above facts,

> boldly assert that the Swami got the 'worst of the fight,' I leave for your impartial readers to judge."

Shastrarth at Haridwar

The Kumbha Fair had left the saddest impression on the mind of Swami Dayanand. He had gone there with great hopes, had put his whole energy into the work that had carried him thither, but for all that, the Fair left his spirits weighed down and depressed. So much idolatry, so much degrading and debasing adoration of the temporal, so much chicanery and fraud, so much of all that is low and mean, he had never before seen in one single spot, and is soul sickened at the sight.

It was not any ignorant and illiterate that clung to and cherished error, that did what should not be done, that followed and worshipped what should not be followed and worshipped, but even learned Pandits, and Sadhus deliberately went in for practices and advocated views that reason and authority alike condemned as objectionable and injurious. Could one individual correct the perverted the judgement of millions, could he cope with any success with the hydra-headed monster of unwisdom and delusion that sat enthroned on the heart of the mighty, myriad-manned Hinduism and regulated its life of thought and action?

The spectre of doubt rose in Dayanand's mind and he felt 'despondent' "The nation is leagued against itself, knowingly courting its destruction, and hard it is to help it," mused he. As might be expected, the fit of despondency did not last long, the great man's soul rose above doubt and despair, and he exclaimed, "I must go on; all that I need is more force - moral and spiritual discipline (tapa)." The realisation, by the Swami, of the need of having more tapa (force) was followed by his distributing among his followers all he had in the shape of clothes and utensils and cash, sending out of his money Rs. 35 together with a copy of the Mahabhashya, to his guru at Mathura. Kailas Parvat Swami who happened to be with Dayanand when the distribution took place, asked the meaning of this strange behaviour. Dayanand's reply was, that he wanted to be perfectly independent and unencumbered, to be absolutely simple in life, and to teach unhampered and unfettered. All this took place about a week or two after the Fair had come to an end.

Swami Dayanand had now nothing but his simple robe on, and his kamandal, and he began to be much alone. But it would not do. Many people who knew him, sought him out, and disturbed his devotions. One day, some one, a selfish Brahman, no doubt, writing on a slip of paper in Sanskrit the words - The Vedas are nowhere compared to the Bhagwat, pasted the slip against the door of Dayanand's hut. When the offensive words caught the Swami's eye, his heart filled with indignation and he commenced denouncing and exposing the Bhagwat again. Not that his in any way affected his recently-formed resolution. He would wander along the banks of the Ganges, he said, till his tapa was complete, and during these wanderings he would speak in Sanskrit alone.

Leaving Haridwar, Swami Dayanand repaired to Rishikesh, and, after staying there for four or five days, he returned to Kankhal, and following the course of the stream, arrived at Landhora. He had not eaten anything for the last three days, and felt terribly hungry. When he found that he could hold out no longer, he asked a peasant for something to eat. The man gave him three bananas (fruit of the eggplant), and with these he appeased his hunger. Self-denial and self-control of this kind was practised day after day, and with the greatest cheerfulness.

At night the Swami would lie down on the bare ground, on sand, wherever it was to be had. If anybody wanted to speak to him, he would answer him in Sanskrit only. Now and then a shastrarth would be held, and on such occasions also, the remarks he had to make would be made in Sanskrit alone.

He would not stop long in one place: on the country, his movements were always rapid, and if he was here today, tomorrow he might, be found miles away. But wherever he went, his virtue and profound learning drew crowds. He taught Gayatri to all who came to him, and gave the Yajnopavit to the "twice-born" in large numbers. At Miranpur (a village 20 miles from Roorkee) he had a discussion with the Pandits for two days.

At the request of the Thakur Sher Singh of Karmvas (a village) the Swami, assisted by some forty pandits from Anupshahar, Danpur, Karnvas, Ahmednagar, Ramgarh, Jahangirabad, etc., helped in the performance of a "Yajna" on a grand scale. So well was everything managed and so faithfully the ancient ritual followed, that the function produced the happiest effect on the mind of the population in the neighbourhood. A desire to tread once more in the footsteps of the sages O yore was aroused in the mind of the Twice-born classes, and Brahmans and Ksahatryas and Vaishayas thronged around the Swami from all sides, with a prayer to be invested with the "sacred thread."

Nothing could give him greater pleasure than to comply with such a prayer. But at the same time he did positive work, he took care that the negative was not left undone. The preaching of the Gurumantra and the investiture with the sacred thread and similar other things were uniformly followed (provided the Swami's leisure permitted) with a merciless exposure of the Puranas, and of the Tantras, Vammargism, polytheism, and so on.

"Whatever makes you forget virtue in the most comprehensive sense of the word, he would say, addressing the people, in the course of his observations, "whatever makes you take to drinking, to adultery, to stealing, to lying and so on, the same is the destroyer of the soul, and must be shunned."

At Anupshahara discussion on idol-worship took place with Shastri Hira Vallabha. It lasted for about six days and as the condition of the shastrarth was, that whichsoever of the parties was defeated, the same should accept the beliefs of the other, the Shastri, on finding the victory declare itself for Dayanand, rose from his seat, and, in the presence of the full assembly, acknowledged, in Sanskrit, that the learned Sannyasi taught nothing but the truth, and that the worship of stocks and stones was false.

After this taking up the chauki on which the thakurs (idols) were placed, he flung it into the Ganges. On the same day, on Pandit Tika Ram, who was a priest in a temple situated on the bank of the stream, severed his connection with the temple and idols for good, and got employment for which his literary attainments fitted him. Also four more individuals renounced idol-worship, and, casting away their necklaces and rosaries, became the worshippers of the one true God!

Well has Mehta Aminchand sung:

> "The Dandi has appeared, the hypocrites have betaken themselves to their hiding-places, the vain and conceited are in a fright, the vile and the unjust (with them).
>
> "Shining with the effulgence of knowledge, has the sun come forth, dispelling the gloom and ushering in the light.
>
> "The Swami, known by the name of Dayanand, has come into meeting, with the thunder-roar of the lion.
>
> "He advocates truth and denounces fraud, thus holding up the signs and symbols of superstition to the contempt and ridicule of the world.
>
> "The idle talkers, the disbelievers in God, and the believers in Mythology, are rending the air with their cries.
>
> "Great atheists have become theists and wait upon him with folded hands.
>
> "By his Veda-given strength and his cogent argument he has transformed Kaliyuga into its opposite.
>
> "By the force of unbroken austerity and by the splendour and might of his spiritual power, he has struck terror into the hearts of he wicked.
>
> "He is Yogishwara, a great Rishi, perfect in self-knowledge, one who is triumphant everywhere by the might of his truth."

Shastrarth at Kanpur

The pasting up of the foregoing manifesto in different parts of Kanpur, and the presence of the author of the manifesto in the population of that town, produced the result that might naturally be expected. The entire Hindu community was in a ferment, and the representatives of orthodoxy, its leaders, were in a state of positive alarm.

A man named Brahmanand Saraswati was put forward to try conclusions with the 'heretic' Sanyasi, and duly waited upon the latter with a large following, but all his arguments taking the form of invective and anathema, the discussion proved nothing but a disgusting farce, and evidently extremely disappointing to his admirers, as, without much delay, they appeared at the Swami's quarters with their favourite Pundit Haldar Ojha, perhaps the most astute and learned champion of the Puranic Faith in their city, at the time.

It was a tremendous gathering that was to hear the shastraarth, being composed of no less than twenty thousand persons, or thereabout. The official element was fully represented. Mr. W. Thaine, Joint Magistrate of Kanpur, and a tolerable Sanskrit Scholar, being nominated *madhyastha*. The discussion commenced at 2 pm. (31st July, 1869), and parties spoke in Sanskrit only.

At the sunset Pandit Haldar Ojha, addressing the Swami, declared that the manifesto he had issued was grammatically faulty. To this the Swami replied that the Pandit was talking after the manner of school-boys and not after two serious and grave men of advanced years, who, in the hearing of thousands, were to speak on a subject of greatest importance. "If you think," he added, "my manifesto grammatically faulty, come to me tomorrow, when we are both at leisure, and I will make everything clear to you."

The rebuke had its effect and the Pandit came to the point without any longer beating about the bush. Asking Swami Dayanand if he believed in the Mahabharata, and getting an answer in the affirmative, the Pandit quoted a verse from the book, saying that a "Bhil learnt archery by practising in the presence of an image of Dronacharya," and the observed that idol-worship was justifiable on the authority of the great Epic.

To this the Swami replied: "I want you to quote a passage which enjoins idol-worship. That which you have quoted contains no injunction whatever: all that it says is, that a certain Bhil did such a thing, as the ignorant and illiterate will always do. The Bhil was not a Rishi or a Muni, nor had he been taught to do what he did by an (saint or sage)."

To this no answer was forthcoming, and the next question, which the Pandit asked, was: "If the Veda does not enjoin idol-worship, where does it condemn it? Let the Swami Show it." The Swami made an exhaustive reply, and as soon as he had done speaking, Mr. Thaine, taking a piece of paper containing something from the Pandit's pen, handed it over to the Swami and asked him to decipher it. The Swami did as desired, thereby removing the Joint-Magistrate's doubt, as to whether the Sanyasi, though such an eloquent speaker, could actually read.

Next Mr. Thaine asked the Swami: "What do you believe in?" "In the one only God," was the reply. Upon this dropping a courtesy to the Swami, he rose and, taking up his hat and stick, left the assembly. This was a signal for dispersion, but the mob, inspired by the leaders, would not disperse quietly. "Hail, mother Ganges, hail!" they shouted out at the top of their voice, and an admirer of the Pandit went so far as to throw piece over his head, bawling out at the same time that the Swami had been defeated!

That the imaginary victory of the Pandit might have all the weight of a genuine fact, a man named Guru Parshad waited upon the Editor of the Sho'la-i-Toor on the following day, with an account of the discussion, for insertion in the Paper. The Editor declined to accede to his request, on the ground that the account was one-sided statement, and that, in the event of its appearance in the Sho'la-i-Toor complications might arise, which might place the press in a serious position and cause it heavy loss. "The officials, you know, were present at the discussion," he observed, "and their testimony would have weight in a Court of law." Guru Parshad told him not to fear, adding that, if it came to the worst, he should be ready to spend as much as ten thousand rupees from his own pocket to shield the Paper. The assurance had its effect, and the following lines in connection with the shastrarth appeared in the Sho'la -i-Toor of 3rd August, 1869:

> "In our last issue we announced the arrival in this city of Dayanand Saraswati Sanyasi, and the fact that a shastrarth had been arranged between him and the Pandit Haldar Ojha, to come off on the 31st of July (1869). The discussion did take place on the date specified. From the very day, Dayanand Saraswati, in

> the disguise of a Sanyasi, came and took up his quarters at the newly-constructed *ghat* at Lala Dargahi Lal, Pleader, near the Ganges, a stir has been created in the city and its neighbourhood. The high and low have all come to see him, and he was warned every one against 'idol-worship,' saying that it is unjustifiable.
>
> "Coming to hear of this teaching of the Swami, the rises of the city, as well as its learned Pandits, went to the Swami and gave him proofs of every description, on the authority of the Shastras, in support of 'Idol-worship.' Upon this the Swami declared that twenty-one Shastras alone were of Divine Origin, and the rest nothing but idle gossip and unworthy of being followed.

In as much as it is objectionable in all creeds and among all classes to speak harsh of a deity or God, the practice being nothing short of 'hellish' according to the Hindu creed, it was this unanimous opinion of Messrs. Guru Parshad Shukla and Prag Narain Tiwari that a shastrarth ought to be held, so that proofs in support of idolatry might be furnished.

With this object in view the name of an Englishman, who is thoroughly versed in Sanskrit, etc., was proposed as that of a person who could act as *madhyastha*. It was no other than Mr. Thaine, the Assistant Collector, Kanpur District, who possess a sound and perfect knowledge of Vyakarna, etc., on whom this responsibility devolved. Lachhman Shastri of Atora was also summoned and appointed to act as *madhyastha* of the shastrarth between Haldar Ojha and Dayanand Saraswati.

"The discussion was take place at 2 p.m. on 30th July, 1869 at the hour fixed, the learned Pandits, the *Raeeses*, the official of the city and others present at the *ghat* made up a huge crowd, and the people from the neighbourhood had also thronged there. The shastrarth commenced between Haldar Ojha and Dayanand Saraswati on 'Idol-worship.' Whatever statements the Saraswati made in condemnation of idolatry, to the same the Ojha replied by quoting from the Shruti, Smriti, the Vedas, the Upanishads, the Bharta, the Manu Smriti and other works which, as the Swami in his printed manifesto says, constitute the 'Vedas.' He further showed to the Englishman and the other *madhyastha* the pages on which the authorities quoted were to be found, and they read out the same. From these it was fully apparent that the worship of idols was absolutely necessary for the *Hindus*. After this the Sanyasi was asked to show, from the Shastras, authorities condemning idol-worship. The Saraswati observed, in reply, that these Shastras also contained many false things, upon which the Ojha (in continuation of his remarks) observed that 'the shadow of a *devta* (God) and of a guru (preceptor') should never be crossed. A *devta* having no shadow, the line in the Shastra should be taken as referring to the shadow of an idol.'

Lachhman Shastri, *madhyastha* quoted largely from the Vedas, the Vedanta, the Mimansa, from the Dharma Shastras, etc., and from these quotations it appeared that the worship of idols was right. All the *madhyasthas* accepted this verdict and praised the Ojha. The statements of the *madhyastha* Lachhman Shastri, as also statements and arguments of the Ojha, were acknowledged to be true and sound, and hence the European *madhyastha* gave it as his judgement that since the Saraswati had failed to furnish proofs and to give answers according to the Shastras, it was perfectly allowable for the Hindus to do idol-worship, and further, that idolatry was inculcated in the Shastras as soon as the judgement. Hence the Ojha was victorious and the Saraswati defeated.

As soon as the judgement was given, the *rises*, who were present there, burst into shouts of joy, declaring that the Ojha had won the field. At this time, Mr. Prag Narain Tiwari threw, as charity, rupees and piece over the head of Ojha, and then all returned to their homes. This shastrarth was due to the energy and high-mindedness of Messrs. Shukal Parshad and Prag Narain Tiwari. Both these gentlemen have constructed, in the city of Kanpur, grand and magnificent temples at an enormous cost, and have thus done themselves good in this and fore the next world. It was proper that a shastrarth should take place in this town, and one did take place, resulting in additional glory to 'idolatry.'

As soon as the Paper was in the hands of the people, they went to the Swami and read out the account to him. He observed that he was neither glad nor sorry at what had been written; none but the foolish would recognise victory or defeat as the end of a shastrarth. The reply was far from being satisfactory to the Swami's well-wishers, and, annoyed at the want of fairness which the writer in the Paper had displayed, they waited upon Mr. Thaine, and respectfully asked him what he thought of the account, Mr. Thaine having heard the statement from beginning to end, wrote, the following letter and handed it over to them:

> "Gentlemen,
>
> "At the time in question I decided in favour of Dayanand Saraswati Faqir, and I believe his arguments are in accordance with the Vedas. I think he won the day, If you wish it, I will give you my reasons for my decision in a few days."

Yours obediently,

(Sd) W. Thaine.

"One of the arguments advanced by this gentleman was that God being all-pervading, was present in idols and images too, and hence idol-worship was "right." The Swami's reply was: "God is present in everything, and why should He be taken to be specially present in idols of stone, etc.? And, further, Why should be lifeless and unconscious be worshipped rather than the conscious and intelligent?" The Pandit was silent. -ED.

The above letter was printed with a complete refutation of the assertions in the Sho'la-i-toor, and scattered broadcast in the city. But valuable though Mr. Thaine's letter was, it was hardly indispensable. The worshippers of idols themselves furnished a stronger testimony to the truthful character of the Swami's doctrines. Snatching up their idols, they commenced throwing them in the bazaars or into the river - a procedure unquestionably annoying to the Ojha and his supporters.

Unable to see the images treated with scant respect, the Ojha had a Notice printed and copies of it pasted in scores of places, requesting the people, in Sanskrit, Hindi, and Urdu, to cease from throwing idols in the bazaars or into the river, and to restore them to their places in the temples! The Notice ran as follows:

"Many Brahmans, Kshatryas and Vaishyas, in accordance with the religion of Dayanand Saraswati, giving up their own family faith, are throwing the images of deities into the river Ganges, a practice which is most objectionable. This notice is issued in order to convey to the people, who have accepted or should come to accept the religion of the Swami, the request that they would get any idols they may have, taken into the temple belonging to Maharaj Guru Parshad Shukal, or into that belonging to Maharaj Prag Narain Tiwari. If they cannot find leisure to do it themselves, they should send us information, and we shall arrange to have removed. The sin of throwing away the images or flinging them into rivers is pointed out in Sanskrit." — *Ojha Haldar*

The editorial which appeared in the Sho'la-i-Toor of 3rd August 1869, in connection with the Ojha's Notice, might be given verbatim here:

"Through the wholesome influence of the Swami's company many people have commenced throwing their idols into the river. The Ojha has, therefore, issued a notice, declaring that the practice is objectionable according to the Hindu Shastras, and adding that whoever be disposed to throw idols into the river, the same should have them sent to the Pandit and not incur the penalty attending the sin of throwing them into the river."

Such is the might of truth. No amount of sophistry of underhand dealing or prejudice can suppress it: it must eventually vindicate its majesty and prevail in spite of them. As an illustration of the truth of this fact, we may give here the following story:

"My younger brother," says a gentleman, "having bought some publications of the Swami, brought them home. I took him severely to task for having done such a thing. The books, however, having a winning look about them, I could not resist the temptation of looking into them. And once begun, I could not leave them unfinished. The inevitable result came - I renounced the worship of idols and became a humble follower of the Vedic religion"! The story is one of the many similar ones that might be told!

Shastrarth at Farrukhabad

The leaders of orthodoxy in Furrakhabad, seeing a Sanyasi establishing schools in their midst with avowed object of reviving the study of ancient Sanskrit literature, to the prejudice of the modern productions, and preaching doctrines subversive of Puranic teaching, lost no time in calling upon Pandit Siri Gopal, a native of the Meerut District, to take up the cause of idolatry against the newcomer.

A shastrarth (debate) came off in May 1869. The Pandit quoting a verse from the Manu Smriti, which says that *puja* is due to the *devatas*, etc., contended that the worship of idols was inculcated therein. The Swami replied hat the word *'puja,'* meant honouring or showing reverence, and that in the verse quoted it signified nothing more than the doing of *Agnihotra*, or treating with respect men distinguished for their learning and virtue, the discussion was prolonged as to the meaning of the verse, and it became every moment clearer that the Pandit was unable to uphold his position, his adversary being unquestionably a man of superior learning and deeply read in the Shastras. The Pandit perceived the impression which the Sanyasi had produced, and dreading lest all should be lost, hurried off to Kashi (Banaras), and succeeded in obtaining from them a *Vyavasthapatra* in Sanskrit, supporting idolatry. The document, signed, among others, by Swami Vishuddhanand, ran as follows:

Vyavasthapatra

"The worship of the images of *Shiva, Vishnu,* etc., of *Shivalinga*, the *Shaligram* stone, and so on, which ought to be attended to by men of all the four *varnas,* is lawful on the authority of many a verse in the *Puranas*. To those who, on the authority of the Shruti and the Manu Smriti, prove the worship in question as false, and who further do not believe in the eighteen *Puranas*, in *Gaya*, the *Shraddhas*, and similar other things, we reply that their contention, that the adoration of *Shivalinga*, etc., is not in accordance with the teaching of the Vedas, is a mere assertion.

In the *Devi*, the *Atharvashirsh*, the *Gopal* and other Upanishads of the Atharva Veda, the worship of idols is allowed, even as the worship of the Linga is allowed in the *Upanishad*. And in the *Devi* and *Atharvashirsh* it is written that man who worships the *Atharvashirsh*, not knowing him, regains purity after ten million recitations! Recitations unite a deity with a new idol, and the chanting of *mantras* for endowing the idol with paranas (life), does establish, in the image, the *pranas*. And in the *Gopaltapni* it is written, the Narayan Dev said, 'Just as there are seven regions on the summit of the Meru Mountain, even so there are seven regions or cities in this resolving world, the true region among these latter being the *Brahma Gopal Puri - Mathura.*'

On the authority of this quotation there are, on this earth, twelve forests, such as the *Pradhaban,* and twelve images of the twelve *Lingas - Bhadreshwar,* etc. Here (i.e. in this world) whatsoever people worship the forms or figures, they cross the ocean of death and obtain salvation. Again, it is written in the *Adbhudhshanti* of the *Vinshiti* Brahmana of the Sama Veda, that the temples of the gods tremble, and that the idols laugh, weep, sing and feel pain.

Similarly, it is written in the *Kaushak Grah Parishishta* of the Sama Veda that the images of gods dance, shine and move. It is also written there that eight months after the weeping and roaring of the idols in a *Shivala*, the King dies and the fact is undoubted. It is further written there that the King is destroyed when the flags erected in honour of *Devraj* (chief deity) fall or are broken, or when the wild beast invade the temples, etc.

"And in the *Ashvalayam Grah parishishta* there is the injunction that in the *Naugrah Yajna* a copper image of the sun, a crystal image of the moon, and a ruby or sandalwood image of *Mangal* (Mars), should be established, on a *singhasan*. Further after giving instructions as regards the establishment of particular idols, the book says that the householder should do *havan* daily and worship the deities, for by worshipping the deities alone does the householder obtain good desires. Again it is written there that the householder is at liberty to worship *Hari-Har, Ganpati, Skandh,* or any other deity he likes. Deities are summoned into the and dismissed from idols. One having established them in fire, in the sun, in one's own heart or on a raised platform, should worship them. The idols which do not possess the exact forms of the deities they represent, into or from them their respective deities cannot be summoned or dismissed.

The deities are near unto the idols which represent their exact forms. As regards movable idols, the presence or disappearance of deities in or from them is a matter of imagination one ay or the other, and with respect to the every-being, the deities can be made to come into or depart from them at pleasure.

The worship is done by the worshipper standing before the idol facing the east, his won face being towards the west, and the temple in which the worship is done should be facing the east. And in the *Villw Upanishad* it is written that Shiva said to Sanka, 'Just as there are leaves on the tree, even such leaves should be offered unto me.'

"Now we shall speak of the worship of Mahadeva: 'The worshipper after having bathed and cleaned himself, and having made an idol of clay or some other thing, should take his seat on a spot plastered over with cowdung, etc." These words clearly prove that Bodhayana was a believer in the worship of idols."

"And in the Manu Smiriti the worship of deities, the bringing of fuel, etc., is enjoined. Kuluka, commenting on the verse containing the injunction, says that in the idol, etc., *Hari-Har*, etc., should be worshipped, and gain it is written therein - *Mridangam daivtam*, etc., which also refers to idol-worship. Hence Kuluka also speaks here of a stone-image, etc. It is, further, written therein (i.e. in Manu Smriti), - *'Jirna devayatan*, etc.'

"The shadow of *devas, raja,* and *guru*, etc." Only images can have a shadow. 'The being near to the *devas* and the Brahmans." This too can hold good of images only (i.e., the presence of the word deva shows that idol-worship is sanctioned, for being near to an idol implies the worship of the idol). Again, it is written (in the Manu Smriti): 'Temples should be erected where the boundaries meet.' What do all these thins mean? Only, that the worship of idols is perfectly allowable.

"If it be asserted, in connection with the foregoing quotations in support of idolatry, that the method of doing the worship not having been described, the worship of idols cannot be attended to (for the injunction is as good as useless), then we reply that your objection is equally telling against *Ashtika Agnihotra*, etc., for the Manu Smriti is silent as to the method of construction or performing these also.

If it be asserted that the method of doing the *Agnihotra* is set forth in the Kalpa Sutras, then we say that the method of doing idol-worship has also been described in the Bodhayana Kalpa, and this is why the Manu Smriti says nothing on the point. Bodhayana's Sutra has already been quoted. Hence the worship of *Shivalinga* being a source of progress, has been enjoined in the Shruti, the Smiriti, and in other Shastras, and this is the reason why good men do idol-worship in all the four quarters of the world. This is known to all. To assert that the *Puranas, Gaya, Shradhas,* etc. have no authority to back them, is to give a proof of one's own stupidity.

In the *Taittireya, Aranyaka* it is written: 'Brahmannanitihasan puranani, etc.,' which proves that the *Purananas* are authoritative. Similarly, the words in the *Atharvashirsh* are: 'Itihas purananam.'

"Manu also has said: 'In the *pitrikarm,* he should read to his class-fellow.' In the Mahabharata too it is written: 'Let him know the Veda by means of the *ithasas* and the *puranas.*' In the *Anushashan Parab* it is written: 'That whatever reward is obtained by reading the eighteen *Puranas,* etc.'

"On strength of the foregoing authorities, the *Puranas* are proved to be authoritative. Hence *Gaya, Shradhas,* etc., must be accepted an indisputably authoritative institutions. Similarly, idol-worship is also lawful on the authority of *Shruti, Smriti, Kalpa Sutras,* etc. This had been written briefly."

The foregoing document speaks for itself. It contains two authorities from the Vedas in support of idol-worship, and any passages that it may be said to embody in support of idol-worship from the *Shastras,* either do not, in point of fact, uphold idolatry, or, being at variance with the teaching of the Scripture, are spurious and unauthoritative, and must be rejected as such by all impartial minds. The document, however, was a rare acquisition to Pandit Siri Gopal, the more so, as it had been obtained without incurring much expense, and he could not make too much of it. A copy of the document was shown to the Swami, and he could not help laughing, observing at the same time, "Is that the learning of the Kashi Pandits?"

Siri Gopal had the *Vyavasthapatra* nailed to a bamboo near the place where the Swami was putting up, and the sight attracted thousands of ignorant men, who, at a word from the Pandit, began to drench it with water, being under the impression, no doubt, that the bamboo, for the time being, represented some deity, *Shivalinga* perhaps! When the Pandit was asked to repair to the Swami's quarters and have a *shastrarth* (debate), he replied: "If I go there, I shall be defeated, and if the Swami comes to me, he will be defeated. He has placed his abode under the influence of a charm!" As to the Swami, his answer to those who wasted a *shastrarth* to be held was: "What would be the good of my going and holding a *shastrarth* with a man who cannot so much as tell the masculine from the feminine gender!"

The excitement and enthusiasm of the illiterate mob, however, was tremendous, so much so that the authorities thought there was going to be a breach of the peace. One of the information furnished by Munshi Bakhtawar lal, Superintendent, the Collector was sent the Head Constable to the Swami, to enquire what the uproar meant. The Swami replied that he was not responsible for it, being in his own quarters, and that it was not fro him to bid the mob disperse. Upon this the Constable went to the Pandit and called upon him to clear the spot of the multitude. A few words from the Pandit, and as many from the Police official sternly bidding the gathering to be off, brought about the desired consummation. Two policemen were appointed to prevent overzealous followers of idolatry from breaking into the Swami quarters and creating a disturbance.

The second shastrarth which Swami Dayanand held at Furrukhabad, was that with a Pandit named Haldar, who at the request of the orthodox Furrukhabadis, had come from Kanpur for the purpose. The discussion came off on the 19th June, 1869, and was, as might be expected, on "Idol-worship."

Ere the parties had spoken much, Haldar, who was a Tantrik (believer in the Tantras), and held that indulgence in flesh and intoxication liquors, the unlawful gratification of the lower passions, and other like things, were far from being objectionable perhaps positively essential to the attainment of salvation, leaving the subject under discussion commenced defending "drinking," contending that the use of alcoholic drinks was justifiable on the occasion of a *Sautramani Yajna*.

In reply the Swami pointed out the word *sura*, when employed in connection with such *Yajnas*, did not mean alcoholic liquors, but the juice of healthy and delicious fruits. It was *samaras*, he added, that was imbibed on the occasion of a *Sautranmani Yajna*, and not an intoxicating liquor. The Swami's remarks on "drinking" certainly did not tend to advance idolatry in the affections of an audience!

Finding the ground slipping from under his feet, the Pandit Haldar asked the Swami the definition of "Sanyasi"." The Swami furnished the required definition, asking the Pandit, in his truth, the definition of "Brahman". No satisfactory answer was forthcoming, for, being a Puranic, the Pandit would not commit himself, and drifted into irrelevant matters.

The Swami did his best to bring him to the point originally under discussion, but it would not do. Quoting a *Sutra* of the Mahabhashya, the spokesman for the orthodox commenced a discussion thereon, and the Swami had no, alternative but to send for the book and show to the people assembled how the Pandit was wrong here also. The discussion lasted till one O' clock in the night.

Shastrarth at Bareilly

From Badaun the Swami repaired to Bareilly (14th August, 1879), where he became a guest of Lala Lachhmi Narayan, Treasury Clerk. His lectures commenced, and they were largely attended, the local European officials and the local Missionaries often forming par to the audience. One of the lectures was on the Puranas and similar other books. Mr. Edwards, the Commissioner, Mr. Reid, the Collector, and the Rev. Mr. Scott were present. So long as the Puranas were being exposed, the European gentlemen felt delighted and went into rears of laughter; but when the turn of the Bible came, and the birth of Christ and similar other mysteries where commented upon, the became sober and serious, and not unoften frowned. According to Lala Munshi Ram, Editor-in-Chief of Pandit Lekh Ram's Life of Swami Dayanand, the Commissioner, shortly after the lecture was over, sent for Lala Lachhmi Narayan and told him to warn the Pandit not to be very strong in his language; "for," said he, "if the ignorant Hindus and Muhammadans get excited, the lectures of your Swami Pandit will be stopped." The treasury Clerk in hesitation and fear carried the message to the Swami, but while he was trying to express himself in a roundabout fashion, not knowing how his communication would be received, the Swami grasping his meaning burst out laughing, and bade the Lala be easy. The evening lecture for the day was on "the Nature of the soul."

In importance of truth, the Swami observed:

> "People say – Don't give expression to truth, the Collector will be displeased, the Commissioner will be annoyed, and the Government will make you suffer? O ye simple ones! Let the *Chakravarti Raja* himself be displeased, if he will, I will give expression to truth alone."

And then reading a passage from the Upanishad, which says that the soul defies the attack of fire, water, weapon and of everything else material, however subtle, he resumed in a voice of thunder:

> "This body of mine is perishable, and nothing can be more ridiculous for me than to commit acts of unrighteousness for the preservation thereof. Whoever wishes may destroy it. But show me a warrior who claims that he can destroy my *Soul*. So long as such a warrior is not forthcoming in the world, so long I am not prepared even to think that I shall suppress truth."

The Rev. Mr. Scott had been regular in his attendance at the Swami's lectures from the first, but one day he did not put in an appearance. The Swami, who used to call him by the name of *Bhagat* Scott; asked those around, about the cause of the Missionary's absence. The reply was that it was a Sunday, and the Missionary had to attend the Church. Upon this the Swami said that since the *Bhagat* had not come, he should himself go and see him in the Church. So in the company with some tow or three hundred men he walked off to the sacred building.

When he entered the edifice, the Reverend gentleman, who had but just finished his sermon, came down at the sight of him from the pulpit and conducted him to it, offered him the seat there, and requested him to say something. The Swami complied, and, without taking the preferred seat, spoke fa a few minutes on "Man-worship." The Missionaries of Bareilly came to the determination of holding a discussion with the Swami, and it was at last settled that is should come off on 25th august, 1879. The subjects to be taken up were:

- 'Transmigration of Souls,' the Swami speaking for, and the Rev. Scott against.
- The doctrine of 'Incarnation,' the Rev. gentleman upholding, and the Swami refuting;
- 'Forgiveness of Sin,' (the attitude of the parties in this case being the same as in respect of the doctrine of Incarnation).

The discussion came off in the building of the local Library; in the presence of large gathering, most of the gentry and nobility of the town being among them.

Debate with Christianity on Transmigration of Souls

As agreed upon, the doctrine of the Transmigration of Souls was taken up first.

Swami: "The inherent qualities, activities and tendencies of the Soul are eternal, and the divine, attributes, Justice, mercy, etc., are also eternal. Whoever does not believe this but holds that the Soul and its attributes, etc., are born and accidental, he must also concede that they are perishable. And he must furnish satisfactory and convincing proofs, to himself and others, in respect of the origin and cause of the Soul and its attributes, etc.; for the birth of an effect in the absence of a cause is absolutely impossible. (The fact is, that the good and bad actions of the Soul, by virtue of their regularity of succession, are eternal, and the Deity, to be true to His nature, metes out, rewards and punishments for the same).

And be it known that it is impossible for the Soul to taste of pleasure or pain, except through a *body,* be it gross, or subtle or elemental.

This being the case, the soul must assume a body over and over again, for a free agent is ever doing new actions, and these accumulate and go on forming new destinies (Prarabha). Were a person to contemplate this world with eye of knowledge, the laws of nature in operation and the *Pratayaksha* and other *parmanas* would soon convince him that the doctrine under discussion is true. Only think that Monday, i.e., to day, comes over and over again; the months, the days and nights also are perpetually recurring. The wheat-seed that is sown, reproduces itself in continual succession.

Rev. Scott: "The teaching that is being now offered to us, means that we are to believe that all the Souls that there are, are being constantly born, sometimes in the body of man, sometimes in that of a bull, sometimes in that of a mortkey and anon in those of worms and insects. But this teaching is being gradually repudiated by the enlightened communities. The ancient Egyptians originally believed in the doctrine of transmigration, but subsequently they gave it up. Similarly, the Greeks, the Romans and the English at the outset believed in it and abandoned it in the end.....My question to the Pandit is, what are the arguments in support of this doctrine? When any specially remarkable proofs are given in support of the doctrine, I shall raise objections in refutation of the doctrine. In the meantime, I have to ask a few questions in connection with what has been said, and they are:

- Are Souls other than that of God also from ever?
- Shall we ever be free from birth?
- As regards your contention that all that we see in the world, is there as punishment, it may be asked: Is re-birth only for punishment, or does it proceed from some other cause?
- Another question is: Is the Deity always *sagun* or does He become *nirgun* also? Is this perpetual rebirth the result of

a special exertion of His power, or is it traceable to the operation of some natural law? - some such law, for instance, as regulates the growing of a seed, the ripening of a fruit, or the coming down of rain, etc.?

Swami Dayanand: "Three things are eternal: God, the Material cause of the universe, and the Soul. There will never be freedom from birth. Re-birth is for punishments as well for rewards. God is always *sagun* as well as *nirgun*. His natural law is only this, that He punishes or rewards, in compliance with the dictates of His absolute justice, everyman in proportion to the amount of sin or righteous action committed or performed. The admission on the part of the Padri Sahib that the doctrine of re-birth was originally believed in by his nation proves that it was an article of faith in all lands in ancient times. As to his assertion that every community that is progressing in civilization is gradually abandoning the doctrine, I would put him the question - Are all ancient things false or are some of them true also? And further, Is modern teaching true in all its entirety, or is there something untrue in it too? If the Padri Sahib should assert that the old teaching is not fit to be believed in, then the teaching of the Old Testament – the Pentateuch, etc., as well as that of the New Testament being old, when contemplated in connection with the present age, should no longer be believed in now, does not prove the thing to be true or otherwise....

"As to the Padri Sahib's words, that I should furnish proofs in support of the doctrine of Transmigration of Souls or rebirth, I got the reporters to write down at the outset that the actions, etc., of the Soul, and the attributes of justice, etc. of God are eternal. If the doctrine of Karma is to be rejected, then how would you account for God's creating in this world the wise side by side with the obtuse, the poor and indigent side by side with princes? For, doing such thing as a mere matter of whim savours of partiality, and partiality on the part of the Deity would utterly defeat the ends of His justice. When action has fruit, God is certainly just and otherwise: he never commits an act of injustice."

Rev. Scott.: "According to the assertion of Panditji all the Souls are eternal. This being the case, there is no difference in the eternity of the Souls and that of God; in other words, two existences are eternal, which, in away, means, that there are two Gods. My objection is, that this teaching is totally oppose to what is taught in the Old Testament – Pentateuch and the Gospel, and I want to enquire, in what teaching there is greater comfort: whether in the consciousness that our Souls will keep wandering, through eternity, in a state of bewilderment – sometimes in the bodies of oxen, sometimes in those of monkeys, sometimes in the repulsive frames of worms and insects, and occasionally in tenements of higher type, in a never-ending succession; or whether it is more consoling to believe that people who are striving after righteousness and do become pure, will, at last, reach a resting-place, where they will be safe form rebirth and secure from all suffering.....How, again, can God be *nirgun* and *sagun* both at the same time – with attributes and without attributes? What thing is there that is wholly destitute of properties or attributes?

"If (according to this position of yours) God does not possess the attribute of justice, how He exercise this attribute....? Moreover, if rebirth is for punishment, what punishment can there be in being made to be born again? The monkey, for instance, does not know what sins he committed (that brought down his soul into the frame of a monkey). Similarly a Padri or a Pandit, coming to assume the repulsive shape of a worm or insect, has really no punishment inflicted upon him, for it is wholly unknown to him what sins he had committed. Has anybody ever been able to remember, or can he remember, that he was a monkey at such and such a time, or that he was a jackal on such and such a occasion? When nobody in the whole world is conscious of ever having passed through such bodies, how can rebirth serve as punishment in the case of nay one whatsoever? We believe that pain is sometimes for punishment and sometimes not."

Swami Dayananand: "The fact that both (God and Soul) are eternal, does not make them equal so long as they are not equal in their attribute, powers, and so on. As it is, God is infinite, the Soul is finite; God is omniscient, and the Soul is partially knowing; God is ever pure and in a state of salvation, the Soul is only occasionally pure and sometimes in bondage and sometimes free; this being the case, both cannot be equal.

"The fact that a thing is opposed to the teachings of the Bible, does not prove that, if really true, it is false. For in the Old Testament, etc., the things that are true have, through delusion, been often declared as false, and vice versa. The teaching of that book alone can be true, in which from its beginning to its end not a single untruth is to be found. Such a book is nowhere to be found in the world except the Veda, of Divine Origin, because the teachings of the Veda alone fits in with the attributes, actions and nature of God. ..God, by virtue of His own attributes, such as omniscience, etc., is *sagun*, and He is *nirgun* when viewed as destitute of the properties of unconsciousness matter and of the characteristics of the Soul, - such as birth, death, doubt, delusion, ignorance, and so on. From what has been said, it follows as something indisputable, that there is nothing in the world which is not *sagun* and *nirgun* at the same time.

"When the sin committed by the soul exceeds the amount of merit (punya), it has to assume the body of a monkey, etc. when its merits and demerits are equal, it is born as man; and when merit exceeds demerit, it appears in the world as a sage, etc."

Rev. Scott: "Not all the ancient teaching is false, nor is the new teaching true in all its entirety. But when enlightened communities, after prolonged though and reflection, give up a thing as false, the proof is conclusive that it is false. The Old Testament is not all new compared to the Vedas. It does not at all speak of rebirth, the point at issue at this time is not whether the teachings of the Old and the New Testament is or is not false. For all that, however, the fact is insignificant that while civilized communities are firm in their belief in the Old and the New Testament, the Hindus, in proportion, as they are advancing in education, are abandoning the Vedas. If necessary, I could cite a thousand instances. If, it be asserted that all His actions are good, then where is the impossibility that the Soul also, through His grace, be so fructified as not to go down into the bodies of monkeys and jackals. As is written in our sacred Book, man has to die only once, and after that he is to be regenerated (for everlasting life).

"As regards *nirgun* and *sagun*, I have no faith in the explanation which the Swami has given of the words. *Nirgun* does not imply in a thing the existence of *gunas*. When God is *nirgun*, He cannot be *sagun*, and the case being such, who arranges for births then? I ask again: if the Soul's rebirth is for punishment, it ought to be in a position to remember why it is being punished, otherwise the purpose of punishment is utterly defeated. I enquire again, Why it is that nobody remembers that he was a monkey or a jackal in his previous birth?"

Swami Dayanand as to the first question of the Padri Sahib, the Soul is *alpagya* (possessing partial knowledge, etc.), and hence it cannot remember thing connected with the previous birth or births. The Padri Sahib ought to ask himself, 'Why do I put such a question?' For even in the present birth, a person cannot remember things connected with the first five years of his age. And when a person is in sound sleep, he cannot remember even a single thing connect with his waking-hours. And from perceptions of an effect one may be sure about the cause of that effect; the wise without an exception, concede that such is the law.

"When the fruit of merit and demerit (pap-punya) is clearly observable in the world in the form of happiness and suffering, of elevation and degradation how can one deny the existence of cause – the actions of previous birth, of which all these are the result?

"I can site the names of hundreds of men who have told me themselves - the author of the Bible in India and other scientific men of the present day, that they have given up believing in the Bible. Colonel Olcott and others also say that they do not follow the teaching of the Bible. An our educated people – F.A.'s, B.A.'s, M.A.'s, LL.D's thousands of them have no faith in the Bible, and they are all educated. This will show that the illustration the Padri Sahib gave in the interests of the Bible, does not meet the requirements of the case. There is no birth of God, for He is infinite and all-pervading, and no material frame can contain Him. He is ever in a state of salvation, and never does aught of which bondage is the result."

Rev. Scott: "The illustration of a child which Pandit gave, asserting that (when grown up) he cannot remember anything, is false, for a child does remember something at least. And the question that naturally suggests itself in this connection is, since our Souls are from eternity and since, like the child, we have become grown-up (through the lapse of years), why should not we remember something like him? But in point of fact we remember nothing. This argument deserves consideration.

"It is impossible that, being from eternity, we should have, on assuming a body, forgotten everything. And rebirth in such a case can serve no end. And a regards sleep, it appears from the (Swami's) reply that things connected with sleep are remembered. Some people hit upon great idea in sleep. Here I want to bring forward a strong objection. This teaching or rebirth encourages the commission of sin. For people say to themselves, - 'Let us do whatever we like, it will be some time before we suffer for it, and after all, a desirable kind of rebirth may fall out lot. And they further way to themselves (in their helplessness), "This succession of births is everlasting, what are we to do?" We do admit that there must be some reason for the suffering which comes to people in the world. Sometimes it is sent to the wicked as punishment, and sometimes to the wise that hey may have training of different kinds."

Swami Dayanand: "By citing the example of a child, I meant to say that the pleasure or pain which he enjoys or suffers, he cannot recall to memory of himself; he remembers it occasionally when reminded of it by somebody else.

"And the inherent qualities of the soul remain ever unchanged, it is only the accidental ones that increase or decrease. Hence the Souls is always the same, but the stock of its knowledge and information grows and grows after the fifth year (from the date of its birth) has expired. If anyone were to ask the Padri Sahib or myself now, What did you talk with such a one ten years ago? Can you recall the words and the letters you sued in their proper order?" the reply will be, that 'we can't remember or reproduce what we said, correctly'.

"If the Souls are not from ever, where have they come from? Although people do not know, for certain, what and what crimes this and that prisoner committed, yet they can infer that it must be for some crime or other that the prisoners in question are in jail, and they can take the lesson from the condition in which the prisoners are, that they (people) should never do what the prisoners did, as otherwise their state would be that of the prisoners. The

Padri Sahib has not grasped my meaning. I spoke of *Sushupti*, and not of the ordinary sleep in which one dreams. *Sushupti* is profound slumber in which nothing is remembered and no idea is hit upon or recalled. Those who have faith in no rebirth, their teaching increases sin in the world, for 'there is not rebirth,' say they, 'let us do what pleases us.'

"And this postponement of the case of a departed non-believer in birth is something hard and unreasonable. His departure from this world takes place today, and his Soul remains in custody uncared for till the day of judgement. The door of the Court is shut, and God is sitting idle. The Soul that goes into Hell, is Hell's time to come, and the actions performed by the Soul are limited, but the rewards and punishments meted out for the same are eternal in duration! This is very unjust of God. And suffering, in the absence of hope, cannot generate man. What is the cause of suffering? If suffering is sent to man as a warning, then it is for his good, but the lesson from that suffering comes only through wisdom. As to the assertion of Padri Sahib, that the Souls will enjoy bliss in a certain place for ever, will he specify the place and its geographical position?"

Rev. Scott: "As to the assertion that some qualities are retained by the Soul and some disappear and that hence it is that things in connection with rebirth are not remembered, I maintain that since some qualities are retained by the Soul, we should remember something at least in connection with our previous birth. If I had a talk with Panditji somewhere during the current year, I could not fail to remember some things at least. The illustration of sleep is out place, for if things are sometimes not remembered in sleep, they are still very often remembered. This being the case, why don't we remember things connected with our previous birth? The example of jail that ha been given, that too does not meet the requirements of the case, for it implies that punishment has only one object. In point of fact, punishment has two-fold object, - the improvement of the sufferer and to serve as a warning to the spectators. But rebirth furnishes warning only to the spectators: the man show is suffering the punishment, does not know at all why he is suffering it. As to the question where the Souls have come from, the civilized nations of the present day hold that just a seed proceeds from a seed, a tree from a tree, and nobody says that the tree existed previously, even so is one Soul born of another Soul, and one body of another body. For all this, however, it is incomprehensible in what particular manner the body comes into existence, and in what the Soul. But is not a fact that the Soul which occupies a body at present was in some other body before; it of recent birth. And when the Soul departs from this world, it will be dealt with impartially, according to the character of it actions. Hence God is not unjust: on the contrary, the fact proves Him just. As to the question where the Souls stay, we don't pretend to be omniscient that we should specify the locality where bliss is to be enjoyed. The almighty God can give the Soul a resting-place, what does it signify if we know it or not?

Swami Dayanand: "There is a stock of accidental qualities present in childhood, but it is small; the essential qualities of the Soul, however, are always the same, never varying. This fact the Padre Sahib has not been able to thoroughly grasp. To illustrate, the heat that comes into the water from fire, that is *naimittic* or accidental, but the heat that is in fire, that is essential or inherent (*swabhavik*) to it. The essential qualities or attributes of the Soul neither increase nor decrease, but the accidental qualities do increase and decrease. As to the observation of the Padri Sahib that although the sight of the prisoners in jail produces a fear in the minds of the spectators, warning them not to do what brought the prisoners in their present sorry plight, this lesson is not at all conveyed to the souls that are made to be reborn (by the Deity), for these Souls do not remember what they are suffering for, I beg to say that when people can infer a cause form an effect, why can't a sufferer draw a similar inference in regard to his sufferings.

"Suppose that a physician gets an attack of fever, and an ignorant man also. The physician, by the assistance of his knowledge, will know the cause of the fever, but the ignorant man will be unable to hit upon the right cause. Both however, are conscious of suffering, nor can even the ignorant man fail to conclude from his suffering at least this much, that intemperance or imprudence in some way or another has given him the fever. Hence the punishment he is suffering is for his future benefit. For he says to himself; 'If I do anything objectionable, the result of this will be pain to me, as it is to such and such a one.'

"If the Souls are born from Souls and bodies from bodies, the it's not God that is your Maker. This shows that what you say is far from being true. And, according to your theory, the Souls and bodies that came to be in the beginning, from what Souls and bodies did they proceed? If you assert that the proceeded from God, then God must be like unto horses, trees and stones, for an effect is always of the nature and character of its causes. And then effect is always of the nature and character of its cause. And then the postponement of the departed Soul's case for an indefinite period. The suffering with which this delay must be fraught must far exceed the pain that could come from actual punishment. If the Soul is to undergo the suffering inseparable from a postponement of its case, for what actions then can it be sent to Heaven or condemned to Hell? – there are virtually no actions to receive a reward or punishment for.

"If you are not omniscient, why do you contend that there is no rebirth? All this does not prove your theory of single birth, but does prove the doctrine of rebirth."

The Debate Continued

The discussion on the 2nd day, 26th August, was on 'Incarnation.' The opening speech was from the Missionary, and the upshot of what he said was, that whoever pretended that he knew everything about God was in error, and such being the case, no one could reasonably maintain that God could not assume a body if it so pleased Him. In reply the Swami observed that in saying what he had the Padri Sahib had done anything but proved his contention, which was, that God does incarnate Himself. The real questions that should be answered were:

- "what necessity is there for God to take a body?
- Is it or is not, His pleasure subject to any restriction?
- Is He incorporeal or corporeal?
- Is He all-pervading (witnessing all), or is He confined to a particular locality, etc.?"

The missionary's answer, stated the popular belief as to the omnipresence or all-pervading character of God, adding that no one could positively say what Divine omnipresence really meant.

What he (the Missionary) affirmed and maintained was that God did incarnate Himself, He passed in all His entirety into the body assumed, and yet remained outside of it also, for He could do it, and there was nothing to be wondered at this. To entertain the idea that the assumption, by God, of a body was something that detracted from His greatness and glory, was to labour under misapprehension.

To this the Swami made answer, that if God was all-pervading, His entering a body or coming out of it was an impossibility. The Missionary (he said) had not shown how it was necessary for God to assume a body. As to the assertion that God had made man in His own image, it was worth knowing in whose image He had made other creatures, - lower animals, etc.

There were further questions and replies, till at last the Missionary leaving the point of issue remarked that the incarnation of Jesus Christ fulfilled a Divine purpose, which (he said) was fully evident from the fact that the Bible was being gradually accepted by the civilized nations. He added: "The Bible has been translated into hundreds of languages, and millions of copies of this book are printed and distributed. Who says 'I don't believe in this book?

And Finally on Forgiveness of Sins

"Hence it is clear that an incarnation of God was possible. Belief in such an incarnation of God was nothing oppose to reason: on the contrary it was only proper that such an incarnation should take place. The great necessity of such a thing coming to pass he (the Padri) had described, and the words of the Bible were true!

The Third discussion on the subject selected for the purpose came off on 27th August, 1879. The contention of the Missionary was, that Divine forgiveness of sin was possible under certain circumstance, for instance, when a man came to have faith in Jesus Christ; while the Swami maintained that forgiveness of sins was impossible, for to hold the contrary view was virtually tc declare that God was the encourager of sin in the world. But, indeed, God was no such thing. He meted out punishments and rewards for all actions in all their fullness.

4

Visiting Religious Fairs

Truth was for all and its discovery could lead to the formation of a common divine faith. In 1879, at Danapur in U.P., a few European ladies and gentlemen came to see Rishi Dayanand. A very interesting conversation took place. The Rishi said: "Like the sun, moon, earth, rain, air and all other things created by God, the divine faith should also be the same for all. There is some truth in all religions. They all agree that speaking the truth and non-stealing are good principles. If a seeker were to collect all such good principles on which all religions agree, it would be a divine religion."

Prayag Khumba Fair

Hearing that the Kumbha Fair at Allahabad was approaching, Swami Dayanand left for that place, and having arrived there took up his quarters in the open air on the bank of the Ganges. The Pandits and Sadhus waited upon him in numbers, and vidyarthis also flocked to him from all sides. His lectures on idol-worship, on *tilak* and *kanthi*, etc., attracted large audiences and revolutionised the religious ideas of many. The Pandits resented his scathing criticism, and some of them even made bold to hold with him a shastrarth on idol-worship, but the attempt ended in a signal failure. They cited *mantras* from the Vedas, alleging that they were chanted to endow the images with life, but when, in response to a call form the Swami, they translated the same, they found that the passage had nothing to do with their contention.

The Swami further pointed out to them how the mantra - *Natasy pratima asti,* inculcated the very reverse of what the Pandits asserted it did; it was an empathic refuation of the worship of images and insisted upon the adoration of the one God only, in spirit. The Pandits grumbled and finally retired growling. Some of the orthodox here went so far as to tell the Swami that were he in their part of the country, they world have him buried alive. A heavy laugh from the Swami was the answer, and resuming his seriousness, he spoke to them exhaustively on "Dharma and Adharma."

Kumbh Fair, Haridwar

On his way to Haridwar, Swami Dayanand made a halt of about a week at Jwalapur, a town in the neighbourhood of the place he was bound for and inhabited mainly by the *Pandas,* and it was on 27th February, 1879, that he ultimately found himself at Haridwar. He put in the grounds of Moola Mistri, just in front of the garden of Sharvan Nath and the quarters of the Nirmals, not far from the Collector's tents. The accommodation provided was entirely of a contemporary nature, being almost exclusively that which could be had under the *shamianas* and in the tents created and pitched. Simultaneously with his arrival he had notices pasted up on almost all the most frequented *ghats* and in all the thoroughfares, announcing his arrival and embodying full particulars as where he had put up, what hours he could be interviewed, when his daily lecture should each day commence, what was the character of his mission, what were his beliefs, and so on.

Fall from and Restoring the Pristine State of the Aryas

The 5th, 6th and 10th mantra of the 71 Sukta of the 1st Mandal of the Rigvedas, as also a passage from the Taittiriya Arnayake, were quoted and explained in the manifesto issued, and the whole ended with the following words of appeal:

"It is really most extraordinary that while earth, water, fire, air and sky, the sun and moon, the year, the nights, the seasons, the paksha, the day and night, the pahars, mahurats, gharis, pals and kshans, the eyes, nose, ears and other parts of the body; the medicines, the plants, eating and drinking, and all other things which play a part in the maintenance of life, should have remained in Aryavarta exactly as they were from the time of Brahma down to the age of Jaimini, we Aryas (the inhabitants of the land) should be so markedly changed. Fellow-beings! If you would only think deeply you would see that Dharma can never be that which is productive of pain and suffering, nor Adharma that of which peace and happiness are born.

"The great cause which has brought about our fall is the same as has been referred to above, - namely, our going against the teaching of the Veda. That which can restore us to our pristine state is nothing else than re-conforming our lives to the behests of Scriptures. This can only be done by following the plan which those natives of Aryavarta who are Sabhasads of Arya Samajes and genuine Aryas, have to suggest. This plan is (1) that a *mandli* (band) of Updeshaks should be created – of individuals, who are well-versed in Sanskrit, who are of thoroughly patriotic instincts, who are philanthropic and ever ready and willing to confer, in their simplicity and purity of heart, the blessings of knowledge on all true suppliants for the same – men who are righteous in thought, word and action, and learned; (2) that schools and colleges should be established wherein the Shastras be taught. Whoever is in a position to assist in carrying through this most noble undertaking, the same should come forward and engage in the undertaking. If this is done, the people will rapidly improve."

The foregoing lines from Swami Dayanand's pen are too clear to misconstrued the regeneration of Aryavarta, it was his conviction, could be best achieved in two ways, - by means of preachers, and by the agency of schools and colleges. His ideal updeshak was a person of loft character, learned, and having the welfare of this motherland at hear, and the pathshalas he as for establishing were, primarily and in the first instance, to be pathshalas where the Vedas and the Shastras were to be taught.

It was a tremendous affair, this Kumbha Fair at Haridwar. The cord was immense, appalling in it proportions. There were no less than two lakhs of souls present at Haridwar as early as the 12th April, 1879, and thousands upon thousands were arriving daily from all parts of the country. For some nine or ten miles along the banks of the Ganges, nothing but masses of surging humanity could be seen. What could the fifty or sixty Aryas among a gather so vast expect to count for? For much, on the principle enunciated by the great sage and legislator in his well-known *shloka* which says that a learned Brahman is superior to thousands of his brethren, who are destitute of the qualities and excellences of a Brahman.

The single personality of Dayanand alone – a personality, the reproduction of that of the true Arya Rishi and teacher of the primeval times, outweighed, in moral and spiritual wealth, the collective individuality of the legions of priests, Sadhus and Sanyasis, in the midst of whom he was placed. This will be fully evident from the fact that no one of even the greatest men present at the fair – Swami Vishuddhanand, Satwa Swami, Sukhdeva Giri, Jivan Giri, etc., had the courage to take up the gauntlet thrown down by the Swami.

Of course the great Vedic Teacher must attend to the work he had come for, irrespective of all consideration as to whether he was being appreciated or not. His lectures on the "Purans" were in the spirit of a Luther, only more learned and profounder in argument. The Brahmans, the Sanyasis, the Bairagi Sadhu, the Nirmalas and representatives of a score of other "orders" frequently came to hear his lectures, but could not, for the life of them, relish the same. Some of them, gnashing their teeth in rage, would declare to his face: "We wish we could make an end of you. You have snatched away the bread from our mouth and spread false doctrine in the world." And choked with passion they would retire.

Although men of real learning and worth shrank form encountering Swami Dayanand, orthodox leaders of an infinitely inferior stamp were not wanting who would rough it out with him. Pandit Shardha Ram of Phillur was conspicuous among these. He established a Sabha of his own, and got his august body to write the following letter to the Swami:

> An invitation for a shastrath by the Hindus on the Vedas and Shastras.

"Salutations to the sacred Ganesh! We, the Sadhus and Pandits and other Sabhasads, in council assembled, write to Swami Dayanand Saraswati, and beg to inform him that for the last three or four days we have been daily holding meetings, from 4 p.m. to 6 p.m., at which religious subjects are discussed for the differentiation of truth from falsehood. Be it known to you that ever since the *Aligarh Sat Dharmavlambi Sabha* came to be established near *Jhona Akhara,* in the vicinity of Mayadevi, invitations have been sent to you regularly, asking you to come over. Now we send you the present letter. If coming into this meeting, you speak, it will lead to two results. In the first place, you, who have hitherto been lecturing on the Vedas and Shastras, in retirement, would, by speaking in the presence of learned men, enable them to judge whether your utterances are in conformity with the teaching of the Vedas and Shastras, and, in the second place, if your utterances turn out to be in accord with the teaching of the Vedas and Shastras, you would find us ready to accept and preach the doctrines you promulgate. The union this brought about will materially conduce to the well-being of Aryavarta. Do please attend Sabha, and if you cannot come, kindly mention the reason.

(Sd.) Pt. Gobin Lal,
Devi Band,
Pt. Lekh Raj, etc.

Swami's Reply

To this letter the Swami replied as follows:

"I have never declined, and can never decline, to hold a shastrarth: I am ready for one at all times. But the shastrarth which you propose should be arranged for by some Magistrate, and it should be attended by Pandits only and by no illiterate men. The place where it should be held, should be such as might not be regarded as especially yours or mine. The place where your Sabha is being held, is one by coming where I apprehend personal violence.

The thought of losing my life does not grieve me at all, but it grieves me to think that in case I loose my life, the work of reform I am carrying on will cease, and it is only for this that I guard my body; hence I don not think it advisable to attend your Sabha."

The Swami further had the writers of the letter informed that he should hold a shastrarth with them only if Swami Vishuddhanand should declare that hey could understand and grasp the Vedas when pitted against him (Dayanand) and that, in the extent of such a declaration forthcoming, he would choose Vishuddhanand as *Madhyastha*. The orthodox took Swami Dayanand's letter to Swami Vishuddhanand. Lala Jamiyat Rai, Master, Normal School, who was present at the time of their arrival at Vishuddhanand's quarters, says that as soon as that sturdy Sanyasi was the epistle of his great opponent, and knew the errand on which the representatives of the orthodox Sadhus and Pandits had come, he fell to abusing the messengers, Pandits Shardha Ram and Chaturbhuj, in a violent manner, declaring it to their face that, compared with Dayanand, they did not understand so much, as a single letter of the Vedas! Swami Vishuddhanand also wrote a letter to Swami Dayanand, and it was to the following effect:

> "Many ignorant and illiterate persons have gathered together with the intention of creating a disturbance. You should not at all listen to what they say."

Pandit Bhim Sen read out this letter in the evening in public to an audience of some ten thousand men, and what the effect of the communication must have been on the minds of the hearers, may be better than described. Pandit Shardha Ram, however, was not going to take his discomfiture to heart. On the contrary, he had the hardihood to write a letter to the *Koh-i-Noor*, saying that Dayanand had refused to hold a shastrarth with his party. More that this, he prevailed upon some creatures of his to declare in his Sabha that though they had, by bearing Swami Dayanand's *updesh* accepted his faith, the were now as orthodox as ever. "We have found out our mistake," said they, "and we beg that we may be readmitted in the *Sanatan Dharma*." Their repentance, was, of course, accepted, and they were conducted to the steps of Haridwar with great pomp, to be purified and reclaimed. No pains were spared to give the expiation as wide a publicity as possible, but alas for the clever Pandit! The trick was expose by a member of his own fraternity. It was Pandit Gopal Shastri, who did the thing. Truth came out!

Swami's Health

The Swami's health during the period the fair was at its height, was anything but good. He was suffering from acute dysentery. Writing in a letter dated 2nd April, 1879, he said "that he was having as many as ten or twelve motions every day, and in another (dispatched 12th Baisakh, 1936), that he had 400 motions up till then. But though afflicted with the terrible disease and considerably weakened, he would never let the interest of *updesh* suffer in any way. Lala Jamiyat Rai, noticing the amount of his daily work on the occasion of the fair, says that he would get up early in the morning and, after an hour or two spent in bathing and prayer, etc., would take his seat under the *Shamianas* and converse on the Shastras and Dharma with the Pandits, Sadhus and other people that came to him till 11 a.m., and sometimes till 12, then the Sabha was held at 1 pm, continuing till 5 p.m. After that the Swami, the Pandits and other Arya gentlemen would meet together and hold religious conversations among themselves. In a word, almost the whole day was passed in teaching and preaching." Probably it would have been better for the Swami if he had left the fair early; but whatever the state of his health, he chose to remain almost to the last, to preclude the possibility of men like Pandit Shardha Ram getting a chance to worked any real mischief, for he was aware that if he left Haridwar before the termination of the fair, the Puranic Pandits would not fail to make capital out of it; they would proclaim to their admirers that Dayanand had run away from the field!

While at Haridwar, the Swami was not unnoticed by the Officials. The Commissioner of Meerut Division, the Collector of Saharanpur, and the Conservator of Forests one day came to see him. The Swami being engaged in *upasna* at the time of their arrival, they had to wait till he was free. His devotions being over, the interview came off. A long conversation on the "Nature and attributes of the Deity" took place, and the European gentlemen were highly delighted with the arguments and observations of the Swami, and before taking their leave, they saw, of their own accord and free will, that the Swami had the benefit of Police attendance, so that there might be no disturbance at his lectures.

5

Preaching of Faith at Various Places

Agra

Hearing that a grand Durbar was to be held at Agra (November, 1866 AD), Swami Dayanand felt that he could not miss such a splendid opportunity for the determination of truth, and consequently left for the place in the company five vidyarthis. The Durbar came off, and was a magnificent affair, all the Native Rulers of the country wit their followers being present on the occasion. The Swami commenced his updesh (lectures), publishing at the same time; in Sanskrit, and eight-page tract, sowing the puerile character of the teachings of the Bhagwat. Thousands of copies of this publication were distributed free among the gathering to the real delight of all true enquires, particularly of those who could understand Sanskrit.

In the meantime, receiving from the Maharaja of Jaipur an invitation fro a discussion with Rangacharya, the Swami left for Mathura to have an interview with his guru before obeying the call from His Highness. The meeting between the teacher and the pupil was most cordial. Laying two gold mohars and a muslin-piece at his preceptor's feet, and presenting him, moreover, with a copy of his tract on Bhagwat, the Swami at last asked for leave to depart, informing the great man that he should next preach at the approaching Haridwar Fair,

Swami Virjanand, with his heart overflowing with joy at the work that was being done, blessed his noble disciple, wishing him the fullest measure of success in his mission. The two were not destined to see each other in life again!

From Mathura, the Swami proceeded to Jaipur. The Maharaja expressed a wish to see him early, but before the wish had time to be realised, some on informed His Highness that the Swami was an enemy of Shaivism and of idolatry. On hearing this he was deeply offended, and determined not to admit the Swami to an audience. It was, therefore, nothing strange that the Swami, ignorant of the change that had taken place in the Maharaja's mind, should, on reaching he place, be informed that His Highness was 'out'. The swami guessed the truth, and observing that a Sanyasi like him could afford to dispense with the company of princes, returned to his quarters.

Ajmer

The next place which Swami Dayanand visited was Ajmer (30th May, 1866). Here, as usual, he commenced exposing the Bhagwat, proclaiming it as an immoral book out and out and false in its teaching. He denounced the temples also, and fearlessly gave it out as his opinion that religious necklace and rosaries were nothing better than so much wood. The Pandits of Ajmer were horror-struck at the views of the Swami, and went into paroxysms of rage over them, but, being unable to meet him to argument, they could do no more than send him the following writing:

- A Sanyasi should not stay more than three days in an village or city.
- He should never drive a carriage.

These were the questions though not in the usual interrogative form, and the Swami replied to them in writing, pointing out, at the same time, the mistakes with which the composition of the Pandits bristled.

At Ajmer the Swami had a discussion with the Rev. Grey, the Rev. Robinson and Rev. Schoolbred of Biawar, on "God, Soul and the Laws of Nature, and the Vedas." The discussion lasted for full three days, and the Rev. gentlemen found it hard to face their antagonist. As an interchange of civilities, the Swami saw Mr. Robinson at his own house.

On this occasion, the Padri asked the Swami if it was true that Brahma, influenced by lust ran after his own daughter. The Swami replied that the story was a libel on one of the greatest of Rishis, that if the deed, of which the story spoke, was ever done in the world, it must have been done by a depraved mortal, scarcely deserving the name of "man".

Rev. Robinson was a great admirer of the Swami. He gave him a certificate, stating that the Swami was profoundly versed in the Vedas, and that he had never seen so learned a man in his entire life. Such individuals, wrote the Padri, were rare in the world, and their company could not but be productive of good to all.

The document enjoined upon all who wished to see the Swami to treat him with all possible respect. The Swami also called upon Mr. Davidson, Deputy commissioner of Ajmer, and in the course of conversation, said to him: "People of false creeds are plundering your subjects. The King being like a father, it behoves the representatives of Government to take steps to remedy the evil."

The Deputy Commissioner's answer to this was that the policy of Government was perfect neutrality in matters of religion. The Agent to the Governor-General in Council was anther European gentleman with whom Swami Dayanand had an interview at this place. The Swami talked to him on the necessity of protecting the cows, setting forth, in detail, the benefits which Government and the people would derive from the adoption of the measure recommended. The Agent admitted the force of the Swami's arguments but said he was sorry, he could do nothing in the matter.

This worthy gentleman gave the Swami a letter, saying that it would secure him an introduction to whomsoever it was shown. He further sent a letter to Raja Ram Singh of Jaipur, in which he expressed regret at His Highness having given but an indifferent reception to a man of the Swami's stamp.

Aligarh

Taking leave of Farrukhabad and passing through Kasganj and Chhalesar, the Swami reached Aligarh on 26th December, 1873, in company with Thakur Mukand Singh, and some other Rajpoots, and accepted the hospitality of Raja Jaikishen Dass, C.S.T. Enquirers from the town and the surrounding villages came in scores, and *Dharma charcha* (discussion on religions topics) was kept up till late in the night.

On 27th December the Swami gave his first lecture at Aligarh, addressing a mixed audience of Hindus and Muhammadans and of Officers, Civil and Military. The lecture was followed by several others, all largely attended by representatives of every creed. As a matter of fact, the Swami had company all the day long, the Pandits and Moulvis and others having full permission to see him at any time and to have their doubts removed. The local celebrity, Pandit Meher Chand, who, before the Swami's arrival at Aligarh, had been boasting that the Swami would not face him, kept away from the Swami's meetings during the entire period of the teacher's stay at the station, calling his adversary a nastik and what not, and refusing to listen to the suggestion of his townsmen that he should go and have a shastrarth with the man whom he had so often worsted in his absence!

Allahabad

Swami Dayanand set off from Dumraon on 8th January, 1873, and after making a day's halt at Mirzapur, where the affairs of the Pathshala received his attention, left for Allahabad, which had its due share of updesh, and it was not had well nigh gone that he reached Kanpur Here he stayed for about a month, living in a solitary hut on the bank of the Ganges, some two miles from the town, and delivering lectures at the various centres of the locality, in accordance with the suggestions of the leading men thereof.

Lala Ghanya Lal, Alakhdhari, noticing on the authority of a correspondent, the Swami's work at Kanpur, regretted that so true a reformer and teacher should be abused and hooted by the deluded, ignorant and priest-ridden kanpuris.

Amritsar

Lahore was, for several months, the headquarters of the Swami, and during months he would be frequently away from the station to the neighbouring towns and cities in the interests of *prachar*. He visited Amritsar twice during 1877, and again on 15th May, 1878, staying up to 11th July, 1878. During his first visit h put up in the *kothi* near the Ram Bagh Gate of the town, being the guest of the late Sardar Dayal Singh of Majithia, who had hired the *kothi* in question at a rent of Rs. 40 a month. The interested priesthood had not been sparing in their efforts to give currency, at Amritsar, to the false and ridiculous rumours which their kith and kin had been so assiduous in spreading at Lahore. But the charm of novelty had worn away and, believing the idle reports set afloat by the advocates of idol-worship as nothing better than old women's tales, the people came pouring daily to the reformer and listened, with the deepest attention, to all he had to say to them.

His exposure of the Puranas and his lectures on other subjects displayed a vastness and depth of learning and a power of reasoning which absolutely surprised and fascinated his hearers, and made many of them set him down as an "incarnation" of the Deity Idol-worship became an object of hatred to the intelligent and thoughtful, and the scenes enacted at Lahore were repeated, the idols and images being handled unceremoniously and either put away in lumber-rooms or 'shied' into the thoroughfares. A month's preaching was sufficient to establish an Arya Samaj, with about fifty Members, Babu Ghanya Lal, Pleader, being elected President, and Bawa Narian Singh, Pleader, Secretary. The exact date of the establishment of the Samaj was 12th August 1877.

The champions of idolatry did all they could to persuade the famous Pandit Ram Datta of Amritsar to hold a shastrarth with the Swami, but a clear refusal was the reply. The Pandit frankly acknowledged that he had not studied the Vedas, nor had the ability to enter into a contest with a man of the stamp of Dayanand. Pandit Tulsi Ram, another well-known and able Pandit was also approached, he too begged to be excused from acceding to the wishes of his admirers. Indeed, the Pandit meeting the Swami one day, in the bazaar, prevailed upon him to accompany him to his house, where, on arriving, he extended to him a most cordial welcome and treated him with the greatest respect. On visiting Amritsar the second time, the Swami has notices circulated, challenging the orthodox Pandits accepted the challenge, and several days were spent in settling the conditions of the proposed shastrarth should take place in the *tawela* of Sardar Bhagwan Singh, and, long before the hour fixed for the commencement of the discussion, the place was full to overflowing, there being over five thousand persons present. The Swami waited and waited, but no Pandit put in an appearance, and at last thinking it advisable to spend the time for some purpose, he rose to address the meeting.

He had not, however, proceeded far in his lecture, when Babu Mohan Lal, Pleader, coming into the meeting, announced that he was a messenger from the Pandits and that they desired to come into the meeting. "They should be welcome," was the reply, and the Pandits came, surrounded by a pageant indulging in loud shouts of triumph (Jai! jai!). One might expect that the shastrarth would begin without further delay; but no, the paper embodying the conditions of the shastrarth was again taken in hand by Pandit Chandra Bhan, and heated discussion as to the merits of the conditions ensued. While the time was being uselessly wasted, some bad characters, hiding themselves behind the multitude, took to shying stones and pieces of bricks at the "unorthodox."

One of these came directly towards the Swami, but as he was seated surrounded by several gentlemen standing, the progress of the missile was intercepted, and it failed to do him any injury. Being unable to throw the stones with precision, it was natural that the miscreants should often hit those they did not intend to, and the result of this was that the entire assembly was transformed into a disorderly mob. Many were seen covered with blood, and a fray seemed imminent. Such a contingency was wholly undesirable, and the friends of peace, taking in the situation, exerted themselves as they had perhaps seldom exerted themselves before, and the apprehended disturbance was prevented.

Ever mindful of his mission, even in the midst of trials and suffering, the Swami had a fresh challenge went to Babu Mohan Lal for a shastrarth, but the Babu replied that he was the representative of the Pandits only for a few hours of the of the previous day and that he had nothing to do with them now. "They are," he added "wrangling and disputing among themselves, and nothing appears to farther from their intentions than to hold a shastrarth." The Swami waited for twenty days more for a more satisfactory answer on behalf of the Pandits, but it was waiting in vain. At last, he saw no other alternative than to have all the circumstances connected with the promised but eventually-shirked shastrarth printed and published for the information of the general public.

Mr. Perkins was the Commissioner of Amritsar during these days, and, either of his won free will or in the interests of state policy and under instructions from the higher authorities, he expressed a wish to see the Swami. The interview duly came off, and a conversation ensued. Among other things, the Commissioner, who was a thorough Christian, and who, on retirement from service took up preaching work, observed that the Hindu Religion was a like a 'weak, untwisted cotton thread,' read to snap in two at the slightest pressure and on the slightest tension.

The Swami replied that the fact as otherwise, that the Vedic Religion (misnamed Hindu religion) was strong as iron, yea even stronger than that.

There is reason to believe that before the interview came to an end, the Commissioner was fairly convinced that the mission of the Swami was perfectly harmless, and that it was not, in the remotest degree, of a character to justify the reckless manner which the orthodox chose to behave while expressing their disapproval of it.

At Amritsar too individuals were not wanting who, not understanding the Swami, often made him requests which he could never grant. One gentleman besought him not to be so hard on 'idol-worship,' and, of course, the request had to be refused. Another wanted him to become his son's guru, and begged him to give the young fellow the *guru-mantra*. The Swami expressed his inability to comply with this request also, adding, "Let your son and yourself repeat the *Gayatri Mantra,* for there is no greater *mantra* than that. You may become a member of the Samaj and learn how to do it."

Lala Murli Dhar, Drawing Master, at present President of the Gurdaspur Samaj, and certainly one of the noblest men belonging to the Arya ranks, was also among those who wanted, the Swami to become the their *guru*. In this instance too, the Swami's reply was fully characteristic of him, and the Lala was told to accept the 'Paramata' as his guru and to repeat and recite His *guru-mantra* only – the Savitri!

Amritsar had long been a centre of the Missionary activity, and it might be presumed that the Padris would no mind risking a discussion with the Swami specially as the Swami was yet new to the Punjab and the Padris did not know (as Mr. Foreman and others came to know later) what sort of man they had to deal with. They put forward Pandit Kharak Singh, but judge of the surprise of his supporters when, instead of arguing against the Swami, he commenced assenting to every proposition and admitting the force of every argument which the Swami laid down and advanced!

Seeing how matters stood, the Missionaries wired to Dr. am Bannerjee of Calcutta, but he final answer from that erudite gentleman was, that he could not obey the mandate. Of course, under the circumstances, no discussion could be held!

Badaun

A Sabhasad of the Badaun Samaj had come over to Muradabad to take the Swami to Badaun, and although the Swami was still weak, he did not like in the interests of reform, to disappoint the gentlemen who wished to see him so much. He reached Badaun on 30th July, 1879, and stayed there till 13th August, lecturing almost daily. The City Pandits one day waited upon him, and a discussion took place between himself and them on the "Nature of God, Incarnation, and the right to study the Vedas."

The Pandits repeating the well-known mantra of the Yajurveda - *Sahasra Shrisahpursha*, etc. declared that God, having so many heads, etc., was not merely incorporeal, and that He could incarnate Himself at will. The Swami's reply explained the true meaning of the mantra, saying that there were in the all-pervading God innumerable heads, innumerable eyes, innumerable feet, and so on. Similarly, he brought forward various arguments, proving that Divine incarnations were an impossible thing, and he quoted authorities showing how the Vedas were meant for entire mankind and not for any particular class.

The Salono festival came off while the Swami was yet at Badaun. Seeing the Brahmans going form house to house with red thread and asking largesses the Swami sorrowfully remarked:" Ignorance has brought about the extinction of all our *sankars*. This festival had for its object the *raksha* (protection) of *Vidyarthis* (students), and the enforcement of righteous practice. But today all men, old and young, are tying the red thread round their wrists!"

Banaras

Returning to Mirzapur the Swami proceeded to Banaras, which he reached on the 19th November, 1879. He stayed here for six months. During this period the Vedic press was established, and much was accomplished in connection with the Veda-Bhashya and other works on hand, nor was the *updesh*-work neglected. The orthodox Pandits were challenged to come forward for a discussion over again and again, but there was no response there was, however, no dearth of men the exact prototypes of excellent Pandit Shardha Ram, in Banaras. One of these, by name Jugal Kishore, had a printed notice put up, saying that the gentlemen, whose names were given at the bottom of the notice, had waited upon Swami Dayanand, but finding that his conversation was oppose to the teaching of the Vedas and to the lessons which practices of men of righteous conduct yield, they thought of having their doubts removed by the *Brahm Amrit Dahrshini Sabha*. "The accordingly, (said the notice), waited upon the Sabha, and their doubts having been thoroughly removed by the same, they underwent and expiation by the advice of Pandit Jugal Kishore, and got rid of their sins by being face to face with the gods....."

In due course the notice came to be read at a meeting of the *Bradm Amrit Darshini Sabha*, and how far it was relished by that Body will be clear form the following article which appeared in the *Arya Darpan*, May, 1880:

"Bawa Narian Singh, Member, Arya Samaj, Banaras, asked Pandit Jugal Kishore to produce the men whose names appeared in the notice. The Pandit, livid with rage, answered that he should produce them at the next meeting of the Sabha,. But as the men referred to in the notice were merely creations of the Pandit's fancy, imagined into realities solely for the sake of amusement, where could he produce them from for the Sabha?

The Pandit was in a dilemma, and at last began to look out for and train stray lads to his purpose, telling them to accompany him and depose so-and-so before the Sabha. But who could accede to the Pandit's request in connection with such an ugly business? The very mention of the word *Prayashchit* is sufficient to frighten people out of their senses, the more so as the confession on a person's part that he performed a *prayashchit* gets him an ill-name. However, the Pandit made a shift to produce one man at the next meeting of the Sabha. When his name was asked, he said, it was Ram Krishn Doobe. (The Pandit must have put him to say that he was called Ram Krishn Doobe, but how long can one remember an assumed name? It slipped from the man's memory).

They next asked him, whether he had gone to the Swami? The reply was in the negative. This reply exposed Pandit Jugal Kishore's nefarious trick, and the people now asked him why he had got a false notice printed and circulated. The Pandit was red with anger and began to talk incoherently, uttering, among others, the words, 'he who has seen Dayanand's face, he is not from the seed of a Hindu!"

Upon this Bawa Narain Singh observed that at the Kashi shastrarth of Samvat 1926, there were thousands of Hindus present, among others, the Maharaja of Kashi, Pandit Balshastri, Swami Vishuddhanand, etc., and that the Pandit and virtually offered them a gross insult, in saying what he had.

"The result of this was that the Sabha, passing a resolution for the expulsion of Pandit Jugal Kishore, turned him out. The Pandit, when being expelled, raised a hue and cry, and mutual thrashing was about to commence; but God be thanked, matter did not take a serious turn, and all ended well."

The Swami delivered at Banaras some twenty lectures in the beginning of 1880. An Arya Samaj was established on 15th April, 1880, and it continues to exist down to the present day, having a fair Mandir of its won, the result, in a great measure, of the zeal and efforts of Rai Bahadur Surjan Das, Executive Engineer.

The Press was established largely by subscription, the members of the Arya Samaj contributing each a specific sum. As the contributions had been accepted on the distinct understanding that they should be considered as a loan, the money was in time returned to the donors. The late Lala Sain Das, however, who had contributed about Rs. 250, declined to receive back the sum, which anything but pleased the Swami, who insisted upon repayment, remarking that the donor could spend it in charity in some way or another.

Bareilly

At Bareilly, Swami Dayanand was staying in Begam-bagh of Lala Lakshminarayan. He learnt his host was keeping a prostitute. He condemned him and said: "Listen, my friend, I will not be partial to anyone and will never hesitate to tell the truth." The prostitute was sent away that very evening. Thakur Das, a goldsmith, had taken a second wife while the first one was alive. He asked Dayanand one day to initiate him into yoga. The Swami said sarcastically: "Marry one more woman; your yoga will be complete."

In the Punjab, an interesting incident took place. Dayanand, after public notice, was giving a discourse. Many Europeans and Indian Missionaries came to listen him. General Roberts, the Commander-in-Chief of India, also walked in. The Rishi continued to attack the contradictions of the Bible and its tenets. General Roberts listened all that. After the lecture, he advanced and shook hands with. Dayanand, appreciating his absolute fearlessness.

Many princes of Rajputana were his disciples. But Dayanand would not spare even a prince. When the Rishi entered the palace of a ruler he found him seeing off a prostitute. Immediately, in the ruler's own palace, Dayanand said: "Kings were like lions and they should have no connection with bitches." The royal head, bent down in repentance and shame, had to listen to the Rishi.

In the Banaras debate, Dayanand had been encircled by a hostile mob of 50,000 people, besides the unscrupulous priests. His very life had been endangered. But the Rishi visited Banaras, again and again, perhaps seven times, and each time he threw a challenge. In short, his crusade for truth was relentless and without a trace of fear. His voice could not be silenced.

Rishi Dayanand was open to conviction. He was quick to admit his error, if any. He was ready to change, if convinced. He used to lecture in Sanskrit. The Brahmo Samaj leader Keshab Chandra Sen advised him to use Hindi language. He agreed. He was asked to put on more clothes than a mere loin cloth. He consented again. On one occasion, a man stood up in the open assembly and pointed out the contradiction in what Dayanand was talking and what his book, *Veda Bhashya,* contained. The Rishi admitted the error, explained how it had occurred, and promised to get it corrected.

Rishi Dayanand held fast to his principles. But he loved people of all religions. Many Muslim scholars used to come to him for debate and discussion. He himself went to deliver a lecture at the Bungalow of Sir Syed Ahmed Khan, then a sub-judge at Banaras. The Lord Bishop of Agra asked for appointment. Swamiji himself went to see him. At. Bareilly, Rev. T. G. Scott, with whom Rishi Dayanand had also held a debate, began to attend all lectures of the Swami. One day, he was not to be seen. On enquiry, the Swami was told that, that day being Sunday, Rev. Scott was busy teaching in the Church.

At once the Rishi said: "Let us go to the Church and hear him." He walked to the Church with some other people. On seeing the Rishi, Rev. Scott came down from the aisle and requested him to give a discourse. Dayanand spoke for about twenty minutes. It is almost amazing to note, and perhaps a testimony to his endearing personality that his rivals holding different view him. They loved to listen to him, argue with him, and enrich their minds. Not only this, it must be said to the credit of Christian missionaries and Muslim scholars that they showed the necessary temperament for religious debate on most of the occasions. The Puranic priests, however, felt embittered and aroused.

Rishi Dayanand was a man of wit and humour, besides being a great debater. He never lost patience with those who tried to harm him, even physically. He was without bitterness. He forgave easily. He seldom talked about his own person. He refused to be a Guru. He stood for independent enquiry and rational approach. He was invariably punctual.

Rishi Dayanand was a true yogi. Earlier, in order to master this science he went on an extensive search for yogis, He met them at Chanoda Kanyali, on the banks of Narbada. He sought them in Mount Abu, Vyasashram, Garhwal, and Joshimath. He learnt yoga from Parmanand Paramhans, Yoganand, Jwalanand Puri, Shivanand Giri, Gangagiri and others. He practised yoga in the jungles of Chandee across the Ganga at Haridwar.

According to Dayanand the 'ancients' thoroughly understood the laws of attraction and repulsion of all things in Nature between each other. The yoga phenomena were based upon that knowledge. The yogi changes or intensifies these attractions and repulsions at will. A yogi has to relinquish five things, namely: ignorance, egotism, passion, selfishness, fear of death. Yoga was in perfect harmony with the natural laws.

Rishi Dayanand never exhibited any of his yogic or psychic powers. But many people had seen him meditating while his body rose above the ground, or it rested on the surface of water in a lake. Many times, he made correct predictions of events about to pass. But the whole stress of his mission was on truth based on reason. Yoga, according to him, was a very difficult science, and few men were capable of learning it at that time. The impact of Dayanand's personality and role was unique. After centuries, the people heard in the Hindu society that all were equal. The Brahmans, the Shudras, even the non-Hindus, had the right to study the Vedas. All had the right to receive education. The mist of spirits, ghosts and incantations began to clear. For the first time, the people learnt that sins once committed could never be forgiven. The gods could not remove them; pilgrimages could not wipe them; a dip in the river could not wash them.

The amulets, the rosary, the images, the elaborate rituals, the sacrifices would not help. Only good actions, purity and sound reason were the remedies. Everything must relate to logic. Even the ban on cow-slaughter was demanded by the Rishi on economic grounds rather than its sacredness. Similarly, he denounced child marriage, female infanticide and purdah system on the basis of pure logic and humanism.

The hierarchy of religious orders was shattered. 'Religion emerged from the nooks of dim temples and mysterious scriptures. It was viewed in the sunshine of reason and debate. It was understood through massparticipation. People were not mere disciples, only a band of frenzied singers in a temple compound. They were now exalted as discriminating judges. They were not passive onlookers. They were now enthused to decide what was right.

Swami Dayanand threw open the wells of knowledge so that his people could drink for themselves. Dayanand transfused in the languid body of India his own formidable energy, his certainty, his lion's blood. His words rang with heroic lower. He reminded the secular passivity of a people, too prone to bow to fate, that the soul is free and that action is the generator of destiny."

Swami Dayanand connected the important portions our ancient heritage *to* the stream of modern life. Thus, he renovated and invigorated it. It was an age of scientific materialism and economic penetration of the west. Its shadows were falling over India. The Rishi revived Vedic values, and the Vedic way of life to save the nation from the grip of westernism. The result was amazing. A new pride in India's destiny was born. A new confidence in its superior culture was recreated. A sturdy and healthy society, ready to take up any challenge, took position. The nation was at once restored back to its Aryan ideas. It seemed, the hand of an Aryan Luther had touched every part of life in the whole of northern India.

The memory of his struggles, the message of his books, the zeal of his followers and the deep roots of his institution, never faded. The Arya Samaj organisations founded by the Rishi at many places grew from strength to strength. Old customs, rituals and beliefs did not, completely disappear. But the initiative, now always rested with Dayanand's followers. The tide of reform and social reconstruction could never be rolled back. The Hindu woman was restored to her Vedic esteem. The glory of good conduct became significant for all.

The first Arya Samaj was established by Dayanand at Bombay. The real aim as explained in its 28 principles was "to promote the good of whole mankind." These principles were reduced to ten at Lahore in 1877. But the aforesaid aim retained its central importance. Under these principles, an Arya was expected to be always willing to give up falsehood and adopt truth. He was not to be content in his own uplift alone. He was to view his advancement in the uplift of others.

In matters which affected the well-being of all, an Arya was to subordinate his personal likings to the general good; in matters which affected him alone, he was to enjoy freedom of action. Within the lifetime of Dayanand such bodies sprang up all over India. Within two years of the death of the Rishi, there were Arya centres at about two hundred places. A large umber of educational institutions of Anglo-Vedic character were established where modernism was not divorced from nationalism.

Swami Dayanand demolished the authority of tradition and orthodoxy. He believed in reason. The force of reason promoted individual freedom. The Rishi also restored boldly the superiority of Vedic thought and culture. These two factors became the base of Indian nationalism in the second half of the nineteenth century. The spell of the West was broken and the cross-currents of Indian renaissance swept; the minds of our people. The Rishi had taker, the path of risk and adventure for emancipating his people. The people got from him the courage to face death eye to eye if the cause was sublime. And, soon they realised that the cause of cultural and political emancipation of the Aryan land was worthier than any number of lives. It is, therefore, no surprise that many a famous patriot in northern India sprang] from the ranks of Dayanand's followers. Swadeshi and boycott were preached from the Arya Samaj platforms. The British Government began to take severe notice of its activities. But the Arya Samaj always measured upto its responsibilities. Dayanand had forged this spiritual weapon from the interior.

Bombay

The Swami arrived at Bombay on 31st December, 1881, and was received at the station by Colonel Olcott and several Raeeses of the Local Samaj, who has selected a suitable building situated on the sea-shore for his residence. In this building (in Balukeshar at Goshala) the Swami took up his quarters, and the work of *prachar* commenced. Repeated challenges were given to the orthodox Pandits, but none of them came forward for shastrarth. Indeed, Seth Mathura Das, an influential Sabhasad of the Samaj, with a view to finishing a powerful motive to the champions of idolatry to come into the field, had it advertised that he would give a reward of Rs. 500 to the man who should prove that the Vedas countenanced 'idol-worship.'

But it was not only to the Pandits that challenges for a discussion were directly or indirectly, sent: the Christian Missionaries also were asked to avail themselves of the opportunity now offered for separating the grain from the chaff. As an instance in point, we may refer to the letter sent by the Swami to the learned and distinguished European Missionary Rev. Mr. Joseph Cooke, who had bur recently landed in India with the one sole object of popularising the teachings of the Bible among the educated classes.

The gentleman delivered, on 17th January, 1882, an eloquent lecture in the Bombay Town Hall, asserting therein that the Christian Religion was the only true religion in the world, and that it was from God. The educated people of Bombay were fascinated with the speaker's rhetoric, and spoke of him very highly.

To prevent evil consequences following form this underserved admiration, the Swami invited the Rev. gentleman to a discussion, in the letter referred to above. The letter ran as follows: "DEAR SIR,

"You have, in all your lectures declared that

- the Christian Religion is from God:
- that it will spread in the whole world; and
- that there is no other religion of Divine origin.

I maintain that not one of these assertion is correct. If you are prepared to prove your contention, and, if you don not wish that the people of Aryavarta (India) should accept what you say till it has been first proved to be true I am ready and willing to hold a discussion with you. I fix 6:30 pm (Sunday next) as the time of my lecture, in Framjee Cowasjee Institute. If you don't like the hour or the place, you may some other place. A neither of us can speak the language of the other, I propose that the arguments advanced by one party should be translated and repeated for the benefit of the other, and, further, that short-hand writers be appointed to take down all the speeches which (on the termination of the discussion) must be duly signed by both of us. The discussion invited will take place in the presence of gentlemen who accompany the parties. Of these gentlemen, there or four at least, on either side, will be called upon to authenticate the discussion by their signatures, and subsequently the whole discussion will be published, so that the people may know what religion is from God.

(sd) "Dayanand Saraswati"

The only answer which the Rev. gentleman vouchsafed to the Swami's challenge (as to those of Colonel Olcott and Captain Nun) was, that he could not accept it, for the object of the news of the refusal spread through the land, and the Rev. gentleman had to make a change in his plans. He gave up his original idea of travelling through whole India, thought that in visiting Bombay, etc. he had visited the entire country in miniature, secured a comfortable berth in a ship bound homeward, and, re-crossing the blue waters, found himself once more amidst congenial surroundings!

The anniversary of the Bombay Arya Samaj came off on 2nd March, 1882, and was a fair success, the Swami taking part in the proceedings and delivering lectures. The *Upaniyams* (by-laws), framed and passed by the Lahore Samaj, had not as yet been accepted by the Bombay Samaj. At the suggestion, and by the advice of the Swami, they were formally recognised at a meeting of the Samaj, a committee of select gentlemen being appointed to make in them some needed alterations, so as to meet the peculiar local requirements. The Committee appointed consisted, among other gentleman, of –Rao Bahadur Gopal Rao Hari Deshmukh; Rajman Raj Shir Bapoodev; Raman Bhadur Ichha Ram Bhagwan Dass, B.A.; Rajman Sewak Lal Krishn Das; Pran Jivan Das Kahan Das. The changes introduced were slight.

During the Swami's present visit, the zealous and liberal-minded members of the Bombay Samaj purchased a large plot of ground, at the back of the Gurgam Police Court, to build a Samaj Mandir upon, and five gentleman were appointed trustees of the library and the *shala* (house) to be erected on the spot.

This time also the Swami's stay at Bombay was a prolonged one, and there were some reasons for it. One of these was connected with the comments on Jainsim in the Satyarth Prakash, and another, as we have already had occasion to hint, with the changed attitude of the Theosophical Society towards the Arya Samaj. The Jains, headed by Lala Thakur Das of Gujranwala, declared the criticism on their creed to be without a basis, and insulting, which the Swami refused to believe; and the Theosophists had come to adopt *atheism* or materialism as the great article of their faith, and were, by their writings and speeches, helping in the revival of those very superstitions which it was the mission of the Swami's life to uproot. As to how the two parties were severally dealt with by the Swami, will be described in two separate chapters.

Calcutta

Swami Dayanand now thought of visiting Calcutta, and, in pursuance of this resolve, he left Kashi and proceeded to the Capital of the Indian Empire via Dumraon. Mr. Chander Shighar Sen, Barrister-at-Law, in response to whose invitation the Swami had undertaken the journey, was, at the proper time, at the Howrah Station to receive his distinguished guest, and drove with him to Baboo Surendra Mohan's garden, where the Swami was to put up. The Barrister, as well as the owner of the garden was unsparing in his attentions to the Swami, making him feel perfectly at home in every respect.

As soon as it was known that the great reformer was in Calcutta, educated people of every denomination flocked to him in numbers. The *Indian Mirror*, type, noticing his arrival, spoke of him as an iconoclast of a superior type, as a man of unbounded learning who had proved himself more than a match for the greatest Pandits of Banaras, as a teacher who, by his other various achievements, had made himself a name in Northern India. The Brahmo Samaj of Calcutta was in the zenith of its power in these days, and the leading Brahmos were constantly by the Swami's side, being under the impression, no doubt, that he would ultimately come round to their views. But the impression was not long in being dissipated. The Swami took his stand on the Vedas, and everything Vedic had his profoundest sympathy and his earnest advocacy, - a thing, more or less, distasteful to the members of the Brahmo Samaj.

Of course, there must be discussions between Dayanand and the believers in the Brahmo Faith, and the debates took place almost daily, "What do you understand by caste?" a gentleman asked the Swami. The reply was, that caste or varna want social status determined entirely by the individual's worth and actions, and that it was not at all identical with the present arbitrary and false differentiation, in social life, of one person from another from considerations of birth alone.

"Should or should not the *Yajnopavit* be worn?" The reply was, that the members of the "twice-born" classes should, one and all wear it, though it did not signify much if the ignorant individuals, miscalled Brahmans, went without it.

Is God corporeal or incorporeal?" The reply was absolutely without form and figure, being essentially Truth, Intelligence and Happiness.

"Was the author of the Sankhya Darshana an atheist? He wrote - *Ishwarasiddhe*, denying thereby the existence of God." The Swami replied that such misconceptions were entirely traceable to the scant regard in which the present-day Pandits held the commentaries by the sages of yore. The aphorism, affirmed as declaring the belief of the author of Sankhya, was really an objection from a non-believer (in the Vedic Religion), and that there was a reply to it in the next aphorism. Kapila, the Swami added, was a believer in the transmigration of souls, he was a believer in the Vedas, he was a believer in yoga, and he was a believer in the existence of the Soul, and as such he could not teach the non-existence of the Deity. In point of fact there was no discrepancy whatever between the teaching of one Darshana-Shastra and another. Each of the six dealt, separately and independently, with one of the six causes which had been instrumental in producing the world. The Nyaya spoke of the atoms, the Mimansa of action, the Sankhya of the combination of elements, Patanjali of thought and intelligence, Vaisheshak of time, and the Vedanta of a creative Deity.

"Was not *Agnihotra* a kind of idol-worship?" The Swami's answer was in the negative. A function which necessitated a contemplation of the Deity and which was fraught with good to the entire world, could not be identified with the worship of idols.

So markedly attractive was the personality of Swami Dayanad to all true enquirers that his company was sought after both by high and low. Baboo Gyani Indra Lal Roy, M.A.B.L. (Editor of a Bengali paper) referring to this attraction, spoke of the Swami's argumentative power and his erudition in the most flattering terms. "His power of lecturing, his skill in discussion and his thorough acquaintance with the Shastras, " says he, "astonished every one. Crowds of men would approach him in the capacity of true enquirers, and obtaining satisfactory answers to their questions, go away to their homes. They had never heard before any of their countrymen, not conversant with the English language, declare to them, in connection with the *Dharma* and the Samaj (society), a Faith so utterly devoid of partiality."

With Baboo Keshuv Chandra Sen the Swami had a discussion on the doctrine of the "Transmigration of Souls." It must have been an interesting debate, and it were to be wished that we had an account of the same to notice here, but perhaps none has been preserved. There can be no question, however, that Baboo Keshav Chandra Sen, though his religious beliefs differed widely from those of Swami Dayanand, had a sincere regard for his opponent.

This is fully evident from the fact that the Swami delivered, on January 9, 1873, at the Baboo's house, and at the learned Baboo's own request, a lecture on the superiority of the "Vedic Religion." Many of the *Raeeses* and learned men of the town formed part of the Swami's audience on the present occasion. Only a few days after this the anniversary-date of the Brahmo Samaj came round. The Swami was also invited, and Maharishi Devindra Nath Tagore sent his own carriage to bring him, and when he came, the Maharishi received him in person in the most cordial manner possible. The Maharishi, like Baboo Keshav Chandra Sen, invited the Swami to his private place of residence. This was during the anniversary-day. The Maharishi was one of the greatest admirers of the Upanishads, and the Vedas in his palace being profusely embellished with texts from the same and with quotations from the other Shastras, the sight was most edifying to the Swami, and he confessed as much to the Maharishi. The latter requested the Swami to put up with him, but the Swami begged to be excused from availing himself of the offer on the ground that as a Sanyasi he could not live with *grihasthis*.

On February 23, 1873, Swami Dayanand delivered a lecture at the house of Baboo Guru Charan Datta, in which he proved that the Vedas did not countenance idolatry. Pandit Mahesh Chandra Nyayaratna, who was present, rose at he conclusion of the lecture and gave a summary of the lecture to the audience in Bengali. But not proving himself a faithful interpreter and saying many things which the Swami had never said, the hearers were much displeased with him, especially the students of the local Sanskrit College.

On 2nd March, 1873, the Swami spoke in the Hall of the Bara-Nagar Borneo Company on "Havan," and some seven days after that he addressed a large and influential audience on the "Vedic Doctrines" in the Bara-Nagar Night School. The lecture lasted over three hours. The upshot of the speech was that the Vedas inculcated absolute unity of Godhead, that they recognised no artificial system of caste, that child-marriage and other institutions of similar kind were utterly un-Vedic, and that the one only remedy for the evils which were, and had been undermining India's prosperity lay in India's returning to the pure Faith of the ancients - even that taught in the Scriptures. Noticing this speech, the *Indian Mirror* said that it proved the speaker not merely a learned man but one who was also deeply thoughtful - one whose arguments were strong and forcible, and whose manner of speaking was bold and fearless.

This lecture was followed by two or three others, all largely attended. The Swami never lost an opportunity of enlarging upon the importance of studying the ancient Aryan Shastras, and when he visited the Sanskrit college of Prasanno Kumar Tagore, he spoke so warmly for these that the good Baboo actually agreed to include the Vedas in the curriculum of studies for the College. It is also affirmed that he spoke to Dr. Mohindra Lal very strongly as to the necessity of reviving the study of the Ayurveda.

We are told that Pandit Tara Charan Tarak-Ratan Naiyyayak thrice essayed to face the Swami, but each time the attempt failed. He was well aware what it was to hold a discussion with a scholar like Dayanand, and he might well shrink from a contest with him. The Swami visited the Asiatic Museum with a view to purchase copies of the Vedas and the Upanishads, and he did buy some works from here.

It was here at Calcutta that Swami Dayanand realised the necessity of discontinuing lecturing in Sanskrit for the future. He could not but see that he was not always interpreted faithfully, and that by speaking in Sanskrit he could directly reach but the minority. Baboo Keshav Chandra Sen is said to have hinted to him as such, and he resolved that henceforward his public lectures should be, if possible, invariably in *Arya Bhasha* (Hindi). And it was probably at Calcutta that the Swami took to wearing clothes. The whims of society, so long, as they were comparatively innocent and did not encroach upon the principle, might be tolerated in the interests of the great mission so dear to him and all true well-wishers of their motherland.

One day, in the course of conversation, Baboo Keshav Chandra Sen is said to have expressed regret at the Swami's ignorance of English. "If the Vedic scholar like yourself were conversant with English," said he, "what a suitable companion you would make me in my contemplated visit to England?" The Swami in reply observed that he too was sorry at Baboo Keshav Chandra's ignorance of Sanskrit, considering that the pure and enlightened Faith of the Aryan nation lay enshrined in that language. Certainly nothing could be more pretentions, added he, than that the Baboo, *the master of a foreign tongue*, should claim to teach to his countrymen what he himself understood but little.

The lectures which Swami Dayanand delivered at Calcutta were considered, as might well be presumed that they were, worth preserving, and his admirers thought they would print them. The proposal had the heartiest approval of Babool Keshav Chandra Sen, but before it could be carried out, the Swami had left the town. What had among other things, principally influenced the Swami to pay a visit to Calcutta, was to found there a Pathshala (school), on true Vedic lines. While he was yet at Banaras, the following editorial had appeared in the Hindu Patriot (January, 1870):

> "Here is an opportunity for the Dharma Sabha to prove itself useful, which we trust and hope will not be thrown away. The Sabha is an anachronism, but its existence may be tolerated by enlightened public opinion, if it make its existence may be tolerated by enlightened public opinion, if it makes its objects to revive Vedic learning and Vedic religion, the glorious heritage of our proud ancestor.
>
> "We wish our correspondent had given an estimate of the cost of the proposed Vedic School, which ought, of course, to be moderate, and we cannot believe that if the objects of the projected institution were properly explained and circulated, there would be lack of funds. A single Native Prince might give the money required. It would certainly redound to the credit of the Dharma Sabha if it should come forward liberally and second the laudable efforts of the New Reformer. Other wise we would recommend the Brahmo Samaj, as the chief instrument of the revival of Vedic worship under the guidance of the late Raja Ramamohan Roy, to interest itself in this sacred cause, and lend its support and authority to the new Reformer."

Further on the paper said:

> "In conclusion, we would make a strong appeal to the heads of the orthodox class of Hindus to assist Dayananda Saraswati in establishing a Vedic School. Almost all the educated natives are theists at heart, and though some cling to idolatry for the sake of their parents and nearest relations, many have avowedly adopted Brahmoism. It is, therefore, meet that the Vedic religion should be revived, the tide of progress cannot be obstructed, and the members of the Sanatan

> Dharma Rakashini Sabha will ill-succeed in keeping up the present system of Hinduism. They will secure the lasting gratitude of the Hindus if they try to purify Hinduism from the corruptions that have crept into it, and establish the Vedic religion of the educated."

On the appearance of the forgoing lines, the Banaras correspondent of the *Patriot* wrote to its as follows:

> "Emboldened by your words of encouragement we repaired to Anand-Bag in Banaras, and explained to the venerable Pandit the substance of your editorial remarks. The joy of the sage knew no bounds, and with a blooming countenance he thanked you most heartily. He then propounded the following plan in accordance with which the working of the proposed Vedic School is intended to be carried out. As a first step, the services of a good Pandit should be secured for teaching Sanskrit literature. As Saraswati has in contemplation the introduction of a system of training that will lead to a clear understanding of the Vedas, he intends selecting a Pandit from among a few best scholars he is acquainted with.
>
> "Though a native of Gujarat, he was brought up in a Vedic School at Mathura, under the tuition of the great sage, the late lamented Sura Dasa. There are a few scholars of this great man, who will gladly accept the teachership of the proposed School, if remunerated on a somewhat liberal scale. The salary should be from Rs. 75 to Rs 100 per month. After the pupils have been thoroughly initiated into Sanskrit literature, which will take two years to accomplish, the services of another Pandit should be secured at say Rs. 100 per month, for teaching the Vedas. As liberal education has inflamed the hearts of many a youth with the fire of religious zeal, advanced Scholars of the Sanskrit College and Pandits of the Vernacular schools might be induced to enter the Academy with a view to obtain an insight into the Vedic lore.

"In that case, a Night School ought to be organised; and not Eleemosynary aid will then be needed. But as there is every probability of pupils from Nabodeep or other Samajes joining the School, arrangements should be made for supplying all their necessaries, including purchase of books, etc. At the outset, a monthly subscription should be raised sufficient to pay Rs. 100 per month to a Pandit, and to defray the necessary expenses for teaching 10 pupils. In addition to the monthly subscription there should of course be a reserve fund to meet contingent expenses.

"I do not say anything at present about School-building and boarding house, because I think any one of our wealthy countrymen might be induced to spare one of their supernumerary buildings for this noble purpose. As soon as arrangements have been made opening the proposed school, our venerable Pandit Dayanand Saraswati will start for Calcutta in company with a Sanskrit teacher, and will stay there as long as his assistance will be considered necessary to place the long as his assistance will be considered necessary to place the *Pathshala* on a firm footing. It is the intention of our Pandit to make Banaras, which has an academic fame of no recent date, the centre of his educational scheme, with Schools spread all over India; and if the liberal-minded gentry come forward to fulfil the desire of this great man, they will assuredly confer a great boon on India. The branches of the tree of corruption have overshadowed the whole of India, and it is his noble intention to apply the axe of truth to the very root of the tree, which has gone deeper at Banaras than elsewhere. Yesterday, the Pandit left this station for Allahabad where he intends staying for a month."

The Swami's object of establishing a *Pathshala* at Calcutta, however, was never realised, for the people would do little more than showing "lip-sympathy."

Chitaur

Leaving Bombay on 24th June, 1882, and passing through Indore and Ratlam, the Swami reached Chitaurgarh. Who, be he a foreigner or a native of the country, can pronounce this name without emotion! Chitaur is associated with events and memories which can never be forgotten, which must stir every brave heart with admiration (whatever the character of that admiration) to its deepest depths. It is pre-eminently in the noblest sense of the words, the hero and the martyr's spot: it is the patriot's dearest spot on earth. Freedom's cause has nowhere been fought with that unwearied persistence and that the lofty desperation with which it was fought on this spot. The bravest of the brave, the fairest of the fair sacrificed themselves, deliberately, eagerly, with the intense order of a religions devotee meeting death for His God and his faith's sake, on this battle-field, in order that the Rajput honour might be preserved and the Rajput harem be secured against the intrusion of the impure ruthless stranger. Where was it that Queen of beauties, that impersonation of chastity, Maharana Bheem's wife, with hundreds of Rajput ladies of the highest families, cheerfully flung herself into the devouring flames, to be beyond reach of an implacable and licentious foe? Where was it that Fateh Singh, with his newly-married wife and his aged mother, fought and fought till he fell to rise no more? Where was it that the immortal Pratap received the inspiration which armed him with inflexible resolution to uphold the glory of the Sessodia race at every cost.

Everything in and around Chitaur must serve, so long as the Hindu race and the Hindu tradition remain, so long as European civilization does not become extinct, as a memorial of the highest order of chivalry, of unique devotion of duty, of virtue in its sublimest form, of patriotic fervour of the most exalted type. Nothing strange that a man like Swami Dayanand should receive at the hands of the representative of Bappa Rawal, - Maharana Sajjan Singh, the reception did!

Delhi

Departing from Meerut, the Swami reached Delhi on 9th October, 1878, and stayed there nearly a month. The effect of his *updesh* and lectures given and delivered in Shahji's Chhatta, was that an Arya Samaj was at last established in the city. Lala Makhan, Lal became the President, and Lal Hakumat Rai, the Secretary, of this Samaj.

Ferozepur

The next station, which the Swami visited was the Ferozepur Cantonment. He left for the place in company with Lala Gobind Lal Kayastha, sent to bring him on 26th October, 1877, and put up in Lala Banwari Lal's *Kothi* in the vicinity of the old Artillery Barracks, the new house which Lala Mathrua Das, Supervisor, subsequently the virtual founder of that noble institution – known as the Ferozepur Orphanage, had specially built for the residence of the Swami, during the space of a few days, being regarded by the Swami as unfit for him to take up his abode in, in consequence of its being situated in the thick of the population. For eight days running the Swami lectured under the *shamianas* set up in front of Lala's Mathura Das's house, and the result of these was of a most desirable character. The *Hindu Sabha* which already existed in the Cantonment and of which Lala Mathura Das was the President, was, by the unanimous consent and approval of its enlightened and thoughtful members, changed into a "Arya Samaj."

At Ferozepur also there was talk of a shastrarth coming off between the Swami and the champions of orthodoxy, but nothing came of it, none having the courage to come forward and hold a discussion with the dreaded Sanyasi.

Furrakhabad

The Swami did not stay long at Lucknow. After a week's halt during which the *updesh* given did not appear to have led to any definite and tangible results, he left for Furrakhabad. An Arya Samaj already existed here, but it was markedly strengthened by the Swami's presence. The members, with a view to securing permanency to the religious institution which had been founded in their midst, came forward with liberal donations for the purpose, each individual subscription ranging from Rs. 200 to 1,000. Over and above this they subscribed Rs. 1,000 in the aid of the Veda-Bhashya. A new building having been secured for the use of the Samaj, the

Swami delivered his lecture on 5th October, 1879, in the premises of the same. We may be sure that the orthodox Pandits were in none of the most enviable of moods at finding thousands of rupees going in to the coffers of the Samaj, and at seeing that Body making itself perfectly at home in their midst.

When the Swami was about to leave Furrakhabad, the champions of idolatry had as many as 25 questions, duly written and subscribed, sent to the Swami for an answer. It was a clever move on their part. They thought that the Swami would not stop to answer them, and if such a thing actually came to pass, they would have a chance of proclaiming with the beat of drums that the Swami had given them the slip! The unexpected, however, came to pass. The Swami answered their questions on the 7th October, and the Dharma Sabha has to gulp down its disappointment as best as it could.

One of the questions was: "Can a Muhammadan or Christian join your faith, and are you and your followers prepared to eat the food cooked by his hands?" To this the Swami thus replied: "My religion is none; whoever follows the commandments of the Vedas, the same is a follower of the Vedic Religion. Have you, falling into darkness, come to identify Dharma with eating and drinking, with answering the calls of nature, with wearing shoes, dhoti, angrakha, etc.? Listen and reflect, such things are mere usages and customs, peculiar to one country or another?"

While at Farrukhabad, the Swami assisted at many *Yajnopavit sankars,* and it is noteworthy that his lectures here were frequently attended by English Officials also.

Garhya Ghat

While the Pathshalas were being established and worked, Swami Dayanand's energies continued to find an outlet in preaching as before. His advocacy of he primeval Vedic Religion and his chastising of modern superstitions provoked, as it had don't already, the fiercest opposition and frequently so maddened an individual here and as to lead him to attempt the daring Sannyasi's life. The discussion which took place at Garhya Ghat, for instance, and which reduced the Pandits defending idolatry and other similar institutions to a state of utter helplessness, soon brought on the Swami the ire of the Thakur of Aheudesar, who would be satisfied with nothing less than with cutting short a career which was proving itself so fatal to the interests of orthodoxy. The Thakur, who had given a daughter to the Maharaja of Jaipur, was haughty in the extreme, and intolerant of everything which did not seem to fit in with the old order of things.

Accompanied by four retainers, two armed with the sword and two with clubs the nobleman came and sat by the Swami, and commence talking after the style of the person having some wicked purpose in view. The Swami, regardless of what he said, severely criticised the Bhagvat, and, on the termination of the speech, rose and entered a mausoleum. Thinking that he had been foiled, the enraged chief from the Etah District ordered his servants to go and seize the Sadhu and bring him into his presence.

The other people had been listening to the Swami's criticism and counsels took objection to such a queer order and requested the Thakur to rescind it. The latter refusing to comply, rough hands were laid on his followers and they were completely disarmed. Livid with passion at the failure of his scheme, the big man retired, making a virtue of necessity and postponing his vengeance to a future date, which, alas for his hopes, never arrived.

From Garhya Ghat the Swami proceeded to the town of Swaron, at the earnest request of many. In this place lived hundreds of Brahmans, who never care to perform their sandhya and gayatri, and with whom self-interest was always the one thing to be consulted. Having reached his destination, the Swami took up his quarters at "Ambagare," and began his work.

A pandit, named Narayan, was so impressed with his teaching that, being thoroughly convinced that the Vedic Religion was the only true religion in the world, he renounced the Charkrankit Faith, of which he had hitherto, been a zealous follower. The incident produced a sensation in the town, and the sole topic of conversation everywhere was the arrival of a Sanyasi who denounced all modern creeds, whether based on the Purana, or Semitic in their origin.

On the third day after the conversion of Narayan Pandit, the wealthiest and most prominent inhabitants of the town, accompanied by several hundred men, waited upon the Swami, with a request that a shastrarth on "Idol-worshipping" might be held. The Swami cheerfully acceded to the request. Pandit Khamai represented the idolators. The pandit had, however, asked and answered but a few questions when he miserably broke down. The followers of the Chakrankit Faith raised a howl at this, to wipe out, no doubt, the disgrace that had been the portion of their spokesman. Upon this the leading men of the town interfered, saying that the meeting had been convened for holding a shastrarth and not for making a noise. "Argue the thing out with the Sanyasi, if you would," said they, "but do not create a disturbance." No one came forward, the effect of which was that another votary of the Chakrankit Faith, one Pandit Gobind Ram, accepted the Vedic religion.

Finding the shame of the defeat something too much for them (for the common people now began to look down upon them), the Pandits of Swaron appealed to Pandit Angad Ram Shastri, of Badrya, for assistance. This man had the reputation of being the most learned individual in the neighbourhood, being specially well up in Nyaya and Vyakarna. The discussion, as before, was on "Idol-worship." After the Pandit had his say, the Swami refuted idolatry on the authority of the Vedas and Shastras, concluding, his remarks by an exposure of the Bhagvat, which, as he proved, was childish in its teaching, and faulty as regards its grammar and composition.

The Pandit was a great admirer of the Bhagvat, but he was also open to truth. When he heard the criticism of the Swami, he could not but feel that it was just and reasonable, and taking hold of his *shaligram*, which he worshipped daily, he consigned it to the waters of the Ganges, declaring, at the same time, that he should no longer do *katha* from the Bhagvat or any other Purana. His example was not last upon others. Gosain Baldevgiri and many of the relatives of the Pandit himself dealt by their images in the same fashion, installing, in their place, the only one Lord of the Universe, *on the throne of their hearts*. This was the second present of the images to the Ganges.

Pandit Jugal Kishore, a fellow-student of the Swami, happening to hear some of his lectures (while Swami Virjanand was yet alive), carried a most unfavourable report of his work of the great teacher. "He is spreading *adharma,*" complained the Pandit, "for, among other things, he says that the worship of *shaligram* is false." Virjanand answered that the *shaligram* etymologically meant nothing but *a heap of rice,* and it was useless to worship such a thing. "But why does he run down the *kanthi* and *tilak*?" persisted the discomfited Pandit. Swami Virjanand, in reply, asked the Pandit to quote authority in support of his contention. No answer was forthcoming, and the Pandit after some hesitation exclaimed, "If the required authority does not exist, then here goes," and tearing his *kanthi* from his neck he threw it away!

The Swami stayed in the vicinity of Swaron for six months, teaching, preaching and reclaiming people from superstitions. There were readings from the Manu Smriti and the Mahabharta instead from the Puranas, and the Pandits breaking away from the Kaumidi commenced the study of Ashtadhyai, under the guidance of the Swami. The spurious *stotras* lost their charm, and the *Gayatri* became, in scores and hundreds of households, the vehicle of meditation and contemplation.

The apostles of the Chakrankit and other creeds began to be scarce, Rangacharya, of Brindaban, the most famous member of his fraternity, purposely avoiding paying visits to villages and towns where there was danger of his being brought face to face with the man he dreaded. Kailasparvat Swami, with whose name the reader is already familiar, was so very angry at what fell form the Swami's lips that, in loyalty to his orthodoxy, he thought it his duty to write a pamphlet in newfangled creed, and to, in no case, hear his lecture before they had carefully gone through his own production. A glorious testimony this to the sound, irresistible logic of Dayanand!

At Garhi, a village some twelve miles from Swaron, the effect of the Swami's preaching was that a certain Kshatrya, a person of considerable influence, tore off his *kanthi*, and giving up idolatry, became the worshipper of the one true God. This wealthy man had great faith in the Vairagis, and the latter were in such a passion over his desertion that they made up their minds to kill the Sanyasi who had so grievously injured them. Their plots, however, eventually came to nothing.

A great fair was held at Kakaora, and the Swami preached on the occasion as usual, shaking, in varying degrees, the belief of his ever-shifting audience in orthodoxy. A large number of men waited upon him and besought him not run down idolatry and the Puranas, but their prayers were in vain. His reply was: "The things of the world which yield pleasure to you, have no charm for me. To me there is pleasure in the contemplation and adoration of God alone, and in carrying out His commandments. I shall work with the one, sole object of disseminating the true Vedic Knowledge." The Swami challenged any one to come forward and prove that the ancient Aryan Religion was not the purest and noblest of all, but though the votaries of the Chakrant Faith came to hear him in hundreds, not one of them would take up the gauntlet. The Collector, who was present at the fair in connection with his official duties, would now and then come to see the Swami and treat him with marked respect.

Gujarat

Having done with Jhelum, Swami Dayanand arrived at Gujarat on 13th January, 1878, and stayed here over a fortnight. The people of the city, worked up by the priesthood, behaved savagely, showering stories and bricks on the Maharishi. In time a Pandit came, had a conversation with him, and then went his way, Swami's remark on the hostility displayed by the ignorant populace was, "that a day should come when truth must bear down all opposition, and, when the people should rain on the preachers of the Vedic Religion, flowers instead of stones!

Gujranwala

On Leaving Wazirabad (7th February, 1878), the Swami halted at Gujranwala, where he stayed for about twenty-seven or twenty-eight days. He put up there in the splendid buildings beneath which lie the ashes of the father of that great statesman and conqueror, the Lion of Punjab. A series of lectures was commenced. The local Padris – men of great learning and sense – declared their intention to hold a shastrarth with Swami. Nothing could be more welcome to the latter, and a shastrarth did come off in the Christian Church on 19th February, 1878, in presence of, among other influential gentlemen. Messrs. Walker and Hewson, Assistant Commissioners, Mr. Mohan Beru, Lala Gopal Das, Extra Assistant Commissioner, etc.

The subject for discussion was "The Eternity of the Soul." Surrounded by a huge audience, the Swami replied to the objections of the Missionaries, and his replies were so sensible and convincing, has his own criticism on the fundamental doctrines of Christianity so unanswerable, that when the discussion for the day came to a close, the *madhyast*, Lala Gopal Dass, Extra Assistant Commissioner gave his decision in favour of the Swami. As the crush was tremendous it as thought advisable that the next days' discussions should take place in some more commodious building, if possible, to no particular sect.

Subsequently, however the Padris saw it convenient to change their opinion (as well they might), and assembling the students of the Mission School in the Church Hall at 12 pm called upon the Swami and the *Madhyasta* to come over for the discussion. The answer from both the gentlemen was that this was no time for discussion, and that: in accordance with the previous understanding, it should be resumed at 4 pm. The Swami took occasion to further remind the Padris that the room available in the Church could not accommodate a large audience, and that the discussion was to take place in some other place. Far from being disappointed at the reply, the Missionaries received it in a spirit of satisfaction, for it enabled them to tell the people that the field was theirs, since the Swami had not obeyed their call!

Of course the intelligent portion of the Gujranwala gentry was not to be taken in by such a move. They had carpets spread and other arrangements made for the resumption of the discussion in the open, and 4 pm, when the people came, streaming along from all parts of the city to the place of the meeting, an invitation was sent to the Padris to attend. There was, however, no response, and after waiting for three-quarters of an hour, the Swami got up and delivered a lecture on the teachings of the Bible, thoroughly exposing the imperfect and ridiculous character of the same. An Arya Samaj was established with the following gentlemen as Office-bearers and Members:- Munshi Narain Kishen, President; Lala Phoolo Ram, Teacher, Secretary; Lala Atma Ram, Treasurer; Lala Mathura Das, Lala Daya Ram; Bhais Sant Singh and Hazara Singh, — members.

Gurdaspur

In response to an invitation from Dr. Bihari Lal, Assistant Surgeon, Lala Hans Raj Sahini and Dr. Bhagat Ram Sahini, Swami Dayanand left Amritsar for Gurdaspur, by a mail-cart, on 8th August, 1877, and on reaching his destination was received by the gentry of the station, who had advanced a mile for the purpose, with cordiality and respect. The Swami put up in the Doctor's kothi, situated *on* the roadside in the open air, and delivered here a number of lectures on "Idol-worship," the "Existence of God." "Transmigration of Souls," Shradhs and oth*er kind*red subjects.

There was the usual opposition, and the Pandits of the place made a shift to look bold and brave. Indeed Pandit Lakshmi Dhar and Pandit Daulat Ram of Dinanagar, obeying the mandate of Mian Hari Singh, Extra Assistant Commissioner, and Mian Sher Singh, Assistant District Superindent of Police, also an idol-worshipper, actually came to Gurdaspur to hold a shastrarth with the Swami, and the discussion commenced.

But before much had been said on the either side, the two Mians, taking offence at the Swami's remark, flew into a passion and began indulging in unparliamentary language. Dr. Bihari Lal too lost his temper, hot words were exchanged, and the meeting broke up.

The Swami's updesh had, how*ever*, done its work, and an Arya Samaj was established at Gurdaspur on 24th August, 1877, with the following gentleman as Office-holders and Members:- Munshi Suraj Saran, Munsif, President; Diwan Kishen Das, Secretary; Dr. Bihari Lal (Munsif) Lala Ghanay Lal (Shukar). Lala Kaka Mal, Lal Ram Saran Das (Pleader), Bawa Khazan Singh (Shukar), Dr. Bhagat Ram Sahini, Lala Hans Raj Sahini and Lala Gurcharan Das (Pleader), - Members.

Indore

Leaving Chitaur, the Swami arrived at Indore on 21st December, 1881. the Maharaja was absent from the Capital, but the State officials were extremely respectful and cordial in their reception. After about a week's stay here, the Swami left for Bombay, to take part in the anniversary of the Bombay Samaj, as well as to come to a definite understanding with the *Theosophical Society*. The Maharaja on his return to his Capital greatly regretted the Swami's early departure from his State, and sent him a telegram at Bombay, embodying the request that he could come back and see him. The Swami replied that he should come, and the promise was faithfully kept, but h pity of it was, that His Highness was again away from his Capital.

As to how intensely he must have longed to see the teacher and have his fill of *updesh* in some quiet hours, may be judged from the fact that at the Durbar of 1977, it was His Highness only that, in conjunction with a minor chief, had exerted himself the most, though unsuccessfully, to bring together Indian Ruler and Nobles to hear the Swami.

Jhelum

On his way back from Rawalpindi, the Swami broke his Journey at Jhelum, staying there for a forth-night and giving *updesh* regularly, which soon resulted in the establishment of an Arya Samaj in the station, Lala Lachhman Parshad (teacher), who had been till now a Brahmo, being given the Presidentship, and Lala Jawala Parshad, at present Extra Assistant Conservative of Forests, the post of Secretary.

Jodhpur

It was Maharaja Partap Singh who wrote to Swami Dayanand at Shahpur, on behalf of Maharaja Jaswant Singh, his sovereign and brother, to visit the Rathore State, and to preach the noble principles of the Vedic Religion there. The Swami, in compliance with His Highness's request, left Shahpur for Jodhpur on 26th May, 1883. The first part of the journey proved one of the most trying of its kind. The sky had looked heavy and lowering for many hours past, and the rain now came down in torrents.

The men were soaked, and almost the entire luggage came to acquire, under the downpour, a double or treble its previous weight. However, Ajmer was reached at last, and here the Swami allowed himself a day's rest.

Taking the train on the following day (in company with Lakshman Rao Deshmukh, C.S.I., Colletor, Khandesh District, who wanted to study the Yoga Shastra), the Swami got down at the Pali Station, a place some eighteen miles Jodhpur, and where some state Officials were waiting for him, with elephants, camels chariots, a postchaise, and some sowars. Setting out early on the morning of the 28th, and after making a few hours' halt at Ropat, where the Jagirdar Thakur Girdhari Singh entertained the Swami and his followers most hospitably, the party found themselves at Jodhpur on the 29th, long before the sun had risen.

A *Rajkumar*, in due state, advanced to receive the Swami, and conducted him to the bungalow of main Faizullah Khan, where he was to put up. Hardly had the Swami taken possession of the bungalow, when Maharaja Partap Singh and Rao Raja Tej Singh paid him a visit, the former presenting him with a *mohar* and Rs. 25 in silver. After a short conversation, and after seeing that the arrangements in connection with the possible requirements of their distinguished guest and his men were as satisfactory as they could be desired, they said their *namaste* and withdrew.

Marwar, like Mewar, though certainly not on an equally grand scale, nor to the same extent, has been rich in heroes and patriots. The history of Rajputana speaks of the achievements and exploits of the Rathores of the true, genuine type in the most flattering terms, and with justice. The sovereigns of Marwar and the chiefs under them have often done and accomplished that which warriors of the very first order alone could do and accomplish.

Jullundur

Returning to Amritsar on 26th August and staying there for about two weeks, the Swami left for Jullundur, on 13th September, 1877, where he stayed up to the 15th October, 1877, the first lecture here was delivered in the house of Sardar Suchet Singh, but the place proving insufficient for the large audience which the lecture attracted, the next came off in Sardar Bikram Singh's house, where the Swami had put up. All the subsequent lectures also were delivered in this building, the gathering on each occasion fully justifying the change. Men of the old type, the Brahmans, in particular, behaved after their kind, denouncing the Swami as a heretic and warning all they came across to keep away from such a dangerous person!

One of the lectures delivered at Jullundur appears to have been delivered pre-eminently for the benefit of those who had provided the Swami with lodgings. The Swami learning that one of the Sardars was intimate with a woman of abandoned character and being justly displeased that a nobleman of the land should be so completely wanting in self-respect and disgrace himself so far, he fearlessly, and in the presence of the Sardars themselves, entered upon the apparently disagreeable tasks of exposing the short-sightedness and iniquity of those who, in disregard of the dictates of conjugal fidelity, wasted their money and manhood on prostitutes.

His words were strong, but the needed to be uttered, for greater the evil, the stronger the remedy. Some persons, on the termination of the lecture, hinted to the Swami that the obligations of hospitality (it was hospitality, in certain measure) required that be should have refrained from taking to task and satirising the conduct of the Sardars in the pointed manner he had done. The Swami's reply was:

> "I have not come here to flatter or please or to intentionally offend anyone. To declare the truth is my mission, and this mission I am trying to fulfil. It is a matter of perfect indifference to me as to who is pleased with my utterances and who is not."

A discussion took place at Jullundur at 7 am, on 24th September, 1877, between Swami Dayanand and Moulvi Ahmad Hussain on "Miracles" and the "Transmigration of Souls," in the presence of the Sardar. An account of the discussion was published in a pamphlet-form by Mirza M. Wahid, Editor and Proprietor, the *Wazir-i-Hind*. The following lines are from the pamphlet: "At the time appointed for the discussion, the Moulvi, accompanied by the high and low of the town, both Hindus and Musalmans, arrived (at the place where the debate was to take place). The subjects were chosen for discussion were the doctrine of the "Transmigration of Souls' and "Miracles," the former, in deference to the wishes of the Moulvi Sahib, and the latter in deference to those of Swami Sahib.......It was announced by the Swami (before the discussion commenced) that on the termination of the conversation, no one was to indulge the conceit of considering himself victorious or defeated......The questions put and the answers given by the parties (he said) should be taken down and manuscript, after it had been signed by Lala Mehar Chand and Munshi Muhammad Hussain Mahmud, should be published. On the termination of the discussion, however, the Moulvi did a thing which was unworthy of a man of learning... It was this, that the Moulvi, after the conversation was at an end, made for the gate of the *Khankah* (abbey) of Imam Nasir-ud-din, and treating his co-religionists to an exhortation savouring of self-praise, called upon them to spread his (imaginary) fame. The educated and respectable Muahmmadans, regarding this desire for fame as the outcome of childishness, retired from the scene of excitement, but not so the ignorant mob. These declared the Moulvi to have been victorious, and mounting him on a horse paraded him, to their hearts' content, through the streets and lanes of the town, shouting out his praises and his triumphs."

The account of the discussion contained in the pamphlet is authenticated, having been duly signed by Lala Mehar Chand and Munshi Muhammad Hussain.

As far as the discussion on "Miracles" is concerned, it is very ordinary, none of the arguments advance by the Moulvi in support of his contention being strong and worth consideration. The discussion on the doctrine of the "Transmigration of Souls," however, is an interesting reading, but the objections of the Moulvi were almost all much the same as were subsequently raised by Rev. Scott in connection with the doctrine in his discussion with the Swami at Braeilly, we need not notice them here.

The Swami returned to Lahore without seeing an Arya Samaj established at Jullundur.

Kanpur

Leaving Farrukhabad and visiting Kannauj, Bathora and Madarpur on his way, Swami Dayanand reached Kanpur with the commencement of the rainy season (Samvat, 1926 AD 1869), the local paper (Sho'la-i Toor of 27th July, 1869), noticed his arrival in the following words:

"For some days past one Maharaj Swami Dayanand Saraswati has been in our midst. He is putting up at the newly-constructed *ghat* of Lala Sargahi Lal, Pleader, Civil Courts, on the bank of the Ganges. He will not speak in any language other than Sahstri or Sanskrit - neither in 'Nagri' nor in any foreign tongue. He is a recluse, avoiding bustle and crowd. His appearance is that of a true saint. He is wholly opposed to the worship of idols, and to the erection of temples for purposes of idolatry. He maintains that idol-worship is not inculcated in the Vedas. This Swami is a scholar among the Pandits of India, a man of unique erudition. In the Vedic and Shastric grammar and in logic he is deeply versed, and one of the chose Pandits. He gives himself out to be a native of the Deccan. When he was five years old, his father commenced teaching him the Veda. At Mathura he perfected his knowledge of Sanskrit, For some time he stayed at Jaipur also, and there he had discussion on the *Hindu Faith*, after that he went to Gwalior and to Farrukhabad, and there also he had discussions with the Pandits. Now ever since he has been at Kanpur, his fame has been going forth. We hear that a large meeting will be held at the *Ghat* referred to on 31st July, 1869. Maharaj Haldar Ojha, a native of the village Hola, who has been staying for some days past in the newly-constructed temple of Maharaj Guru Parshad and who is perfect in the Sanskrit language, will attend the meeting and will hold a discussion with Swamiji."

Almost simultaneously with reaching Kanpur, the Swami had a manifesto put up in Sanskrit, in which speaking of the contents of the twenty-one Shastras, - the Vedas, the Upavedas, the Vedangas, the Upanishads, he acknowledged them as authoritative, adding that whatever in the Rishi Granths (the composition of the sages) too was opposite to the teaching of the Veda, to Vyajarana and to virtuous conduct, was also rejectable. In illustration of his position he said: "There are eight *gups* (things that injure and debase), which ought to be rejected, and eight true things which ought to be done or accepted." These respectively, enumerated as follows:

Eight Gups

- All the works published by common mortals - the puranas, such as Brahmavaivarta, etc.
- The worship of stones, etc., in the belief that they represent *devtas* (gods).
- *Shaiva, Shaktik, Vaishnav, Ganpatya,* and other orders and sects.
- *Vammargism,* taught in the Tantras.
- The use of intoxicating drugs and liquors, such as bhang, etc.
- Adultery.
- Fraud, conceit, lying, etc.
- Theft.

Eight True Things

- The twenty-one Shastras, - The Rigveda, etc., of Divine origin, or works coming from the Rishis and Munis.
- Serving the *Guru* from the commencement of the *Brahmacharya Ashrama* and the study of the Veda, in keeping with the behests of *Dharma.*
- The performance, in keeping with the Vedic Varna and Ashrama, of the practical duties, sandhya, agni-hotra, etc.
- Conjugal faith, base don't the teaching of the Shastras, the performance of the five daily *maha-yajnas* (great duties), sexual connection with the wife in proper season, regulation of conduct in conformity with the behests of Shruti and Smriti.
- The practice of *tapa* (severe contemplation), etc.) of yama (self-control, etc.), rising gradually to the trance stage of upasna, and the observance of the Vanprasth Ashrama, in the company of, and under instructions from, the righteous.

- Meditation, introspection, indifference towards the temporary and transcient, the cultivation of spiritual knowledge, the non-desire of fruit of action on being initiated into Sannyas.
- A constant effort to subdue and conquer by science, mundane and spiritual, birth and death, joy and grief, lust, anger, avarice, partiality, and the evils of bad company.
- The destruction of all pain - resulting from ignorance, self-conceit, love and hate, fear of the dissolution of the body, from *tamas, rajas,* and *satva* and the realisation, after shaking off the hold of the Five Elements (*panch mahabhuta*), of the nature of *moksha* (salvation) and the bliss attendant thereon.

Lahore

Swami Dayanand left Ludhiana on 19th April, 1877, reaching Lahore the same day, Pandit Manphool, Mir Munshi, Government, Punjab, and Munshi Harsukh Rai, received him at the station, and drove him straight to Rattan Chand's garden, where the Swami had to put up. Enquirers flocked to him from all sides, the general curiosity having been sharpened and intensified by the false rumour which interested people had se afloat, namely, that the newcomer was a hireling of the Christians, and that he professed to be a Hindu, in order to be in a position to deceive the Hindus all the more successfully.

He was, it was given out, secretly helped with money from England, and a stated sum was paid to him monthly, in recognition of his services. The fact, the mischief-mongers said, was evident from his bitter opposition to idol-worship, *shradhs*, incarnation, *tirthas*, and so forth. Such a rumour could have no weight with the educated and enlightened, but he ignorant priest-ridden classes could not but have some faith in it, and accordingly they swarmed round Swami Dayanand, asking questions and getting answers, to be finally undeceived by his true exposition of the Shastric teaching.

Pandit Manphool had withdrawn himself from the Swami's company, disappointed, it is said, at the failure of a certain scheme of his, which, he had thought, he would be able to carry through by the Swami's help. The Swami would, doubtless, have accorded him all the assistance in his power, but the Pandit would not avail himself of it, as it was dangerous to do so, the reformer, according to him, being unorthodox in his views, and not safe to be associated with, - considering that state of Hindu society. But the Pandit was not missed, other influential gentlemen, especially members of the Brahmo Samaj, came forward with their help and made satisfactory arrangements for the Swami's lectures.

The first of the series were delivered on April 25 and 27, respectively, in the Baoli Sahib in the centre of the city, and both were on the "Vedas". The rush being tremendous, the police was in attendance. The lectures made the orthodox wild with rage, but the educated community saw in these everything to appreciate.

Koh-i-noor's Report on His Discussion on the Vedas

The Koh-i-Noor (28th April, 1877) had the following note about the Swami and his work at Lahore:

> "The famous Vedic Scholar, Swami Dayanand Saraswati, who, visiting Ludhiana, arrived at Lahore on 19th April, and put up in Diwan Rattan Chand's garden, delivered, in deference to the wishes of enquirers after truth, Brahmo gentlemen and others, a lecture on the 'Vedas and the Vedic Dharma' in the Baoli Sahib, on the evening of 25th, from 6 to 8 pm Some five hundred men must have been present to hear the lecture. At the outset, the erudite Swami explained, according to the rules of Vyakarana, the etymology and literal meaning of the words, 'Veda', 'shruti', 'mantra', etc.,' adding that the Vedas, like the material atoms of the universe, were eternal.
>
> "Whenever a creation took place, he said, the Vedas also became manifest, and when the universe was dissolved into its primary atoms, the disappeared into the Supreme, like unto the germ of a plant disappearing into its seed. The omniscient God, with view to making us wise and enlightened, had revealed

> the Vedas to the minds (of the primeval sages) Agni, Aditya, Vayu, and Angira, and through these sages to the world. The Vedas being eternal and acknowledge as such by all, it was, on the strength of irrefutable arguments, clear that in the beginning of creation there was only the Vedic religion prevalent in the world, and that the faiths now prevalent owed their existence to this Primeval Religion.

On the Eternal Vedas, the Origin of all Sciences

There were 1,127 *shakhas* of the Vedas, and these were full of numerous sciences. There was no science and art of which the germs or rudiments were not to be found in the Vedas. The facts of the earth's revolution round the sun and the law of gravitation, for instance, were spoken of in the Vedas. The *mantras* of the Vedas left no doubt on the point, although the ignorant had misinterpreted these. In the reign of Raja Bhoj, who live only fourteen hundred years ago, there were balloons which could travel at the rate of 55 miles an hour, and by means of which large numbers, of men, with their families, could transport themselves through space, from one country to another. And during his time a *pankha* was invented which, once wound, would keep moving for a whole month. The Vedic knowledge was three-fold in its character – that relating to *upasna,* that relating to *gyan,* and that bearing on *karmakand. Karmakand* meant a human activity or energy in action of all kinds; *upasna,* communion with, and contemplation of the Supreme – adoration and worship of God, - glorification of His attributes; while *gyan* signified intellectual and scientific enlightenment and perception. But even as activity or energy had a three-fold aspects (i.e., had to do with *upasna, gyan* and *karma*), even so *gyan* had a three-fold aspect. Whatever action or deed was the result of the guidance of a chastened and enlightened intellect (gyan) the same was *dharma* and the reverse for that *adharma*. The word *dharma* was also a synonym of *nyaya* or justice, the one being inclusive of the other.

> "The four Vedas contained about twenty thousand *richas,* which were popularly thought to represent particular *devatas,* but which, in point of fact, were

only associated with the names of *devas*, the wise and erudite sages (who saw into the meaning of the *mantras*). In ancient times these *devas* or wise men were worshipped, that is, were made much of, for when the Shastras says that women should be worshipped, the meaning clearly is, that they should be honoured and made much of, Vishvakarma was an individual of the noble type, the originator and founder of industry and art, and not incorporeal god. Jaimini and other Rishis had given the summary of the Vedic Teaching in the Smritis and Shastras. If anyone of the audience was desirous of realising the nature of *karmakand* more comprehensively, he should go through the 12 Chapters of Jaimini's treatise on the subject.

"Yajna meant *yagya* performed in accordance with the injunctions of the Vedas, and the *yajna* and the 'Homa' used to be performed, both morning and evening, to purge the air of hateful and disease-producing germs, and for the bringing down and purification of rain and water. Having mixed a *ratti* of musk, a *masha* of saffron and other fragrant substances of various kinds in a seer of clarified butter, every man and woman, in these days, would throw twelve *ahutis* into the fire, the quantity thus offered being thought sufficient to purify air and water, rendered foul by the offensive smells thrown out by human beings during the day and night. And the injurious and disgusting gases generated by the droppings and urine of beasts, and the deposits and urine of miscellaneous classes of men, - for the destruction of these a big *havan* was performed forth-nightly, on *amava* and *poornamashi*, and the fragrance diffused by these *havens* purified the harmful vapours containing the gases. And, further, *havans* were performed on a grand scale, six-monthly and annually, to cope with and destroy the bad gases in general. The festivals of Holi and Dewali, so called in these days, were but names for these periodical *havens*. And these ceremonies had existed from times immemorial, and it was due to the performance of these diseases and epidemics, which afflict India in these days, were wholly unknown in times of yore. The performance of such an similar rites meant the exercise of human activity and energy, and it was the pleasure of the Supreme that such exercise should always continue, for it was a fulfilment of the Soul's mission on earth.

"And the general impression that the study of the Vedas was prohibited to all by the Brahmans, - this impression owed its existence to the selfishness of the ignorant. Whosoever would know the real truth, should refer to the real truth, should refer to the second *mantra* of the 26th Chapter of the Yajur Veda. The substance of the mantra might be stated as follows:- (God, speaking to entire mankind, says Yathemaam Vaacham Kalyaaneemaavadaani.

"Just as I proclaim the truth to you, even so should ye proclaim it to all persons, - to the Brahmans, the Kshatriyas, the Vaishyas, the Shudras and that to those that are utterly below the Shudras.'

It was really sad that nobody studied the Vedas for himself, but followed others, like sheep following sheep. When the blind led the blind, both the parties must fall into the pit. Selfishness was reigning supreme in the country.

"The so called leaders (the Brahmans), instead of doing good to those upon whose wealth they throve, wished them only evil. Not understanding the true meaning and purport of the Vedas, they gave out as 'Vedic' what they chose. Release from the clutches of such individuals could be had only by a dissemination of the knowledge of the Vedas.

"It was due to the absence of this knowledge in the land that some ignorant people, not understanding the allegorical language of the Scriptures, had described the allegories as stories in the pages of the 'Puranas'. As for instance, the story of the cohabitation of the Moon with the wife of Gautam Rishi, the running of Brahma after his own daughter with a carnal purpose. 'I end my today's lecture here,' said the Swami in conclusion, 'What more I have to say, I shall say in this very place on Friday."

Akhbar-i-Am's Report on more Sciences of the Vedas

The Akhabar-I-Am (an orthodox paper) said in its issue of 2nd may, 1877:

"For more than a week Swami Dayanand has been at Lahore. This personage wears the *Faqir's* garb and toes teaching, from city to city that the four Vedas are the word of God, containing in them all the sciences of the universe. There is nothing (not fact or truth or principle) which according to him, is not to be found in these Books. The ancient people of India, he says, were well versed in every science and accomplished in every art. They knew how to run railways, and understood the mysteries of the telegraph. They were aware of the existence of America. They had carried to perfection medicine, political science and logic. Many of their books, however, got lost, and disunion reduced them to the (miserable) state in which we now find them. The Vedas, he maintains, do not at all speak of idol-worship of sun, moon, fire, air, etc., allowed in them those who think otherwise are labouring under a great mistake. The Swami is writing a commentary on the Vedas. Many portions of the book have already been published. He believes that the religion which is taught in the Vedas, is the only true religion.

"We, too heard three or four lectures of the Swami. The fact is, that the Swami is a man of genius, and we know of none in India at the present time who possesses his grasp of the Vedas. We cannot, however, say that the interpretation he gives of the Veda Mantras is the only correct one, for other great teachers have also commented upon the Vedas. The Swami's interpretation differs from theirs. The Swami is at one with the educated young men of India of these days in holding that caste is nothing. According to him he is a Brahman, who does the acts of one. If a Brahman neglects his duties, he is worse than a Shudra, and the word 'Shudra' means nothing more than ignorant person.

"The aversion towards promiscuous eating, which is manifested by the people nowadays and which has existed in this country for some time, is unjustifiable in his opinion. There is nothing in the Vedas which lends countenance to this assertion. It is advisable to marry widows, or at least it is not objectionable, if they are married. Little boys and girls should not be married. The promulgation of these enlightened views had made the Brahmans enemies of the Swami. But he does not care for their hostility at all. He is in earnest and absorbed in his works as ever. Those who are real well-wishers of this country and wish from their heart that it should prosper, owe it to themselves to help the Swami to the utmost of their power."

The two lectures in the Baoli Sahib had evidently taxed the patience of the ignorant and selfish element in the Brahman community too far, and, fearing a disturbance, it was resolved by the admirers of the Swami that the Baoli should be left alone in future and the should address the public next in the Brahmo Mandir, Anarkali. This was accordingly done, and the next lecture and another after it were delivered in the Mandir in question.

Brahmo Samaj

The lectures were on the "Revealed character of the Vedas" and the "Transmigration of Souls". In these the Divine origin of the Vedas was fearlessly upheld and thoroughly proved and the arguments put forward in support of the doctrine of the transmigration of souls were unanswerable. The Brahmo Samaj does not believe in a Revelation, nor has it's faith in the doctrine of the transmigration of the souls and it would, under the circumstances, be perfectly natural on its part to desire that some building, other than the Brahmo Mandir, should be made available for the Swami's speeches and discourses. At the same time, the orthodox, smarting under the rebuke administered to them, and the exposure to which they were subjected, pressed round Lala Bhagwan Das, son of Diwan Rattan Chand, with the request, given expression to in grieved and indignant tones, that he would turn the atheistic Sanyasi out of his garden.

"The man condemns idol-worship and runs down your and our deities, and as such, no true believer should, in the slightest degree, be helpful to him.' Lala Bhagwan Das judged discretion the better part of valour and forthwith notified the Swami that his house was to be vacated without delay. There was no other alternative but to comply, and the Swami's well-wishers waited upon Dr. Rahim Khan for the loan of his *kothi,* situated in the Anarkali. The doctor was duly informed for whom the *kothi* was wanted and to what use it would be put, but he was a large-hearted gentleman and cheerfully acceded to the wishes of the Deputation. And the Swami removed to the Doctor's *kothi,* an it was found to be sufficiently spacious and commodious to allow of lectures being delivered there also.

Koh-i-Noor's Report again

The *Koh-i-Noor,* speaking of these lectures, said, in it's issue of 5th May, 1877:

> "Swami Dayanand Saraswati is still in Lahore, and residing in Dr. Rahim Khan's kothi, situated in Anarkali. He now and then addresses the public on the Vedic Dharma, when he feels an inclination to do so. These lectures of his have split the city people into two parties. One of these believes that, that what the Swami teaches is right and useful, the other looks at his preaching as unorthodox and false, and hence inimical to the interests of religion. The first party is

> composed of young men who have received Western education, and of those who are in Government employ; the other of men of the old type and old ways of thinking, advanced in years. We are not in a position to say what the result of all this will be. We notice, however, that the party in sympathy with the Swami is gaining strength, and the other one faring in just the opposite way. Whatever is going on here, is very much the same as was described in some past week."

Biradar-i-Hind's Reports on the Swami's Visit

The *Biradar-i-Hind*, a monthly journal, edited by Pandit Shive Narain Agnihotri, a prominent member of the Brahmo Samaj, contained, in its number for June, 1877, the following in connection with the Swami's work at Lahore:

> "Starting from Ludhiana on 19th April, 1877, Pandit Dayanand Saraswati reached Lahore the evening of the same day, and took up his quarters in the garden belonging to the late Ratan Chand Sarhiwala. The people here had already been waiting for his arrival. When they heard of the arrival of the Pandit Sahib, they streamed forth from their houses to see him. The Brahmos were particularly delighted at his coming, for they had specially exerted themselves to induce him to come here. For four days the people continued to gather around the Pandit in the very garden (where he put up). After the expiration of the period it was thought advisable that the Pandit (the principal object of whose life is to preach and to teach the people) should address the public in a suitable place within the city. At a general meeting held to consider this proposal, the conclusion was arrived at that the Baoli Sahib, being situated in the heart of the town and being, at the same time, a spacious and commodious building, was specially suited for the Pandit's lectures. In conformity with the decision of the meeting, printed notices were issued, and on the date appointed, the Pandit delivered a lecture on the 'Vedas' (in the

building in question). People had come together in large numbers to hear lecture, but inasmuch as the Pandit is a dead enemy of idol-worship (wishing to exterminate it altogether) men of the old school, - Brahmans, who, for a living, are largely dependent on idolatry, and who had, long before the lecture came off, assumed an attitude of hostility towards the Pandit, made a terrific noise, and otherwise behaved most shamefully on the occasion of the lecture. But for the presence of the police in attendance, there was every chance of disturbance taking place. But one took place, and the Swami once more addressed the public in the very same building. However after the two lectures in question, it was resolved that, inasmuch as there was apprehension of a disturbance in the Baoli Sahib, and inasmuch as there was a great deal of noise there, the Swami should henceforward lecture in the Brahmo Mandir. Accordingly the Pandit delivered two lectures in the Brahmo Samaj, perfect order, as might be expected, prevailing there on each occasion, and the people hearing the *updesh* with patience and attention.

"In the meantime, however, the gentleman, in whose garden the Pandit had to put up, and who had, of his own free-will invited him to take up his quarters there, yielding to prejudice and wholly regardless of the fact that he was a Raees, desired the Pandit to vacate his house. Well, there was not dearth secured for his residence another building, better and far larger than the first, and the Swami vacating the Raees's house, removed into the new *kothi*. This new *kothi* belongs to Dr. Rahim Khan, Khan Bahadur, whose courtesy and large-heartedness may be gauge and judged from the fact that, though a Muhammadan by faith, he most cheerfully made over his house to the Pandit the moment the people asked him for the loan of it. This act of generosity on the part of the Khan Sahib was such that the well-wishers of the

Pandit would ever consider themselves beholden to him for the same. The house was so big and possessed such a spacious compound, that it was thought that it was suitable not only for his residence but for his lectures also. This being the case, his lectures commenced to be given in the *kothi* instead of in the Brahmo Mandir, ever since his leaving his old lodgings.

"On reaching here the Swami commenced speaking against idol-worship so strongly that the Brahman community in particular, and the other people in general, came to be in a state of excitement. When the Brahmans saw that many of their 'sheep' had left them and many were daily leaving them, they could contain themselves no longer. Recognising the necessity, they convened a meeting, which was attended by the best-known and select Pandits of the town. These Pandits summoned Pandit Bhanu Datta, Acharya, Sat Sabha, Punjab, to the meeting also, and inasmuch as the Pandit was an acharya of a Sabha whose chief object was, admittedly and in effect, to proclaim to the people the worship of the one formless, and inasmuch as he himself had helped the educated community to entertain about him the impressions that he did not look upon idolatry as anything commendable, and further inasmuch as he was frequently seen with the Swami when the latter arrives at Lahore, the Pandits, with one voice, declared to his face that they thought he too was of the religion of Dayanand Saraswati. Now sooner were these words uttered than Pandit Bhanu Datta, in trepidation and alarm, replied that he was at a loss to understand how such a thing could be predicted of him. 'My faith,' he added, 'is the same as yours and, if you desire to say anything against the Swami, my services are your disposal.' Hearing his answer the Pandits were pleased, and Pandit Bhanu Datta was appointed 'Secretary of the Sabha organised by them.

"When the people came to hear that Pandit Bhanu Data had joined a Sabha whose object was to uphold idol-worship and to prove the same from the Vedas, they, the educated portion of them especially, who were fully acquainted with his religious views, were extremely surprised. We, in particular, were not only surprised to hear the news but very much grieved also, for the Pandit was friendly-disposed towards us in a remarkable degree. Whenever we had occasion to converse with him on idol-worship, he never supported idol-worship. Indeed, only a few days ago, he told us that Pandit Dayanand Saraswati wanted him to remain with him and to assist him in this national work by becoming a missionary and giving *updesh* to the people; but,' said the Pandit, 'I am so very much attached to my family and household that although Swami Dayanand is willing to provide amply for my family, and although I myself like the work proposed very much, I have not sufficient moral courage to close the with the Swami's offer and to work with him in the furtherance of his mission.'

"Our readers will see from this that Pandit Bhanu Datta joined the idolatrous Pandits and became the Secretary of their Sabha through motives of 'policy'. Indeed, he went so far as to stop seeing the Swami from the day he joined the Pandits, and to issue a notice under his signature that a certain Pandit would, on behalf of his Sabha, deliver a lecture in 'idol-worship' and prove that the Vedas allowed the adoration of idols. In addition to this lecture, the Pandit himself, in the meantime, delivered two lectures, in which he explained the nature and character of the gods, and actually supported idol-worship. So far we have spoken of the Lahore Pandits and of the opposition of the Pandit Sabha. As to what are the views of Swami Dayanand, what the nature of the reform which he wishes to bring about by his updesh in different places, how far his teaching produces its effect on the minds of the educated youth, to what extent the principles of the Brahmo Samaj are in conformity with his religious ideas, wherein they differ and why, what is the measure of success which the noble efforts of the Swami have already achieved, and what success they are likely to achieve in future; - on these points we shall speak in a future issue:

And in fulfilment of the promise made in the foregoing article, Pandit Shive Narain Agnihotri, wrote in his journal (1st July, 1877):

"The views of Swami dayanand are catholic and mostly in accordance with the advance ideas of the present day. His mind appears to be capable of vast improvement, and hence it is that although he is conversant with no literature other than that embodied in the Sanskrit language, he has yet, by the help of this literature, and by mixing enlightened and educated gentlemen, liberalised his ideas and made them clear in such an eminent degree that, rising far above the level of bigoted and narrow-minded contemporary Pandits, he has developed into a model of a truly learned and enlightened Pandit, his views are ahead of those of the general mass of English educated people of our country. This man, to all outward appearance, seems to be an enthusiastic advocate of national reform, and an enthusiastic lover of his nation, although it is utterly impossible for us to declare at present how for this enthusiasm is free from the alloy of selfishness. For it is only time and experience that can furnish conclusive evidence on this head one away or the other. For all this, his personality, as far as we can judge of him at the present time, holds out great hopes of progress and reform in the country. As a religious reformer, this man is an inveterate foes of idol-worship. Really, contemplating him side by side with those who are at present body undermining the foundations of idolatry, it would not be improper to set him down as the greatest iconoclast of the age.

> "Viewed in his capacity as a helper of the Brahmo Samaj, in pushing forward the interests of the of the religious crusade undertaken by that body, whose fundamental principle of belief requires that idol-worship in all its phases should be uprooted and the worship of the one only true God should be spread in the world, the man has so much of the angel in him that it is impossible to over praise him. It is not only religious upheaval which this man is desirous of bringing about: he has also in view the reformation of the evil customs and usages such as child-marriage, etc. which are prevailing in the land. He is, above all, an advocate of female education and emancipation, believing that so long as the Indian woman remains ignorant and does not obtain freedom from domestic thralldom, the hope of seeing India make an appreciable progress will never be realised. To be brief, the destruction of ignorance and prejudice from among the nation, the diffusion of knowledge, the creation of national union, and evolving, out of this union, an all-embracing civilization, which will make the Indian Community a model community, is thee first and final aim of this man."

Excerpt from the Koh-i-Noor

The following excerpt from the *Koh-i-Noor*, 16th June, 1877, describes the effect on the public mind of the Swami's utterances at Lahore:

> "The truthful words of the Swami have turned the hearts of numbers from idol-worship. Many have packed up their idols to be put away and never to be thought of again, many having gone to the Ravi quietly have consigned them to the waters, while many others, more daring than the rest and wholly indifferent to the threats of the *Biradari*, have flung them hero-like into the streets. The result of these herculean efforts of the Swami had been of the highest advantage not only to his followers but to the other party also. A

> body of young men, educated and imbued with new ideas and impatient of restraint, has given their wholehearted allegiance to the Swami, and such has been the effect of his preaching that during the current week, a man, taking up his *Chauki* of idols, threw it into the bazaar."

Swami Dayanand had hardly been little more than two months in Lahore, when the enlightened community of the town came to recognise the absolute necessity of establishing an Arya Samaj in their midst.

Strange that over a dozen years, *updesh* in the N.W.P. should have failed to produce in these Provinces the result which a couple of months' stay in the Punjab was sufficient to bring about! No doubt, the educated people of Bombay had been prompt in perceiving an organisation which should, on systematic lines, work for the good of mission; but in the vigour and intensity of feeling, - the earnestness with which the Punjab took up the Swami's work, in the comprehensive realisation of the stupendous significance of the Samajic propaganda, and in the prevision of its far-reaching and enduring consequences, for which the Punjabis distinguished themselves, our good brethren of Bombay were far from bring up to the mark. And they were not to blame.

Lucknow and other Towns

Leaving Bombay on 1st May, 1876, and visiting Farrukhabad for the fifth time, Swami Dayanand arrive at Banaras and put up in the Atamgiri garden. He stayed here for over two months, but no shastrarth was held with the Pandits. It was Banaras that the Swami came to make up his mind to engaged to write from dictation, and giving the usual details connected with the work. The book was to be brought out by the well-known local printers, E.J. Lazarus and Company, in monthly parts.

From Kashi and the Swami went to Jaunpur and thence to Ayudhia, which he left for Lucknow towards the close of September, preaching and holding discussions. The conversation which took place between him and Lala Brij Lal, Raeeses, is worth reproducing:

Imperial Durbar

While the Swami was busy with this Bhumika and with his updesh, he heard of the importance of the coming Imperial Durbar at Delhi, and, wishing to be present on the occasion, if he could help it, he left for the scene of the approaching function in company with Thakur Mukand Singh and other Thakurs. Reaching Delhi, he took up his quarters in Sher Mal's Anar Bag, which had already been put in a fitting condition to receive him. Anar Bag was close to the plot of land on which the tents of the Rajas and Raeeses of Oudh stood, and over the gate of the garden hung a placard with the words – Residence of Swami Dayanand Saraswati.

The Swami had notices pasted in front of the tents of the Rajas and Maharajas, and to draw the attention of these magnates all the better to the contents of his manifesto had a copy of the same sent to each of them, with a request that they would bestir themselves to arrange for a shastrarth between him and the Pandits, so that truth might be known from what was false, and the great land of the Rishis should once more return to the primeval Vedic Faith.

It could be expected that the Rulers and Chiefs would think much of a shastrarth at such a time;: they were thinking of other things and were other wise occupied. The Maharaja of Indore was the only one who did make an effort to convene a meeting of his brother-Rulers and of the Pandits, but the effort was signal failure. For all that however, the work of updesh vigorously went on, and Hindus and Muhammadans and Padris thronged under his Shamianas all day long.

Occasionally, the Raeeses and Rajas of Oudh also would stop to hear him and would have conversations with him. Of the great ones of the Punjab, Maharaja Ranbir Singh of Jammu and Kashmir sent his Vizier, Anant Ram Diwan, and his Musahib, Babu Nilambar, to wait upon the Swami, with a request that he would see His Highness; but before the Swami could comply with His Highness's request, the State Pandits had changed his mind, and the interview never came off.

On the occasion of the Durbar, the Swami, failing to get the Rajas and Maharaja to come together and to hear his lectures, convened a meeting of some enlightened well-wishers and reformers of India, with the object of finding out, by discussion and deliberation, if cooperation in the work of reform was possible among them. The Sabha was composed of the following gentlemen:

Baboo Ghanaya Lall Alakkhadahri, Baboo Navin Chandra Roy, Baboo Keshva Chandra Sen, Munshi Indramani of Muradabad, Sir Sayyad Ahamad Khan, Baboo Harish Chandra Chintamani and Swami Dayanand Saraswati. The Swami's own solution of the problem before the Sabha was in these words: "If we have the same set of principles to believe in, and work on the same lines, I have hope that the country can be soon reformed." This solution could not be appreciated by the others, for there were differences in religious belief which could not be got over, and thus nothing was practically accomplished. Baboo Navin Chandra Roy speaking of the meeting in his Journal *Gyan Darpan* (1885) wrote: Inasmuch as we differed with him on fundamental principles of belief, the sort of union he sought to bring about could not be effected."

Chandapur Fair

Munshi Pyare Lal kayastha, Raees Chandapur, District Shahjahanpur (N.W.P.), with a view to ascertaining which was true *Dharma* (faith), obtained permission from the Collector of his district to hold a religious fair at his native place, and having fixed upon 19th march 1877, as the day of the first meeting, had, printed notices circulated, inviting the most learned and distinguished followers of Hinduism, Islam and Christianity to come and have, by friendly conversation and discussion, truth sifted from falsehood.

In response to these notices, leaders of every religion, of profound scholarship, and well-known throughout India, came. First of all came the famous Vedic Scholar and Founder of the Arya Samaj Swami Dayanand Saraswati, accompanied by the well-known opponent of the Muslim Faith, Munshi Indramani of Muradabad a man who was a complete master of Arabic and Persian, and a critical student of both the Quran and the Traditions. These two gentlemen, deeply interested in religious matters, arrived at Chandapur on 15th March, 1877.

On behalf of the Christian religion came, on 19th March, 1877, the famous logician and profound scholar, author of many learned pamphlets and of commentary on the Bible – the Rev. T.G. Scott, accompanied by Rev. Mr. Noble, the Rev. Mr. Parker, and the Rev. Mr. John Thompson, and several other Missionaries of knowledge. And on behalf of the Muhammadans came, on the same day and at the same time, Moulvi Muhammad Qasim, the Principal of Deoband School, the most distinguished Arabic Seminary in India, the author of a delightful treatise or rhetoric, and the awarder of diplomas to Moulvis, accompanied by Sayyad Abul Mansoor of Delhi, the foremost man in literary discussions, the author of works like the Zinda Javaid, written against Christianity, and the holder of a diploma from His Imperial Highness, the Sultan of Turkey, as a recognition of his scholarship, and by many other gentlemen.

It was suggested to the Swami that if the Hindus and the Muslims formed a coalition and unitedly exposed the Christian Religion, it would be most commendable. But the Swami replied that he was sorry he could not agree to the proposal.

"It appears to me just and proper that no one in this fair should do anything savouring of partiality. To me it seems best that the Moulvis, the Missionaries and ourselves should meet in love and peace and investigate the truth. No one should be hostile to the others."

After this it was proposed that all the parties concerned should repair to the place where the *jalsa* (grand meeting) was to come off, and settle the conditions of the shastrarth; but I being pointed out that the crowd there would be in the way, two gentlemen from each repaired to the tents of the Missionaries, and there, assisted by Mr. Moti Mian and Lala Ram Parshad, Raeeses and Honorary Magistrates, Shahjahanpur, and Mukta Parshad, Raees, Chandapur, commenced their deliberations. But though hours were spent in these deliberations, no unanimity of opinion could be secured as to the conditions of the shastrarth.

The only point settled was the formal recognition of the necessity of holding a *jalsa* for the discussion. Seeing what little had been achieved and that the Padris were for not staying for over two days, Swami Dayanand observed that he and his companion had come to Chandapur on the distinct understanding that the Conference would last for a full week, and in no case for less than five days, and this period, he said, would have sufficed for determining the worth of every religion. To this the Munshi Indramani replied "Swamiji, be sure that the true religion will be found out even in a single day."

After 10 O'clock, it was unanimously resolved that the first spokesman, on behalf of each party, should speak on the question taken up for discussion for half an hour, and that the after-speakers replying to or expressing doubts and objections, should each speak for 10 minutes. The fact was made know to all would-be speakers that every one of them was to be perfectly master of his time, to enjoy, while speaking during the time allotted, complete immunity from interruption.

Opening Address

Munshi Pyare Lal rose and addressed the meeting in some thing like the following:

> "We should, first of all, be thankful to God, the omnipresent and all-pervading Lord. We are all fortunate in that this Supreme Sovereign of the universe has placed us under a Ruler who permits us to talk freely on religious subjects. At the same time we ought to express our thanks to our Collector and District Magistrate, who, influenced by his sympathetic, appreciative and benevolent disposition, had been pleased to allow us to hold a discussion on an occasion like the present on 'god' and other kindred subjects. Language cannot describe the pleasure I feel today. It is a blessed day indeed, and happy is the land which finds so many influential and learned men, representing different faiths, assembled in it.
>
> "Sirs, the world is a *Caravansera*, and life is not a thing to be depended upon. The mercy of God has been specially manifested today, in that so many gentlemen, in pursuance of a lofty resolve, have graced this meeting with their presence. I am confident that they

> will each speak of the beauties of his sacred Faith in words at once gentle and sweet, and will thus enable the audience to acquire, by his expositions, the fruit of salvation. I, Pyare Lal, a Kabirpanthi, pray to God for the preservation (success) of the Jalsa."

Appointing Representatives

On the termination of the speech, the discussion commenced as to how many persons should be appointed as 'representatives,' out of the professors of each creed present. Ultimately, five individuals were put forward by the Musalmans as their representatives, as many by the Christians, and only two by the Aryas, namely, Swami Dayanand Saraswati and Munshi Indramani. The Moulvis and Padris insisted upon the full number (five) of representatives being appointed by the Aryas as well, but the Swami assured them that two were enough.

The Christians, not satisfied with the answer, made an attempt to add the name of Lakshman Shastri to the list of 'Arya representatives.' Swami Dayanand protested against such a conduct, observing that, though the Christians were perfectly free to choose representatives for themselves, they had no right to do so for others. And addressing the Pandit, the Swami said:

"Don't you see their game? These people want to create ill-feeling between us, in order to enjoy the fun!

The Muslims, however, would not listen to the Swami's protest, and the instant he had ceased speaking, a Moulvi came forward, and, catching hold of the Pandit, urge him to have his name enlisted. Upon this the Swami observed that in the event of the Aryas agreeing unanimously to appoint the Pandit as their representative, his name might be put down as such, but it was no concern of the Musalmans to select him.

A Muslim critic, commenting upon the Swami's words, remarked that if such was to be the case, all the Hindus present should also be asked if the were willing to appoint Swami Dayanand and Munshi Indramani as their representatives. To this the Swami made answer:

> "When you have not been elected by the Shias and the Sunnis unanimously, when the Christians have

> not been assigned the position of 'representatives' by the Roman Catholics as well, where is the necessity for you to raise such objections with regard to us? There are many who would be willing to accept us as their representatives, but many there may be who would be unwilling to do so but for all that you have no right to create ill-feeling between us."

Munshi Indramani added: "We are believers in the Vedas and the Shastras, and so are these people; if there are any that do not, they may be constituted into a fourth party in the discussion." The object aimed at by the Moulvis, by bringing forward the objections they did, was to stir up quarrels between the Aryas and the Hindus, and, keeping aloof from the wrangling that must ensue, to enjoy the 'fund' thereof. The Aryas, however, did not think it advisable to add the name of Pandit Lakshman to the list of their representatives, and the Moulvis (perceiving as much) retired, at this stage, to say their prayers. On their return Moulvi Muhammad Qasin said, that he would address the meeting, for a whole hour, on his religion, independent of what he might to say directly on the questions to be propose for the discussion, later on, and that he would remove any doubts that might arise in any one's mind by his speech. To this all agreed.

Ludhiana

Munshi Kanhaiya Lal Alakhdhari, Raees, Ludhiana, Pandit Manphul, Raees, Lahore, and Munshi Harsukh Rai, Proprietor, the Koh-i-Noor paper of Lahore, had come in contact with Swami Dayanand on the occasion of the Imperial Darbar and, struck by his extraordinary attainments, his passionate love of truth, and his patriotism, had expressed a hope that he would visit the Punjab also. Accordingly, as soon as the fair at Chandapur was over, Swami Dayanand, accompanied by Munshi Kanhaiya Lal Alakhdhari, the bold and fearless denunciator of every form of hypocrisy prevalent in Indian Society, whose invaluable writings have been and are still studied by thousands of his countrymen, left for Ludhiana, which he reached on 31st March 1877, he put up outside the city in a garden, and the hospitable Munshi saw he wanted nothing.

The news of the Swami's arrival at Ludhiana brought forth many enquirers, the Missionaries especially, who had frequent conversations with him. The local Christian paper, the *Nur Afshan* (March 1877), had the following lines about him:

"Pandit Dayanand Saraswati Swami, who is a famous Vedic Scholar of India, and goes form place to place preaching, arrived here during the present week. He gives *updesh* daily at the house of Lala Jat Mal, the Treasurer, and from his lectures it appears that he wants to reform the present usages and customs of the Hindu community. He would have them worship and adore the one only God, and leave off all other kinds of worship. Yes, it is his wish that they should believe in the one only Creator, should give up, one and all, idol-worship, and follow civilized customs only, even as their ancestors of old were in the habit of doing. We are confident that his *updesh* will do considerable good to the Hindus."

An Englishman becomes his Admirer

During his stay at Ludhiana, the Swami had interviews with Mr. Carr Stehphen, Judicial Assistant Commissioner. This gentleman was an English man of liberal views, and a great admirer of the Swami. He was so delighted by the Swami's conversation, that he became a subscriber to the Veda Bhashya, and when the Swami was leaving Ludhiana, presented him with some money in an envelope as a contribution towards the expenses of the publication.

Saving two from Converting to Christianity

It is worthy to note that the Swami's presence at Ludhiana was instrumental in saving two men from falling into the hands of the Christians. One of these was a Gaur Brahman (Pandit Ram Saran) of Alwar. He had the misfortune, while proceeding towards Delhi some six months back, of being set upon by robbers and stripped of the little he possessed. Almost naked he reached Delhi. Here he happened to hear Rev. Newton preaching. The Padri reading a shaloka from the Durgapath, the Brahman immediately interrupted him with the remark: " You are reading the verse incorrectly." The Padri, his preaching over, beckoned the man to approach, and learning his history, gave him two rupees to provide himself with clothes.

The simple man was thankful, and easily prevailed upon to accompany the Missionary to Ludhiana, where, he was assured, he should have suitable employment. He was appointed a teacher in the Girl's school to teach the children Nagri on Rs. 5 amonth. Being constantly thrown in the company of the Padris – Rev. Mr. Wherry, Rev. Mr. Newton, Rev. Mr. Rudulph, etc. he had come to hate his own religion, and to discover a partiality for that of the Christians.

The crisis was approaching. He had agreed to be baptised, and the date fro the ceremony had already been fixed, when a reformer from among his own community, a person of commanding personality and strong in truth, lighted upon him and his delusion was at an end. Bidding farewell to the Padris, he went his way.

Refuting a Westerner's Ridicule of Shri Krishna

Dr. Wherry and others, in their conversations and debates with the Swami, sought to uphold Shri Krishna to the ridicule and contempt of those present, but the Swami pointed out to them the loftiness and purity of the great teacher's character by quoting from the Mahabharata and other Arsha Granths, observing at the same time that the Puranas were spurious productions and not to be relied upon. The Swami further made clear to them that neither Christ or Krishna nor any other great man was an incarnation of the Deity.

Mainpuri

On May 5th, 1880, the Swami left Banaras for Lucknow, where he preached for about two weeks and then left for Furrakhabad, staying there till 30th June. From Furrakhabad he went to Mainpuri, whence he departed to Meerut on 6th July, arriving there on the 8th, and five days after he had left Mainpuri, an Arya Samaj was established there (11th July, 1880.)

Masooda

In defence of the wishes of Rao Bahadur Singh of Masooda, the Swami left Ajmer for his principality on 23rd June, and stayed there till 17th August. Some twelve lectures were delivered during.

The Principality containing a large number of Jainis, they were called upon to come forward for a shastrarth. They said they would do it, provided their leader, Sadhu Sidh Karn, could be induced to take up their cause. They sent for the Sadhu, and he came. At first he refused to comply with the wishes of his followers, but at last permitted himself to be prevailed upon so far as to agree to answer any questions that Swami Dayanand should send to him for a reply. The Swami sent him a few questions in connection with the custom of keeping the mouths bandaged, observed by the leaders of Jainism, and the Sadhu replied.

Comments on the reply were duly forwarded to the Sadhu, but they were so very hard to answer was compelled to see refuge in silence. The Jains perceived the weakness of their creed, and many of them waited upon the Rao to have a Vedic *Yajna* performed. The Rao graciously complied with the request, and as many as thirty-two Jaini gentlemen put on the *Yajnopavit* on the occasion of the function. The Rao himself underwent the ceremony, and declared himself to be a staunch follower of the Vedic religion. Yet a second *Yajna* was performed on 14th august, 1881, and at this a goodly number of clerks, belonging to the Bharatpur State, were invested with *Yajnopavit* Here an English Missionary and a Native Padri came from Biawar to see the Swami and they had a long conversation with the reformer.

There were Hindus in Masooda, who, though they have married their daughters into Muslim families, once part and parcel of their *biradri*, refused to receive girls from the latter in their own families. This the Swami considered objectionable for more than one reason, had he gave his advice to the individuals concerned accordingly. The Rao presented the Swami, when the latter was taking his leave, with Rs. 500, in aid of the Veda-Bhashya.

Mathura

After about a month's stay at Aligarh, the Swami went to Hathras, whence, in response to an invitation from Rao Tikam Singh, he proceeded to Mursan, which, after a few day's halt, he left for Mathura (Vrindavan) via Hathras. Pandit Dev Parshad, Deputy collector, was aware of the Swami's approaching visit to

Mathura, Raja Jaikishen Das having written to him about the same, and he selected Radhabagh for the Swami's residence. As to what had been instrumental in drawing the Swami to Mathura, was the refusal on the part of a class-fellow of his (Pandit Ganga Datta) to accept a teachership in the Farrukhabad pathshala till Mathura, the stronghold of idolatry, had been visited and idol-worship there been given a deathblow. "Rangacharya he said, "goes about the city with flambeaux burning before him in the daytime, proclaiming that the worship of idols is right and good. If I am to accept the post in your gift and move from Mathura, I will do that only after you have been in our midst, and exposed the false teachers." The Swami was impressed by this communication from his class-fellow, and found himself erelong at Vrindavan.

When Swami Dayanand arrived at Vrindavan, he found it in a state of unusual excitement. The Raht Fair on the Brahma Utsav was about to take place, and followers of Vaishnav creed had flocked to Krishna's birth-place in hundreds and thousands from the most distant parts of India. A more glorious opportunity the Swami could not look for to make known the Truth. Accordingly, a notice was issued in Hindi, under the signature of Bakshi Mahbu Masih, that Swami Dayananda's lectures would commence on the 5th of March, 1874, the very day on which the Fair was to begin.

At the same time a challenge was sent to Rangacharya to come forward and support idolatry on the authority of the Vedas, to show that the wearing of kanthi and tilak was, as he asserted, inculcated in the Scriptures. Rangacharya replied that he would answer the call on the termination of the Fair. The reply was significant and the Swami rating it at its proper worth, took to vigorously exposing the un-Vedic institutions and usages in the very thick of the Fair. The unanswerable arguments of the Swami were daily reported to Rangacharya, and the latter realising, in the depths of his heart, the utter hopelessness of making good his position against such antagonist, had it given out that he was not feeling well. In proportion the day fixed for the shastrarth drew nearer, the illness of the learned Rangacharya increased, and at last when the day arrived, he would not leave his house and was self-denying enough to forego the pleasure of entering into a controversy, in spite of his promise to the contrary! The erudite Rangacharya is said to have confessed to an acquaintance of his in private that he had no desire to hold a shastrarth, for in the event of Dayanand's being defeated, the "Sadhu" would lose nothing, but if he was worsted in the contest, all his reputation would be gone. Rangacharya caring for the world and its opinion, had doubtless much at stake, and he was wise in his generation for avoiding Swami Dayanand, for the latter was stronger in faith!

The admirers of Rangacharya took up cudgels in behalf of their master, not metaphorically but literally. Some four or five hundred Chovas (strudy, begging Brahmans) armed with clubs, surrounded the Swami's residence, abusing him and gnashing their teeth in rage, but the Deputy Collector was equal to the emergency and no disturbance took place. The effect of such conduct on the part of Rangacharya's followers was that many men gave up idolatry once and forever.

Having done his work at Vrindavan, the Swami came at Mathura, where he stayed for only four days, but something was accomplished even during this small period. Several enquirers were so impressed by his teaching that they threw their idols into river, and gave their allegiance to the one and only God of the Universe – even to Him whose glory the Vedas proclaim! Pandit Madan Datta, in particular, was so charmed by the Swami's truthful updesh that though he had started from home with the avowed object of defending and advocating idolatry, he commenced denouncing if before his very admirers and in the presence of hundreds of Vaishnavas and other non-believers in the Vedic religion.

Meerut

From Aligarh, the Swami went to Meerut (August 26th, 1878), where he put in Lala Damodar Das's *kothi*, near the quarter of the Native Calvary. The Hindus and Muhammadans alike made preparations for a discussion, issuing handbills and exchanging letters with the Swami as an evidence of their earnestness of the Swami, but no discussion actually took place, the opposing parties no doubt, being convinced in their heart of hearts that the wisest plan for them to adopt was to rest content with making a reasonable amount of fuss and show. The Muhammadans would hold a shastrarth on the condition that it should not be reduced to writing, and to this demand of their would-be representative and spokesman the Swami found himself unable to agree.

Meritoriousness of Bathing in the Ganges

The Sanatanists, after they had sent a few questions to the Swami for a reply, declared their willingness to publicly face the Swami. The question of conditions was taken up and half settled. The announcement came from the upholders of orthodoxy that they could never hold a shastrarth with Dayanand till it was satisfactorily determined what *varna* and *ashrama* he belonged to? The uselessness of holding a shastrarth with such a man as Dayanand, was further pointed out in the following words, appended to the announcement: "Our Pandits are profound scholars, and you are an ignorant man. It is ridiculous for the learned to hold a shastrarth with the illiterate."

The questions which the assembly of "profound scholars" had sent to the Swami for an answer were:

- "We hear that doubts have arisen in you mind in respect of 'idol-worship'. If the report is true, then quote from Shruti and Smriti in support of your contention; but if the report is unfounded, then declare the fact in clear words.
- "If you have any doubts in respect of the *Gangamahatam* (meritoriousness of bathing in the Ganges), then quote authorities in support of your contention.
- "Is the doctrine of incarnation right? If otherwise, cite authorities to prove your case."

Replying to the questions in his public lectures, the Swami said that he was absolutely convinced that idol-worship was opposed to the teaching of the Veda. The mantras like the third and the eighth of the thirty-second and fortieth chapters of the Yajurveda proved this beyond the shadow of a doubt, showing further that the worship of idols and images could only be productive of suffering. As to the *Gangamahatam*, the Swami quoted the well-known *shloka* (109th) from the 5th chapter of the Manu

Smriti, and further repeating a passage from the Chhandoagya Upanishad, showed how *tirtha* was a name from *mental purification* - the cleansing of the heart from envy, hate, etc. According to the true Shastras, therefore, bathing in the Ganges or any other river or pond was fruitful of no moral or spiritual merit. It could only benefit or harm the body.

Incarnation of Gods

As regards the question of incarnation, the Swami's answer was, that there were no incarnations of God. God, as taught in mantras like the first mantra of the thirty-first chapter of the Yajurveda, was all-pervading, infinite, omnipotent, free from the bondage of the captivity of every conceivable kind, indivisible, unharmable, absolutely immaculate, the knower of all hearts, and so forth, and, as such, He could not assume a material form.

The beings looked upon as "incarnations" of God by the orthodox, added the Swami, were only mortals, men of an exalted and lofty type, who deserved to be reverenced and followed, and by walking in their footsteps, we too could make ourselves good and virtuous.

The Swami's lectures, which were delivered in three different places in succession, in Lala Geneshi Lal's Press, at the house of Lala Ram Saran Das, Raees, and in the *kothi* of Babu Chhedi Lal, Commissariat Agent, had their effect on unbiased minds, and an Arya Samaj was established at Meerut on 29th September, 1879, with the following gentlemen as Office-bearers:- Pandit Kundan Lal, B.A., President; Lala Ram saran Das, Raees, Vice-President; Babu Anand Lal, Secretary; Babu Chhedi Lal, Treasurer; Pandit Jagan Nath Parshad, Librarian; Pandit Amba Shanker, Assistant Secretary.

Mirzapur

Starting from Furrakhabad on 8th October, 1879, and making brief halts at Cawnpore and Prayag, the Swami arrived at Mirzapur on 23rd October, 1879, and lectured there for four or five days. He was far from being in the best of health yet, but for all that, the *updesh* was given without fail, and religious conversation with the enquirers was being daily pushed on. A Samaj already existed here, doing by itself and others what it was in duty bound to do.

The Swami left Mirzapur for Danapur (Behar) on 30th October, 1879, in company with some members of the Danapur Samaj, who had come to fetch him. He delivered on different subjects some fourteen lectures during the seventeen or eighteen days he stayed there. The lectures were attended by the Missionaries and by other European gentlemen also. Being full of criticism on the Hindu, Muslim and other creeds, they created considerable excitement, and threats of vengeance were forthcoming freely. A Muhammadan youth, thrown into a state of frenzy by the reformer's comments, warned the Swami not be so free with his creed, but the only reply which the Swami gave to the menace was that in is public lecture when he said:

> "So long as Muhammadans had their way, they spread their religion by the sword, but now that India had a better Government and the people enjoyed the blessing of freedom of speech, there was no reason why men like him should not expose absurdities and abused, like rational men, with their tongue!"

At one of the lectures delivered on the teachings of the Bible, General Roberts, the Commander-in-Chief, with his staff, was present. The comments were as strong as ever. On the termination of the speech the General shook hand with the Swami, remarking:

> "When you can speak in this fashion on the Bible in our presence, you must care but little for others."

A real Sanyasi will fear nothing.

The local Dharma Sabha, in its desperation, sent for its famous Pandit Chaturbhuj, to hold a shastrarth with the Swami. The Pandit obeyed the call, but he would not come forward, insisting that the shastrarth, if it was to take place, should take place in a building to be specified by the Dharma Sabha. The Swami suspected foul play, but at last he agreed. His suspicions proved to be true.

Pandit Chaturbhuj did not put in an appearance at all in this new building either, the Secretary of the Dharma Sabha only attending and declaring that he should speak in place of the Pandit. The Swami refused to have anything to do with him, on which that truly excellent man extinguished the lamp, and, giving admission to a large number of Muhammadans from the other entrance to the house, prepared to set upon the Swami and his companions, but he was playing a losing game. There was that in the voice of the Swami which sent terror into the hearts of the miscreants. The party forcing their way through the crowd emerged into the open, safe and sound, although the Dharma Sabha-followers and the Muslims in combination had sen after them showers of stones and bricks.

The Missionaries and other Europeans saw the Swami when he was comparatively at leisure. Mr. Jones one day urging an objection against the Arya Religion, on the ground that the Hindus observed *chhut-chhat,* the Swami replied:

"We do not believe that Dharma lies in eating or drinking with this or that man. All these things have to do with the usages and customs of a country or a nation. They have no bearing on the true Dharma. Those who are wise, they too will not infringe the national usages unnecessarily." At the same time, the Swami, in the course of further observations made on the point, assured the European that the real religion of the Hindus (Aryas) was not 'idol-worship.'

People were not wanting at Danapur, who would misrepresent the reformer through the press. One good man sent a telegram to the *Indian Mirror,* Calcutta, saying that the Swami had kicked an idol! But what sensible man could ever believe such idle and unfounded reports? The unbiased minds at Danapur gave the lie to the telegram by an increased faith in the Swami and in the true and enduring character of his mission.

One person, who, through the fear of the priests and the *biradiri,* has not the moral courage to hear the Swami's *updesh* openly, one day waited upon him early in the morning, in a secluded spot, far from human habitation, when the Swami was returning from his "constitutional." Giving the Swami an insight into his inmost feelings, he touched his foot with his head, in spite of the Swami's declaration that it was useless doing so, and then went his way.

The Danapur Arya Samaj had now been in existence for over a year, having been established in April, 1878, when the Swami was yet in the Punjab. In fact, it was a development of the *Hindu Sat Sabha,* which the station had possessed for some time past.

Moradabad

Leaving Chhalesar on 3rd July, 1879, the Swami arrive at Muradabad anything but improved in health. This was his second visit to the place. The Arya Samaj established here during his first visit had ceased to exist, and a new one had to be established on a firm footing, and such a one came on 20th July, 1879. The orthodox priests gave out that the Samajists had eaten the leavings of the Swami, and the idle rumour proved so mischievous that the Biradiries commence persecuting all who had embraced the Vedic Religion.

The weak-minded left the Samaj, but there were others who were not in the least move by the threats indulged in by their enemies. Munshi Indramani, the great Arabic and Persian Scholar, who had been a member of the defunct Samaj, was nominated President of the present one; Kanwar Parmanand and Thakor Indra Singh were appointed Secretaries; Sahu Shyam Sundar and Raja Jaggan Nath, Treasurer and Librarian, respectively. In addition to these, the Samaj had 38 members.

Though the Swami stayed for 27 days at Muradabad he could deliver only three lectures during the period. Dysentery had robbed him of his strength, and he found it rather irksome to work. One of the lectures was delivered in the Cantonment, under the presidency of the Collector, on *Rajniti* (political wisdom). The collector was highly pleased with the remarks which fell from the speaker's lips on the subject and on the termination of the speech spoke of him in very high terms.

The well-wishers of the Swami at Muradabad finding how weak he was, placed him under the treatment of a Vaid, summoned specially for the purpose from Badaun., but the Vaid's medicines did him no good. At last the European physician, Dr. Dane was called in. His treatment proved highly beneficial, and before long the Swami was restored, evidently, to perfect health. On the completion of the recovery, Rs. 200 were offered to the Doctor, but the good man refused to receive any remuneration, observing that he could not accept anything from one who was labouring for the good of humanity.

A remark which fell from the Swam's lips at Muradabad, no doubt as a protest against words, intentionally or unintentionally uttered by some one, ought to yield a lesson to all who are, or who may become, members of the Arya Samaj. Addressing the Samajists the Swami said:

> "It is wrong for anyone of you to say that you believe in the religion of Dayanand; what you should say instead is, that your religion is *Vedic*."

Multan

The Swami was yet at Gujranwala, when he received a letter from Dr. Jaswant Rai, requesting him to come to Multan. Coming back to Lahore on 4th March, 1878, he stayed there for a week, and then left for Multan (12th March, 1878), where he passed some thirty-seven days. It being the days of Holi, and law and order being at a discount with the greater part of the population, and the rules of common morality being deliberately set at defiance, satisfactory arrangements for the lectures of the Swami could not be made in the city, and hence, at the request of some Parsi gentlemen, he delivered three lectures in the Cantonment on subjects like the "*Yanopavit*, Child-marriage," etc. The Parsis behaved most hospitality and on the Swami's returning to the city they presented him with one hundred rupees in cash and some choice 'sweets.' The worst of the Holi was by this time over, and the people being in a better and more reasonable frame of mind, the Swami's *updesh* commenced and he never let a day pass without addressing a public meeting.

The substance of these lectures, as of those delivered elsewhere, is embodied in the *Satyarth Prakash*. Some of them touched the enemies of truth and reform sorely, and though no Pandit came forward for a shastrarth, the Goswamis of the town one day mounted on their horses and ringing gongs suddenly appeared at the place where the lecture was going on. They set up an awful howl and indulged in sundry other demonstrations of hostility, but a sharp reprimand made them shut up and depart. Smarting under their discomfiture, they came again the following day, this time accompanied by their followers armed with clubs and knives, and shouting out *Jai Gopal! Jai Gopal!* This time their argument was unanswerable, for no one could say to what length the blind mob might proceed in its frenzy. The lecture was stopped and the meeting broke up.

The Multan Brahmo Samaj felt the Swami's presence in their midst in a manner nothing much to congratulate themselves upon. Many of its members hearing the *updesh* of the Swami lost faith in Brahmoism, and felt a strong desire to become members of the Arya Samaj (established, 4th April, 1878). "We have all our questions answered, and our doubts removed by this Vedic Reformer," said they one to another, "and why should we then delay accepting the religion he preaches?" Why indeed! But before they had time to take the step which their reason and conscience prompted them to take, they were confronted by those who, though they were unable to say anything weighty in defence of Brahmoism were for sticking where they were, and they said to the admirers of the Arya Samaj: "It will reflect discredit on you if you give up your old Faith in this manner. If another man should come tomorrow and convince us of the truth of his doctrines, shall we change our religion again?" a very good argument no doubt, the more so as it came from those whose motto is, "accept the truth where you find it," but the argument, whatever its worth, served its purpose, and the Multan Arya Samaj had to begin its life only with seven members.

Some one in jest observed to the Swami: "You have got only seven members in all?" The Swami was adequate to the occasion and he wittingly answered:

> "The Muhammadan Prophet had but his wife to help him at the outset, but only observe now, for all that, his religion had spread in the world! We have seven men to start with, and why need we be anxious?"

Sardar Prem Singh was the President, Kishen Narain, the Secretary, of the Multan Samaj. The Samaj is still in existence, and doing useful work.

Nabira

From Raipur the Swami went to Nayanagar (Biawar), and stopped there for a fortnight, doing his work as usual, and after that he left for Nabira (via Masooda), where he arrived on the 6th October, 1881. Many of the people in this State were Yajurvedis, though the chiefs' sons recited the whole of the Samveda to the Swami. This is really something to rejoice over, but the pity of it was, that Mahidhar's commentary was in fashion in the State.

The Swami, however, was not wanting in duty: during his twenty days' stay in the principality, he was constantly exposing the mischievous character of the commentary, and explaining to the people the real meaning of the *mantras* misinterpreted and traduced by Mahidhar. The library of the Maharaja, containing valuable books the Swami made a good use of it, especially in comparing the Samveda with the Nighantu, and correcting the Samhita (Vedic Text).

Poona

The nominal shastrarth being over, Swami Dayanand left for Poona, where he stayed for about two months. Poona is nothing if not a stronghold of idolatry in Southern India, and the Swami's presence there was deeply resented by some of the idol-worshippers who, in the heat of excitement, went so far as to put up hirelings to create breach of the public peace and to make themselves a positive nuisance to the reformer and his admirers, to the disgust of the really brave and refined portion of the Poona Community. It was inevitable that they should suffer for their misdeeds and two of the miscreants were sentenced to six and nine months imprisonment, respectively.

This had a very wholesome effect upon their fellows, making them behave peaceably in future. The Swami delivered fifteen lectures in all at Poona, five of these more or less historical in their character, one biographical, and the rest dealing with moral and religious subjects, such as God, the Veda, Revelation, the Transmigration of Souls, etc. These lectures were, in substance, published in the Marhatti language, in the form of a book. In a journal (*Loka Hitavadi*, February 1883) conducted by a Marhatta gentleman a complete account of the Swami's visit to Poona was published. The following passage occurs in the account:

> "In response to an invitation from the influential and learned portion of the Poona community, Swami Dayanand arrived here, staying during the months of June and July (1875). We had occasion to hear some fifteen lectures in the local Hindu Club building. These meetings were always full, and fascinated with the style of speaking of the unique orator and moved by the updesh which his speeches contained, the truth-loving people of the town received him in a manner at once cordial and respectful. One day the seated him on an elephant and took him through the various parts of the city. The greedy, mischievous, hair-brained, thoughtless, selfish and vindictive individuals, in the Poona community, however, could not bear to see this honour shown to him, and they did what the should have abstained from doing. Under these circumstances, the availing of the assistance of the Police became a matter of necessity."

From the journal it appears that Gopal Krishna Bhandarkar, who enjoyed the reputation of being a distinguished Sanskrit scholar, had come to fall out with the Swami on some point, and was ever writing against him and helping the opponents of the Vedic Faith.

Towards the close of August, 1875, Swami Dayanand returned to Bombay to consolidate, by his presence and cooperation, the good work begun. This time, as was perhaps only natural, he put up in the Samaj Mandir. The Samajists and other gentlemen had all the benefit of *Dharmacharcha* (religious conversation and discussion) they could expect to enjoy by associating with the foremost Sanskrit scholar of his time, of a true thinker and genuine reformer.

The Swami told them to be perfectly free with him, and he was never tired removing their doubts regarding the Divine origin of the Vedas and on other points. The Brahmo gentlemen, with their minds surcharged with ideas embodied in the works of

Western Sanskrit scholars, would, again and again, bring forward objections, on one thing and another, connected with the Vedas. One of these concerned the interpretation given to the word 'Agni'. They said they could not understand how it could be taken in the sense of 'God.' The Swami's reply was that the word was taken in that sense as well as in the sense of 'fire,' etc., in the Brahmana Granths, and he quoted the passages bearing on the subject.

The internal evidence of the Vedas also on the point was condensing. The word occurred in the eighteenth *mantra* of the *Ishavasya Upanishad*, the fortieth chapter of the Yajur Veda, and all the commentators, whether ancient or modern, had interpreted it there as God. Further, in the commentary on the Nirukta, the learned Pt. Satyavrat Samasrmi of the Asiatic Society, had clearly stated that the word 'Agni' meant also 'God.' And so on.

It was absurd to suppose that the Vedas taught 'element-worship.' *Mantras* like - *Indram mitram varunam agni, etc.* the eight mantra of the fortieth chapter of the Yajur Veda, and others, too numerous to detail, rendered such a supposition utterly groundless, and left no doubt as to the truth of the fact that the adoration of the one only God was taught in the Vedas, and of naught else.

After some eight months' stay at Bombay, Swami Dayanand resolved to visit the N.W.P. again, but just as he was about to depart, a learned of Nadiea Shanti came forward for a shastrarth on – "Idol-worship." The meeting was duly held, a still more learned Pandit, name Bhojaji Shastri, occupying the chair of *Madhyastha*. Bhojaji's verdict, before the breaking up of the assembly, was that Pandit Ram Lal had failed to prove idol-worship from the Vedas. The Pandit himself acknowledged as such. His own words were: "The Swami is a Sanyasi, he cares for none. He has studied the Vedas and other Shastras thoroughly, and he is very wise and wields great powers. Whatever he says, is in accord with the Shastras. We have not the strength to oppose him, for we are householders. We have to consult our interests in many things. If we were to say anything against "idol-worship," our living would be gone, and then how would things get on?"

The effect of this shastrarth was of a very wholesome character. On the 14th April, 1876, a notice appeared from Bhai Jiwan nothing to do with "idol-worship." For, as the effect of Swami Dayanand's updesh, he had renounced it for good. The notice promised a reward of Rs. 125 to any one who prove idolatry from the Vedas and convince the convert to the Vedic Religion that, is giving up idolatry, he had made a mistake. Who would attempt such a hopeless task?

Pushkar

Starting on the 6th November from Delhi, the Swami arrived at Ajmer on the 7th. His visit to this place is associated with an act of underhand dealing which deserves a mention. It was, while preaching in the Punjab, that the Swami received a letter from certain gentlemen, resident in Ajmer, embodying a request that he would pay them a visit, the inviters of the letter undertaking to defray all expenses in connection with the visit by means of a subscription they intended to raise. The Swami replied that he would come.

A subscription was duly raised by the Ajmer, gentlemen on the receipt of the news that the Swami was coming to them. Before, however, the reformer had time to reach Ajmer, some member of the priesthood, probably in his desire to "settle old scores, sent him a letter in the name fan admirer of the Swami, telling him that it was unnecessary for him to come, since no subscription could be raised in the interest of his visit! The Swami communicated the contents of the strange epistle to Munshi Samarthdan at Ajmer, and the Munshi instituting enquiries and ascertaining the real facts, submitted his report to the Swami. The villainy was apparent, and the Swami duly came to Ajmer, reaching there on the date already specified.

Without making a halt at Ajmer, the Swami proceeded direct to Pushkar, a famous *tirtha* of the Hindus, situated at a few miles' distance from Ajmer. The annual fair was taking place, and the work of *prachar* could not be neglected on an occasion like the present one. The Swami put up at the *ghat* of Maharaja Jodhpur, popularly know as the "Window of Nathji," and he stayed at Pushkar as long as the fair lasted. Notices were issued, inviting all true enquirers to come and hold religious conversations, but nobody came forward for the purpose. The *updesh*, however, was regularly given, and we may be sure that it did not fall on deaf ears. As soon as the fair was over, the Swami returned to Ajmer, and kept lecturing here till 1st December, 1878. His lectures were attended by the gentry and nobility of the town, and by the local Officials, such as Rai Bhag Ram, Extra Judicial-Assitant; Sardar Rai Bahadur Amin Chand, Judge; Sardar Bhagat Singh; Rao Sahib Masooda, etc. The first named gentleman was long a member of the Ajmer Samaj.

The following lines are form a gentleman's diary regarding the Swami when at Ajmer:- Swamiji must be about fifty years of age. I saw him lying on a bed with his *langot* on. It appeared that he was suffering from dysentery. For all this, however, his appearance, by virtue of his *brahmacharya* was such as to furnish little ground for anyone to suspect that he was ill; he possesses a well-knit body, and is tall of stature".

One of the lectures the Swami delivered at Ajmer was on the teachings of the Bible. Mr. Rev. Grey, and some other Missionaries, were present at this lecture, and being anything but pleased with what was being said, they, finding their opportunity, intimated to the Swami that they were ready and willing to hold a discussion with him in connection with any objections he might bring forward against the Biblical teachings provided that he had these objections handed over to them in advance for consideration.

The Swami agreed to the condition, and getting some sixty-four out of the numerous objections he could raise against the dogmas of Christianity, had them sent to the Rev. gentleman, through Rai Bhag Ram. After the Rev. gentleman had considered them for full ten days the 28th of November, 1878, was fixed for the discussion. The public announcement that a discussion of such a character was going to take place between the Missionaries and Swami Dayanand attracted thousands of men to the place of meeting. Three reporters were in attendance.

When the objections against the bible were read out to the audience, Rev. Mr. Grey insisted that only two or three objections should be made the subject of discussion, and that no objection should be spoken upon, if possible, more than once. It was pointed out, in reply, that the restriction imposed was unfair, and that, though it did not signify much what objections were discussed and what left out, it was material that the objections that were selected for discussion should be discussed thoroughly. The Rev. gentleman would not listen to this, and so the discussion being nominal led to no definite result; the more so as the Missionary declined to resume it after the first day had closed. Whatever, however, was said by the parties, was published in the *Theosophist:*

Lecture on the Teachings of the Bible

Swami: "Genesis 1:2, says:- 'The earth was out form and void.'

Now, God is omniscient. His knowledge is perfect. That which He has made by His knowledge, cannot be imperfect or void and without form. Man's knowledge is limited his works are therefore without any form or order. But such can never be said of the works of God."

Missionary: "The phrase *without form* does not mean imperfect, it means uninhabited. As, for instance, the book of Ayub 2: 24, - 'They shall have to wander in trackless wilderness.' The word which signifies *without form* here means 'wilderness' there.

Swami: "In the verse preceding it, it is said that *'in the beginning God created heaven and earth. And the earth was without form and void; and darkness was upon the face of the deep.'*

This passage shows that the words *without form* cannot mean 'uninhabited'; there was no necessity of using the word void or uninhabited again. If God alone created the world, could not He have created it by His knowledge from the beginning with some kind of form?"

Missionary: "All languages have synonymous words, generally coming one after another; as, *bood-o-bash* in Persian, the two words being synonymous: in like manner, it is right to say in Urdu that the earth was barren and a waste."

[*Observation:* The Swami was going to say something more, but the Missionary said that only two questions and answers could be put and given on one point; or else the questions being many would not be finished that day. Upon this the Swami said that it was not necessary that all the questions should be disposed of in one day; some should be discussed that day, and others in tow, three or in as many days following, as it would take them to be discussed. The Missionaries did not consent to more than two questions being asked and two replies being given on a point. The Swami remonstrated against this, observing that so many men had come together in order that they might hear something, and that if nothing worth their trouble was said, they would go home disappointed; but all was to no purpose. The Missionaries were obstinate.]

Swami "Genesis 1:2 – "And the spirit of God moved upon the face of the waters.'

The first verse tells us that God created heaven and earth; but the creation of water was not mentioned. Whence, then, did water come to exist? Is God of the form of spirit, or is He corporeal like us? If He has a body, He can have no power to create heaven and earth; for the atoms are more delicate than the limbs of the body, and consequently, it is impossible for limbs to hold and unite them, to create things with. Also, He cannot be omnipresent or all-pervading. When His spirit was floating on the surface of the waters, where was His body?"

Missionary: "When He created the earth, water was included in it. God is spirit, and so is He called in the Bible from beginning to end."

Swami: "The account of God in the Old and the New Testament make shim corporeal in many places; for, His coming down to Eden for Adam, His descending on the Mt. Senai, His talking with Moses, Abraham, had his wife Sera, his going into their tent, his wrestling with Jacob, and the like adventures of His show that He must possess some sort of body, or assume it on such occasions."

Missionary: "These things do not concern the verse, and are mentioned as the outcome of ignorance. Suffice it to say in reply the Jews, the Christians, and the Muhammadans, who accept the Bible, are all unanimous in declaring that God is spirit."

Swami "Genesis 1:26 – 'And God said, let us make man in our image, after our likeness

This verse clearly proves that God is like Adam in form. God had body and soul like Adam according to this verse. How could he make Adam after His likeness, if He had no form?"

Missionary: "This verse makes no mention of body. God created Adam holy, intelligent, and happy. He is a holy, intelligent, and happy Himself, and made Adam like Himself. When Adam sinned, he fell from the likeness of God, as is manifest from the 24th and 30th questions of the First Cathechism. Epistle to *Corinthians 3: 9 and 10: - "Don't tell lies amongst you, for ye have cast off the old Adam with his works, and put on a new life, which is like your Creator's in knowledge.*

This shows that man was made like God in knowledge and holiness. We are made anew. *Corinthians 3:17 and 19 – 'God is spirit; God is spirit, wherever the spirit of God is, there is peace. We distinctly see the glory of God, and change into His form from glory to glory by means of His spirit.'*

This shows that the faithful or believers are change into the likeness of God, i.e., in knowledge, holiness, and happiness; for being endowed with certain qualities, man's body is never changed."

Swami: "The creation of Adam after the image of God proves the corporeity of God. Had God made Adam holy and happy, how could he have broken the command of God? If he broke the law, it is evident that he was not wise or knowing. His statement that when he tasted of the fruit of the tree of knowledge, his eyes were opened, proves that he got knowledge afterwards. If he had knowledge before he tasted the fruit, it is unreasonable to say that he got knowledge after the commission of the act.

"God at first blessed Adam with prosperity. But when he broke the divine law by eating the forbidden fruit, he became endowed with knowledge and knew that he was naked. He covered his body with the leaves of *goolar*. Only reflect a little that if Adam was like God in knowledge, holiness and happiness, he should have been omniscient and ever-happy, and should have experienced no pain whatever: for, he was like God in the qualities above-mentioned. He could not have fallen from his state. If he fell, he could not be like God; for, God never falls off from His knowledge and the like divine attributes. Since Adam, being like

God in those three qualities, fell from them, the believers will suffer the same fate, unless they have more knowledge than Adam, and consequently, than God! If they have equal knowledge with Adam, they will fall, as fell he who was like God in those respects."

Missionary: "The first answer will suffice most of the objections. As regards the disobedience of Adam, he was holy at first, but became sinful after he disobeyed God. It is incorrect to day that he acquired knowledge afterwards; because when he tasted the fruit of the for forbidden fruit, he simply cane to know of evil, of which he did not know before. That his eyes were opened and he knew that he was naked means that being sinful he became ashamed. As for the assertion, that had he been like God, he would not have fallen, I say that he was made after the image of God, but he was not equal to God. Had he been equal to God, he would not have fallen into sin. As for the question, if the believers were more holy than Adam, I say that the question is not one about more or less holiness, but about form or likeness, - as to whether the image of God was material or not. If the image in question was material, the believers, when regenerated by the grace of God, would change their corporeal frame."

Swami: "Gen.2:3 – 'And God blessed the seventh day, and sanctified it: because in it He had rested from all His work which God created and made.'

God can experience no fatigue in creating the world, being almighty, all-pervading, truth, intelligence, and happiness. Then how can He have the necessity to rest on the seventh day? If He rested at all, He must have worked very hard during the previous six days. If He blessed the seventh day, what did He do with the foregoing days? We can't believe that it takes God more than a moment to create the world, or that He is ever fatigued.

Colonel Olcott's Opinion on the Debate

Colonel Olcott's opinion on the discussion at Ajmer is worth a perusal. It was given in the following words:

> "The account of the discussion given above shows what policy the Missionaries pursue in India. As far as possible, they avoid discussions with native Scholars, and confine there preaching to the low classes and ignorant in the Missionaries Schools and Colleges

> also the teachers do not like answering the questions of intelligent youths on matters of religion in *class: they would have students come to their houses if they would have the same answered.* It is no secret to the impartial Europeans who have visited India that the Missionary propaganda here has had to face bitter disappointment. The gentlemen of philanthropic impulses who donate millions to the Padris are in reality wasting their charity. Many Anglo-Indians are in absolute sympathy with this view of ours. It is our intention to publish from time to time whatever evidence on the point is forthcoming."

From Ajmer, the Swami went to Masooda, in deference to the wishes of the Rao thereof, and stayed there till 9th December, 1878, delivering lectures throughout the brief period of his stay. On the 10th December, 1878, he visited the Nasirabad Cantonment, and, after a halt of four days there, during which the *updesh* was regularly given, he left for Jaipur, where he received a most cordial and respectful reception from the Vazir, Sardar Fateh Singh. The Maharaja would have seen the Swami but for the dissuasion of the orthodox priests about him; but for all that, the Raj Officials, at His Highness's desire, saw that the State was not in any way wanting in hospitality towards the reformer.

Rawalpindi

Returning from Ferozepur and making a halt of but a single day at Lahore, the Swami left for, and reached Rawalpindi on 8th November, 1877, and stayed there for about two months. The *kothi* of Seth Jamsetjee a had been selected for his residence, and in that he took up his quarters, and commenced a series of lectures. After he had delivered about twenty lectures, he was removed into Sardar Sujan Singh's garden, where *updesh* was resumed. He would lecture for two days running, and rest on the third. An Arya Samaj came to be established in due course, Lala Ganesh Das, Contractor, being appointed President, and Bhagat Kishen Chand – Secretary. Some persons urged Sadhu Saptgiri to hold a shastrath with the Swami, but he refused to humour their wishes. The Samaj established in the presence of the Swami has been doing useful work ever since.

Rewari

Proceeding from Jaipur to Rewari the Swami reached the latter place on 24th December. He had come to Rewari in response to an invitation from Rao Yudhishtar Singh, son of Rao Tula Ram, and during the fifteen or sixteen days he halted there, he delivered eleven during the fifteen or sixteen days he halted there, he delivered eleven lectures on various subjects of importance. The lectures were largely attended, the Rao's relatives, who had come from the neighbourhood of the town, also being present among the audience. Taking leave from the Rao and other Rewari gentlemen, Swami Dayanand arrived at Delhi, whence, after delivering there a couple of lectures, he went to Meerut, which he soon left for Haridwar via Saharanpur and Roorkee, to attend the so-called last Kumbh Fair on the banks of the Ganges.

Shahjahanpur

From Bareilly the Swami went to Shahjahanpur, where he stayed till 17th September, 1879, delivering during the period six lectures. The *updesh*, however, was daily given, the enquires coming in large numbers. The orthodox sent for and prevailed upon one Pandit Angad Shastri, who had at one time served as a teacher in the Pililbhit School on a salary of Rs 15 a month, to hold a shastrarth with the Swami.

The Pandit proved an ideal orthodox disputant. He would not come forward, declaring that the conditions of the would be shastrarth were unsatisfactory, and that till they were amended and altered so as to be perfectly acceptable to his friends and brethren, the shastrarth could not commence. What the Pandit seemed to be rally striving for was the bringing about a public *jalsa*, in which the mischievous element at his beck and call should have a chance to display their activities and should accomplish, by dint of noise and abuse and force, that which he had not the learning and the brains to achieve in a fair contest.

The Swami perceived his aim and would not give him a chance to carry out nefarious purpose, insisting that the conditions of the contemplated discussion should be, in an equal degree, cognizant of the interests of both the parties. The Pandit's letters to the Swami were generally full of unparliamentary expressions, but the Swami could bear fouler language than that, and his replies were always thoroughly courteous in tone. Of course, the shastrarth never came off.

It was at Shahjahanpur that the Swami conceived the idea of writing books of a purely educational value, and it was also here that he gave the idea a practical shape.

Shahjahanpur already boasted an Arya Samaj, of which Lala Bakhtawar Singh, Editor and Proprietor, The Arya Darpan, was the Secretary, and the Swami left the station for Lucknow on 18th September, 1879.

Shahpur

The first time the Swami saw Raja Nahar Singh of Shahpur, was at Chitaur, in Samvat 1938, and it was the Raja's request on that occasion that the Swami would visit his State as early as his leisure permitted him to do so. Now was the time when the Swami could accede to His Highness's wishes, and the Raja perceiving as much, had sent some of his courtiers to Oodeypore, and these escorted the Swami into the Capital of the State. After a week spent on the way the Swami reached Shahpur on 9th March, 1883, and was received by the Officials of the Durbar with the greatest possible respect. His Highness would have advanced in person to receive him, but the Swami would not consent to this.

On the very day of the Swami's arrival at Shahpur the Raja accompanied by all his dignitaries and nobles, waited upon him at dusk, and the conversation that ensued (on dharmic subjects), lasted for some two hours. Fort he first five days this attendance at *updesh* was repeated, but after that it being settled that the daily visit should be of a more profitable character, His Highness commenced devoting two out of the three hours he was with the Swami to the study of the Shastras, and he had, following this plan, gone through the Manu Smriti, the Yoga Sutras, and some portion of the Vaisheshak during the two months and-a-half of the Swami's stay in his dominions. Very often accompanying the Swami in his walks, His Highness also learnt from him, practically, the method of *pranayam* (controlling or restraining of breath for and during contemplation).

At the moment of parting, the Raja presented the following address to the Swami:- "The repeated and most humble Namaste of the Ruler of Shahpur State to Parmahansa Parivirajkacharya Shrimat Swami Dayanand Saraswati, - I agree to furnish an *Updeshak* (preacher) to belong to the Vedic Dharma Updeshak Mandli. He shall continue to receive a salary of Rs. 30 a month from my Treasury from today. The duty of Updeshak shall be to uphold and preach the Vedic Religion and expose and denounce false creeds.

"Although Your Holiness has stayed here for some two months and –a-half, yet my soul still hunger after spiritual food. But it having become evident that the Maharaja of Jodhpur is longing to see you, and hear the Vedic Updesh from your lips, so that he too might know truth from falsehood, and Your Holiness being disposed to gratify His Highness's longing, I, too, under the circumstances, do not insist upon prolonging your stay in this place: on the contrary, I think it is better Your Holiness should go, for the reason that your personality is for the good of millions and not for that of one or two men. I have hope that you will come here again and thereby confer honour upon me.

(Sd.) Nahar Singh

"Raja, Shahpur"

"4th Jeshth, 1940.

His Highness gave a donation of Rs. 250 in aid of Veda-Bhashya.

It was a Shahpur that Ishwaranand received sanyas and was directed to go to Kashi to prosecute his studies there.

Udaipur

In defence to the request already made more than once, the Swami after a short halt at Chitaur, left for Oodeypore, the Capital of the State, and arrived there, in company with Swami Atmanand Brahmachari Ramanand and Pandit Bheem Sen, on 11th August, 1882, putting up, as desired by His Highness, in the Naulakkha Bag.

A few days. Company was more than sufficient to strengthen the conviction in the Maharana's mind, that the individual before him was an extraordinary individuality, an individual who could clean and purify, shape and mould, other individuals for highest purposes, - one whose society could not be sought after too much by men in every condition in life, by great men and princes especially as them must always, more or less, serve as 'models' to hundreds and thousands of souls, upon whose destinies they presided, and they could but do them harm if they were bad models. His Highness saw much of the Swami as his leisure would permit. He visited him at his quarters morning and evening, in the morning generally accompanying him in his walk, and in the evening studying with him.

Before long His Highness had gone through particular portions of the six Darshanas, some portions of the Manu Smriti (particularly those dealing with Rajniti), a portion of the Mahabharata (Van parva, etc.), and the rudiments of *Vyakarna* (grammar). His chiefs and courtiers were always present when the Manu Smriti and other works were read and explained, and they heard everything with the deepest attention, with a mind disposed to learn. In a letter written by the Swami (4th March, 1883), the following lines occur: "His Highness visited me almost daily, and had satsang with me for four or five hours, in a spirit of love.

He read with me the principal portions of the six shastras, the three chapters of the Manu Smriti on government, all the valuable verses in Vidarparjagar, etc., some Vyakarna, and the rudiments of the method and are of paraphrasing." The Swami also taught the Maharana *upasnavidhi* (the method of performing upasana), and gave him a clear idea of his daily duties, a timetable having been prepared for the purpose.

As the result of the updesh, His Highness was a new man, - regular in his devotion, self-controlled, and never permitting women of ill-fame so much as to appear in his presence, and thoroughly aware of the evils of polygamy. At his request the Swami assisted him in the performance of a grand havan near the Nilkanth Mandir), which lasted for several days. The four Vedapathis were present, the *hotris*, etc., were in attendance, and everything was being attended to as it ought to be. The final *ahuti* was thrown by His Highness on the Vasant Day. Need we doubt that henceforward the *Agnihotra* was daily performed in the palace?

One great reform which the Swami's updesh brought about in the Mewar State was the introduction and use of the Devanagri character in all State offices, - a reform the value of which can never be over-rated.

The Swami, with a view to securing permanency to the interests of the Vedic Religion in the State, conceived the idea of establishing a Vedic Pathshala at Udaipur, but before a fund could be started to give a practical shape to the idea, the scheme, for one reason and another, fell through, and nothing was accomplished. The Swami was, further, for opening a school or college in the place, where the children of the nobility and gentry might be practically unstructed in their *nityakarma* (daily duties), and where they might be trained in the use of arms. The Maharana approved of the proposal, and it was greatly appreciated by his chiefs also. A plan of the needed institution was prepared and duly inspected and examined by the dignitaries of the court, but before long, after the Swami had taken his leave, the Maharana fell ill, and the disease terminating fatally, all came to naught.

And anecdote of the Swami is related in connection with his stay at Udaipur, furnishing one more illustration of his stern, uncompromising devotion to principle. It is said that the Maharana, in the course of conversation, one day counselled the Swami, in a humble but serious tone, to give up denouncing idolatry as a 'matter of policy.'

"Your holiness knows," added His Highness, "that this State is spiritually subject to the Linga Ishwara Mahadeva. In case you cease from running down idol-worship, I shall give you the Mahantship of the Mandir wherein the Linga reposes. You then be master of lacs of rupees, and the State will be spiritually subject to you." The indignation of the Swami at the proposal may be better imagined than described, and his reply was:

> "Neither this insignificant State of your nor your Mandir has power to alienate me from God and His eternal Word. You should not say to me what you have, I do not care for your lacs at all."

The Maharana was, perhaps, not wholly unprepared for the outburst to which he had been treated, and he hastened to remark: "Your Holiness, I was only trying you!"

There was another anecdote of a different kind, but sufficiently interesting to be reproduced. The Swami was one day talking to distinguished audience, when a Native Christian interrupted him, and insisted upon having an answer to his question without delay.

The Swami desired him to wait a little, but would not. " Well, what is your question?" said the Swami. "Whence do we come, where are we and where shall we go?' "You come from *pol* (void), in *pol* you are, and into *pol* you will go," was the answer! The man began to grumble, but the Swami quietly said: " You have had your answer. Now sit down and find out for yourself whether it is the right one or not."

Doubtless, the effect of the Swami's *updesh* on the Maharana had been of a most satisfactory character. The Swami in a letter, dated 7th October, 1882, said:

> "I have seen few individuals possessing so much gentleness and goodness of heart, of such ennobling and grateful disposition, so gentlemanly and courteous, so cheerful, intelligent, etc., as His Highness, the sun of the Aryakula (Arya race)."

Pandya Mohan Lal Vishnu Lal, noticing the change that came over His Highness by reason of his associating with the Swami, says: The Maharana, through the updesh of the Swami, became a completely regenerated man." There is no exaggeration in these words, His Highness respected and revered the Swami as he had really respected and revered no one before. When receiving updesh, he would insist upon occupying a seat much lower than that of the Swami, observing; "Your Holiness is my guru, and I have no right to occupy a seat as elevate as yours." It was only when the Swami would no longer be crossed that His Highness consented to take a raised seat, and the Swami had reason on his side. Said he to the Maharana: "If I don't show respect to Your Highness, how can your subject respects you as they should?"

It might, perhaps, be expected that the Maharanis would not, if possible, lose the chance of seeing the man for whom their lord and master had such unbounded regard and respect, and of whom he always spoke in no common terms of praise. They made their wishes known to His Highness, who conveyed their request to the Swami. That Sanyasi at first would not consent to accede to the request, but finding that His Highness was bent upon having the longing of his consorts gratified, at last yielded to his importunities, saying: "If them must see me, let them come when I am in a trance." The condition was accepted, and the Swami was deep in his samadhi, wholly unconscious of the world around, when the august ladies came and had a look at him. The fact was that the Swami wholly and absolutely dislike to have a woman introduced into his presence. "The Brahmachari," he said, "must not look at a woman if he would have Brahmacharya remain perfect!"

It was at Oodeypore that the Swami made his final Will, constituting thereby the Propkarni Sabha to act, after his death, as the executor of his Will. The Will was read, and confirmed at the court of the Maharana in full Durbar, and a fund also was started with a view to enabling the Sabha to carry on the benevolent work entrusted to it. We shall notice the Will later on.

When the Swami was bout to leave Oodeypore, the Maharana presented him with an address written with his own hands, in which His Highness gave expression to his sense of gratitude for the updesh and instruction he had received, observing that he could never repay the debt he owed the Swami, and adding that he should request him to stay longer but for the consciousness on his part that the great teacher's personality was for the good of all.

"I, however, hope" were the concluding words of the Maharana, "that you will come again and make me happy.' A *nazarana* of Rs. 600, in aid of the Ferozepur Orphanage, and another of Rs. 2,000, in aid of the Ved-Bhashya, was presented, and was accepted. The companions of the Swami also had suitable presents. The Swami left Oodeypore on 1st March, 1883.

Various Bengal Towns

Wandering about for a whole year along the banks of the Ganges, the Swami was again back at Kashi, in March, 1872, and having spent some days here, running down superstitions and declaring sublimity of the Vedic Faith, he proceeded to Bengal.

Passing through Dumraon, he reached Patna, in September, 1872, and having stayed here for about a month, during which period many discussions on a small scale took place and hundreds of people heard him exposing idolatry and other institutions, the Swami repaired to Monghyr, where he lectured for fifteen days. From Monghyr, he went to Bhagalpur, arriving at his destination on 20th October, 1872. Here several discussions took place with the Brahmans and the Christians.

One day a Bengali Christian gentleman, hearing the Swami's updesh, burst into tears, remarking, "Had I found any one like yourself, O most revered Sir, a score of years earlier to resolve my doubts, I would never have permitted myself to be torn from my brethren and my ancestral religion. In those days, I waited upon on Pandit after another with my questions, but not one of them would or could answer them to my satisfaction."

The Maharaja of Burdwan also came to hear him, and discussion with the Padris took place in His Highness's presence. His Highness was alleged to have a decided leaning towards the Christian Faith, but he heard the discussion in silence, and then retired. He requested the Swami to stay in his palace, but the Swami begged to be excused from acceding to his wishes, saying that he preferred retirement.

The Bengali Headmaster of the local school also waited upon the Swami one day, in company with some twenty of his pupils, and began to speak upon the merits of his Faith. The Swami gave him an exhaustive reply, disabusing, in the course of the reply, his mind of the impression that all the four *varnas* were one and the same thing and that promiscuous eating was anything desirable. The conversation lasted until 10 pm.

The following day, there was another discussion with the Brahmos, in the open air, under a grand *shamiana*. The Maharaja was present at the discussion, although, as formerly, he never said anything for or against the position of any party during the period the debate lasted. The Brahmo gentlemen finding themselves pressed hard finally said: "If our great one in Calcutta accepts what you say, we shall accept it too." After two months' stay at Bhagalpur, the Swami left for Calcutta, on December 15th, 1872.

Various Bihar Towns

Swami Dayanand left Calcutta on Ist April, 1873, and reaching Hooghly put in the garden belonging to Vrindavan Mandal Zimindar. The news of his arrival produced the usual stir in the town and brought numbers of people to see him. The well-known Professor Rev. Lal Behari Dey waited upon him and had a talk with him on "Caste" were perfectly reasonable and sound, and frankly acknowledged that his own ideas on the subject had been rather confused and erroneous.

At Hooghly the Swami delivered several lectures, the one on the 7th April being given in the presence of the principal men of the town. Pandit Tara Charan was not far from the place where the meeting was held, but he would not venture near the Swami, though getting on the top of a neighbouring house he held forth to his admirers on the unorthodox character of the Sanyasi's teaching. When the Pandit's conduct was reported to the Swami, he regretted that he should have behaved in the manner he had done, for he was perfectly at liberty to give expression to his views at the meeting and to have the truth threshed out. The leading men of Hooghly agreed with the Swami, and they besought Pandit Tara Charan to hold a shastrarth with him. The Pandit at last consented, and the discussion came of on the following day – 8th April – on "Idolatry."

The Pandit commenced by reciting an aphorism from, as he declared, the Yoga-Darshana of Pantanjali, and commenting upon it declared that the mind could not be concentrated without the help of material objects, and hence the necessity of idol-worship in *upaasna*, according to the aphorism of Vyasa! Swami Dayanand replied that no such aphorism was to be found in Patanjali, and if it was Pantanjali's, it could not possibly be Vyasa's.

He then recited the real Sutra and, repeating Vyasa's commentary thereon, said, that what the commentator meant was that the mind should be concentrated on the forepart of the nose. The discussion proceeded, and eventually Pandit Tara Charan, finding himself hard pressed, became reckless and exclaimed: "All worship is a lie." The audience was astounded, while the Swami smiled and said: "You confess then that idolatry is false?"

The Pandit, it is asserted that Swami in private and he was an admirer of Classical Sanskrit Literature and an enemy of the modern productions in Sanskrit, and the he fully believed that idol-worship was false out-and-out; but he could not, he added openly avow what he believed in his heart, out of consideration for his worldly interests!

Departing from Hooghly on the 16th of April, 1873, the Swami arrived at Bhagalpur, where he stayed for one month, and then left for Patna. At Patna he delivered several lectures, and it was towards the close of May that eh proceeded thence to Chhapra, where he became a guest of Rao Shiv Gulam Shah Bahadur, Zimindar, whose reception of him was markedly respectful and cordial. The interested portion of the Chhapra community taking their cue from their brethren of Patna, who had proclaimed the Swami to be a "German Christian," gave out that he was an infidel.

The sensible and enlightened residents of the place, however, could not be hoodwinked, and they called upon the local Pandits to hold a shastrarth with the newcomer. The Pandits declined to accede to their wishes, on the ground that the man was a nastik (infidel or atheist, that they would have to undergo a *prayashchit* (expiation) in case they say his face. The Swami coming to hear of this objection, observed that he difficulty was not insuperable, that a screen might be hung between himself and the Pandits, which would prevent his being see by them, and they hung back silent and sullen, till one of them, Pandit Jagannath, took up the gaunlet and specified the day on which the discussion should take place.

The day came, and a screen was actually hung between the parties. The Swami put the Pandit some questions from the Smritis, in Sanskrit, and the Pandit replied; but so wretched were his answers that on the Swami's pointing out his bad grammar, he was wholly non-plussed and refused to proceed with the discussion.

The Swami had no alternative but to address the audience himself, and his lecture lasted for full four hours, convincing all thoughtful and impartial-disposed minds that idolatry-loving Pandits were completely in the wrong. The Pandits, however, were not going to take their defeat silently. The shouted out that the Swami was misinterpreting and disgracing the Vedas and hence one who was to be shunned and avoided by all true-believers. Some of the more zealous, in their disappointment, went so far as to openly assert that they would stone the atheist to death if they should get at him after about two weeks' stay at Chhapra, during which he visited the local school also, the Swami left for Danapur, whence he proceeded to Arrah, where he spent over a month, making known his mission to all who came to him. From Arrah he went to Dumraon, where he became a guest of the ruler of the principality, putting up in the state Bungalow near the Railway-station. The Maharaja, with his courtiers, met him and had friendly chat with him on various subjects.

No shastrarth worth the name was held here – only a short discussion took place between him and the State Pandit, Durga Datta, on "Vedantism and idolatry," in the presence of the Chief and his grandees. The Swami, when refuting the Neo-Vedantism, pointed out the true meaning of such expressions, as *Ekamedvadvtiyam Brahm* and giving the *Niaruktak* interpretation of the mantra - *Brahmanaoasya* etc., which Pandit Durga Datta had advanced in support of idolatry, showed that the Scriptural passage hand nothing to do with the worship of the creature in any form whatsoever. The Pandit then quoted from the *Jabal Upanishad* in defence of idol-worship, but the Swami's reply was: "This Upanishad is a spurious composition. Shankracharya, whom you profess to follow, does not, does not at all recognise it." To this no answer was forthcoming.

The Pandit, however, knew how to retrieve his defeat. In his own summary of the discussion, embodied in "the history of his triumphs" (Digvijai), published in Samvat 1941, after the Swami's death, he wrote: "When Dayanand saw that he was unable to answer any further, he smiled and said: Pandit Durga Dattaji, you are a wonderful one. I am only a man, by you are omniscient and thoroughly conversant with all the Shastras. I, a mortal, cannot hold a discussion with you, the Brahm!" Very modest this of the pandit! And pray, why was not Dayanand as a good "Brahm" as the Pandit himself, according to the Pandit's own way of thinking?

Various N.W.F.P. Towns

The true *Yogi* and every other real working will see action in action, and will go on working wholly unmindful of rewards; but even such an individual, whatever the order or class to which he belongs, cannot help bring moved and affected pleasurably when truth triumphs over ignorant and misguided opposition. Swami Dayanand was pleased at the result of his efforts in the Punjab, for the message he had come entrusted with from On High had been welcomed and accepted.

While Swami Dayanand was yet at Multan, he had received a letter from Lala Umrao Singh of the Thomson Engineering College, begging him to visit Roorkee. The Swami's reply was, that he could not comply with the request contained in the letter immediately, but hat he should do it as soon as his leisure permitted him to. The reply was somewhat disappointing, but Lala Umrao Singh and his friends saw their wishes realised sooner than perhaps they had expected they would. While leaving the Punjab, the Swami addressed from Amritsar a letter to the Secretary of the Arya Samaj, Gujranwala, which speaks for itself. The letter was to the following effect:-

"Secretary and Sabhasadhs – we wish you happiness. Be it known to you that we intend to set out for the N.W.F. Provinces on Thursday, the 11th July, 1878, and, passing through Jalandhar, Ludhiana and other cities, shall proceed onward. It is just possible that we may stay, for a matter of three or four days at Amballa. Henceforward we shall be able to converse with you through letters alone. Let us hear from you constantly, and, on our part, we shall write to you from time to time. What we now want to say to you is, that you should strive daily to further the progress of the Samaj.

"You have undertaken a great responsibility, and your advancement and happiness lie in carrying your undertaking to a successful termination. The Samaj her id progressing daily; many influential people of the place have become its members. The Pandits of this place had come to the determination of holding a shastrarth, but on their coming into the Sabha they neither spoke nor replied to any question; having merely shown their faces they went away. And some of the people of this place, who were partial to the 'popes' (idol-worshipping priests), had slandered and misrepresented the Arya Samaj to the authorities, but the results of their efforts, thanks to the power of truth, was that nobody now dare raise a finger against the Samaj, Namaste to all the Sahbasads – (Signed) Dayanand Saraswati, Amritsar."

Busy giving *updesh,* the Swami reached Roorkee 925th July, 1878), and put up in Lala Shambu Nath's bungalow in the Civil Station. The Muhammadans of the station ran away with the idea that the Pandit had been invited to Roorkee to vex them and to oppose their famous local preacher and disputant who, as the Muhammadans were well aware, had been, for some time past, attacking the Christian and Hindu Faiths with vigour.

No wonder that the educated people of Roorkee heard the Swami's lectures with astonishment and in deeply appreciative and enraptured frame of mind. These lectures and the reply to Colonel Olcott's letter from America read out to the audience gave them an insight into the Swami's teaching and made them feel that a nobler teaching could be had now here. It was, of course, natural that the Muslims of Roorkee should find but little to appreciate in his speeches on "Revelation" and on the teachings of the Bible and the Quran as contrasted with those of the Vedas.

While his lecture on the comparative merits of the Vedic doctrines and the doctrines of the Quran and the Bible was in progress, our Muslim friends, we are told, looked angry and threatening, almost ready to resort to violence, emboldened perhaps, in some degree, by the fact that the Police in attendance was not over-active in the discharge of their duty (why? The reader might well guess for himself.) Apprehending a disturbance, the gentlemen, who had arranged the meeting, put a slip of paper into the Swami's hand, requesting him to be sparing in his criticism of Islam. Without heeding the advice, the lecturer went on speaking in his wonted manner, bringing forward objection after objection against the creed, and quoting profusely from the Quran I support of his objections. Everything, however, ended peacefully, nobody seeing anything reasonably to find fault with what had been said.

Pandit Umrao Singh has the following to say regarding the utterances of the Swami at Roorkee:

"On the 4th day the Swami's lecture was on 'Western Philosophy, Theory of Darwin, Effects of English Education and on some other subjects. At the same time the speech dealt with the 'Christian and Muhammadan Metaphysics and the Absurdities of the Puranas.' Of English Philosophy the Swami, in his own parlance, spoke as the *keet preet* (worms, insects, etc.) philosophy. He enlarged upon the advantages and methods of education, and briefly dwelt on the virtues of the British Government and on the boon of freedom of speech which it had bestowed on its subjects.

Criticising Darwins Theory on Evolution

He refused the Darwinian theory that man was descended from a monkey, He said that the thing was impossible, and brought forward unanswerable arguments in support of his contention. One of these was, that if man was really a descendant of monkey, then it was, as it were, a fact – a law which according to the followers of Darwin and other philosophers of his school, was unceasing in its operations under any conditions whatsoever. If the law was of a constant and permanent nature, ever working itself out, how was it that for thousands of years past, no monkey's young one had developed into a human being? If in times gone-by a money copulating with a fish (for instance) brought into being a strange creature, and if that strange creature copulating with some other creature brought forth another strange creature, and if the process of copulation on the same principle continuing, the last strange creature helped to bring on the scene, as the result of copulation with a nameless creature, a human being; if all this happened formerly, why was it that similar result had ceased to be brought about in the later ages? Did the last strange creature leave a will that no animal in future, especially a monkey, was to act after the fashion of his ancestor.

The Swami further observed that the copulation of an animal of one species with that of the another, did not result in off-spring. Similarly he advanced many other arguments. The English-educated young men of the station were surprised on hearing the Swami's arguments, confessing that they had never heard such arguments before. And these young men were also under the impression that the principles of physics, chemistry and of other sciences, which they studied in their colleges, had been discovered and brought to light by the Europeans, and that no other people were aware of these before. When however, the principles in question were dwelt upon by the Swami in language remarkable for its connectedness and its intellectual depth, as if the speaker was reading from a scientific treatise, the wonder was all the greater. When a gentleman observed to the Swami that the principles and theories he had spoken of were the discoveries of modern times he deplored the fallen state of India and added:

> "Any (true) theory or principle which you think to me of modern origin, name the same, and I will prove to you that it is taught and set forth in the ancient Shastras."

Upon this the people commenced asking him many questions as to the fixedness of the sun and the motion of the earth, as to the nature of rain and clouds, of elements of chemical simples, of fixed and moving stars, of the heavens, of the planetary system, of the moons, of earthquakes, hurricanes, etc. and the Swami would reply to them from the Shastras, with incontrovertible proofs in support of his replies. His answers were so absolutely convincing as to remove all doubts on the points touched from the minds of the questioners. For no sooner was a question uttered than a *shloka* in reply was forthcoming. The mere literal meaning of the *shloka* was sufficient to satisfy the enquirer, and to impress the greatness of the Shastras on his mind.

Various Rajputana Towns

Swami Dayanand had already been more than once to some of the States in Rajputana, but there had been do regular *prachar* during these visits in the States in question, and it was with the intention of ding systemic work, - of preaching and disseminating the principles of the Vedic Religion in conformity with the methods followed in the Punjab and some other parts of India, that he determined to revisit the tract immortalised in his *Annals and Antiquities of Rajasthan.* And in pursuance of his purpose, he left Agra on the 10th March, 1881, for Bharatpur, where he stayed up of his stay. On 29th he left for

Jaipur, where more than a month was spent, and though the number of lectures delivered here was the reverse of 'large', yet the *updesh* being daily given at his quarters, an Arya Samaj was at last established in the place.

Wazirabad

Starting from Gujrat on 2nd February, 1878, the Swami arrived at Wazirabad. A Samaj had already been established there, and the President, the late Lala Labdha Ram, then an Apprentice Engineer and subsequently an Executive Engineer, and the Secretary, Lala Sukh Dyal, and other members of the Samaj gave a hearty welcome to the Swami, and according to the arrangements already made, conducted him to the Balai Kothi in Raja Faqir-ulla's garden to take up his abode there.

The Swami delivered five lectures in all here. A Shasrarth was held too, but some of the good men, instead of listening to the discussion with patience and attention, sought only, in pursuance of a premeditated plan no doubt, to create a disturbance. On the Swami's asking the Pandit who was arguing with him to point out in the Vedas the mantra, the commentary on which he (the Pandit) had first repeated, and on the latter's utterly failing to do it, a boy standing by commenced shouting 'fie! Fie!' The contemptuous exclamation was meant for the Swami, but before the rowdies could come up to them the Swami just flourished his club, and there was an instantaneous stampede towards some place of safety! But it would seem that the courage of the mob had not yet completely oozed out, for no sooner did they find that the Swami and the other Aryas had retired to the upper story, than they sent up a shower of stones.

The Swami's Clerk, Bihari Babu, descending to remonstrate with them on the folly of their conduct, worst element among them, instead of respecting his person as that of a messenger, fell upon him in a body, and commenced thrashing him unmercifully. The Swami being informed of the matter rushed down the stairs to succour the man. The mere sight of him and his leonine shout were sufficient to strike terror into the hearts of the miscreants and they took to their heels. The Arya Samajists thought of putting the breakers of the peace in court, but the soothing words of the Swami calmed them down, and the proposal was dropped.

6

Interesting Facts and Anecdotes

- The Swami would not let women come into his presence. The ladies of Lahore, however, accustomed to a different order of things, and wholly failing to appreciate the Swami's attitude towards members of their sex, thronged to the Swami's lodging in numbers and insisted upon having an updesh. Unwilling to disappoint them, he had separate accommodation provide for their benefit, and in his lecture strongly emphasised the fact that it was improper for women to take part in the meetings of men, adding; "Women generally go to the Sadhus and Faqirs for children and for the acquisition of wealth. But the Sadhus and Faqirs, who promise such things to women are great scoundrels. It is meet that women should have their own Sabhas or hear updesh from their husbands, who, according to the Shastras, being their gurus, should be alone served and waited upon by them. They should never go to the Faqirs, either for offspring or for wealth." And he also said: "the men who permit their women to go anywhere and everywhere, and have no control over them, are worthless."

- One day Pandit Shiv Narain Agnihotri asserted that the Sama Veda contained the story of owls. The Swami, taking up the Book, quietly handed it over to the Pandit, and asked him to find the story for him. The Pandit kept turning over the leaves for some time, but finally returned the book, observing that he could not find the story!
- One day Babu Sarda Parsad Bhattacharya proposed, in a public meeting, with the full occurrence of the other Arya members present, that the title of "Patron of the Samaj" be conferred upon the Swami. When the proposal had been thoroughly approved by the meeting, the Swami smiles and observed:

"The word 'patron' is suggestive of 'gurudom', my mission is to weaken and break up sects which recognise 'gurudom', and not to found a new sect and become a guru myself. If my head is turned by the title tomorrow, or if my successor becomes proud and haughty by reason thereof, you will be confronted with a great evil, and this evil will be the same as the new creeds have been confronted with! Hence, the proposal that has been made, should never be repeated in the future."

The Babu still insisting that the Swami should at least accept the title of *parama shaik* (supreme helper), and latter answered:

"If you call me *parama Sahaik*, by what name will you call the almighty *Paramatma*?

This anecdote contains lessons of the highest value for the Arya Samaj, and may Heaven help us never to lose sight of these. Slavery and thralldom of the worst kind ever follows in the train of 'gurudom', it utterly enfeebles men morally and intellectually and spiritually, and of what use is a community that is undone in so many ways?

- Once Pandit Manphool said to the Swami: "If you give up refuting and denouncing idol-worship, the people would cease to be angry with you and what is more, the Maharaja of Jammu and Kashmir will also be pleased with you!" The Swami answered:

> "Shall I strive to please the Maharaja of Jammu and Kashmir, or shall I strive to carry out the mandates of *Ishwara* - the Sovereign of sovereigns – embodied in the Vedas?"

This reply was conclusive for the Pandit, and it is said he never saw the Swami after this.

- While putting up in the *kothi* of Nawab Nawaszish Ali Khan, the Swami one day delivered a lecture on Islam. While the lecture was going on, the Nawab walking about at a distance, listening to it, a person approached the Swami and said: "Maharaj! None will lend you his house to step in, neither Hindus nor Muahmmadans nor Christians. Now that the Nawab Sahib has kindly placed his *kothi* at your disposal, you would run down Islam even in his house!" The reply of the Swami was, "I cannot barter my religion for the luxury of staying in comfortable lodgings. In declaring the truth I fear no one, though the declaration might cause me trouble and inconvenience."
- During his stay a Lahore, Swami Dayanand had interviews with Colonel Holroyde, Director, Public Instruction, Punjab, and one with Sir Charles Egerton, Lieutenant-Governor, also. In the course of conversation with His Honour, the Swami observed that:

  > "I could not understand how Englishmen, with all their boasted civilization, could believe in such a book as the *Bible*"

His Honour begged to be excused from making a reply, as (said he) he was not prepared to talk on religious subjects with the Reformer. The Swami, of course, did his duty.

- During the days when *prachar*-work was being pushed on in the garden belonging to Nawab Ali Raza Khan, near the Masti Gate, a Padri and his lady visited the Swami. A conversation ensued, during which the Rev. gentleman said: "What proof have you that the Aryas were originally wealthy and in the enjoyment of comfort, and degenerated and fell in to poverty afterwards?" In reply the Swami observed that the annals of ancient Aryavarta bore witness to the truth of his assertion, and that the Rev. gentleman, being conversant with history, could verify the fact for himself. As to the cause of the fall of the ancient Aryas, it was their great wealth that brought them down.

"I have been', said the Swami, "an early riser from my childhood. In the beginning.

I saw that Englishmen would get up early in the morning, and, taking their children with them, would go out for a walk. The excess of wealth, however, has made them indolent since. They are seen stretched on their beds in their *Bungalows* till the sun is up, and I cannot but perceive that, like the old Aryas, the days of your fall is also coming."

- Dr. Hooper came one day to hear the Swami's lecture at Dr. Rahim Khan's house. On the termination of the lecture, the missionary put the Swami a question in Sanskrit. On the termination of the lecture. The audience who were about to disperse, retained their seats. The Swami requested the Doctor to come forward and take a chair. The latter replied that it did not become him to sit on a chair in the presence of such a man as the Swami, for the Swami was the "sun of knowledge." The question which he (the Doctor) wanted to ask, he had come to ask in the capacity of *jigyasu* (enquirer), and not in the spirit of one who would discuss and argue. Having said this, the Doctor remarked that since the Vedas spoke of *Ashvamedha* and *Gomedha Yajnas*, it was evident that in the Vedic period, the people were in the habit of offering sacrifices of horses and cows. What had the Swami to say about it? The Swami's answer, in substance, was:

  "All these stories have been invented by the *Vamamargis*. The Vedas nowhere speak of doing Yajna by sacrificing kine and horses. *Ashvamedha*, according to the Shatapatha Brahmana, Nirukta and so on means the just and impartial treatment of his subjects by a King; while *Gomedha* means the cleaning of grain, the purifying of the five senses, the mind, and so forth."

The second question which the Rev. gentlemen asked was: "What have the Vedas to say on Caste?" the reply was that caste-distinction, according to the Vedas, rested on worth and merit. Upon this, the Missionary asked: "If I be a possessor of noble qualities and virtues, can I become a Brahman?" The Swami answered: "Most certainly. If your worth and actions are such as to entitle you to claim the position of a Brahman, you can become one."

- One day a Padri hearing his criticism on the mantra - *Hiranyagarbha*, etc. remarked that the ancient Aryas knew nothing about God, adding that the spiritual upheaval of the word was due to the Bible. "Wherever," the Bible has been carried, the people there had become civilized, and the teachings of the Bible influence an area of land over which the sun never sets."

  The Swami replied that it was not due to the Bible that the results of which the Missionary spoke had been achieved, but to the teaching of the Veda which the Western people practically followed. The non-recognition of early marriage, observing of *brahmacharya*, love of knowledge, monogamy, travelling of distant countries, patriotism, etc. (inculcated in the Vedas) had made the Western people what they were. The people of India had made the Western people what they were. The people of India had come to mistake for the Vedic religion a totally different faith which was worthless, and had ceased following the behests of the Vedas. But the Europeans, though not acquainted with the Vedas, yet followed their commandments. This was the reason why the Indians were going down, and the Europeans 'going up.'

- The Swami was in Lahore when the anniversary-festival of Brahmo Samaj came round. The Swami was invited. He went in company with a large number of Arya gentlemen after the proceedings of the weekly meeting of the Arya samaj was over. When the Swami entered the Brahmo Mandir, Pandit Raghu Nath Gupta, pracharak of the Brahmo Samaj of India, who was at the time conducting the Service, descended from the pulpit and falling at the Swami's feet, embrace him and said: "In reality the Brahmo Samaj and the Arya Samaj are one." The Swami replied:

"Although there is a difference between the Samajees at present, the day will come when the two will become one."

- The *upaniyams* (by-laws) of the Arya Samaj were passed on 6th November, 1877, the Swami happening to be present in the Samaj at the time, the members requested him to give his opinion on some points. The Swami replied that he had no right to do it, as he was not a member of the *Antrang Sabha*. And he never gave his opinion till, for special reasons, he had been elected a member of the Executive Body!
- The body that had suffered most by the establishment of the Arya Samaj was the Brahmo Samaj. Its ranks were considerably thinned, and, in their annoyance, the remaining members of the Samaj called upon their brethren of Calcutta to help them. The Calcutta Brahmo Samaj sent the Lahoris a number of *mantras* with their interpretation, claiming to prove that the Vedas were not revealed. The Lahoris lost no time in holding a public meeting and asking the Swami to explain the *mantras*. The Swami accepted the challenge. As the Brahmo gentlemen were ignorant of Sanskrit, they constituted Pandit Bhanu Datta their representative. The Pandit read out the mantras, with their interpretation. Before rising to reply, the Swami asked the Pandit if he too, who unlike the Brahmos, knew Sanskrit, thought the interpretation to be right. The Pandit replied in the negative, adding that the objections which the Brahmo gentlemen had brought forward, had no weight in his opinion. The answer sent the audience into roars of laughter, and it was a 'stunner' for the Brahmos. As Brahmo gentleman then undertook to repeat the objections, and after he had done speaking, the Swami got up and explained how the words, *Ganga* and *Yamuna*, were not proper names, but the names of two arteries, paling a conspicuous part in Yoga to convince his hearers

thoroughly, he read the chapter from the beginning, explaining each mantra and proving conclusively that the chapter dealt with the *Science of Yoga*, and not with the so-called rivers, Ganga, Yamuna, etc.

Interview of the Swami

The Colonel and Madame Blavatsky set off from New York on 17th December, 1878, and met the Swami at Saharanpur on 29th April, 1879. Writing of the interview, the Colonel says that the interpreter told him that Swami's conception of God was exactly the same as that of the Vedantis of their *Parbrahma*. We confess we find it rather hard to believe that the interpreter should have helped the Colonel to run away with a wrong idea, considering that a book embodying a complete refutation of Vedantism had already been published by the Swami, and considering further that the Swami's beliefs as regards the Nature and character of the Deity has been only too clearly set forth in this letter of 21st April, 1878. Whatever the Colonel might say to the contrary, the Swami still saw no reason to suspect that the Americans were materialists or any such thing: on the contrary, he believed them to be thorough believers in God and in the Vedas, as the following letter of his, addressed to the Secretary, Arya Samaj, Shahjahanpur, shows:

"*Om Tat Sat.*: Happiness and peace to the Secretary, Arya Samaj, Shahjahanpur:

> "Be it know to you that we are going to communicate a happy news in the interests of all concerned. The news in question is that we had an interview on 1st May, 1879, at Saharanpur, with colonel H.S. Olcott and Madame Blavatsky, who sent letters from America to our Samajes. We found them wiser and far more talented than what their letters had prepared us to expect them to be, and they appeared to us perfectly cordial and gentlemanly. We enjoyed there company for two days at Saharanpur, and all the Arya Samajists showed them due respect. The minds of people were extremely delighted at hearing their lectures. After the (expiration of the period of two days), they accompanied us to Meerut.

"All the members of the Samaj gave them a fitting reception, and their lectures were charming that all felt pleased at hearing them. And the lectures were so attended by the gentry and nobility of the station, by the Officials and the Europeans, for five days running. And whoever brought forward any objections against the true Shastras, the same had an appropriate and right answer. In other words, the Americans thoroughly convinced everybody that, all that is good and scientific can be had from the Vedas alone, and that all creeds repugnant to Vedic Teachings are based on cunning and deceit. After the lectures, the above-mentioned gentleman and the lady left for Bombay (7th May, 1879.)

We shall stay here for some days more yet. Our contact with the above-spoken-of individuals (from America), will be instrumental in helping the regeneration of India and other countries. Just as an extremely good medicine destroys a disease all sooner with the assistance of good diet, even so our meeting with the Americans will, by spreading the Vedic Religion in Aryavarta and other countries, destroy, in a comparatively shorter space of time, the disease of untruth. And the disposition and character of the above-spoken-of personages appears to us to be of a very superior type, for these people are ready to exert themselves, to the utmost of their power, to help the Vedic Religion. As to the report set afloat by Babu Harish Chandra Chintamani, that these people are conversant, with the 'black art,' and practice tricks like fraudulent men, - this report is unfounded. For that which is called necromancy of magic is really nothing more than physical science. The ignorant look upon the achievements of physical science as those of magic.

"The Americans have chosen to have recourse to physical science to dispel the doubts of the ignorant, and to lead them to the right path, and there is no harm in their having done so. Men like Harish Chandra, however, see something objectionable in all this. Thus Harish Chandra had so filled their minds with doubts that we are unable to specify the extent of the mischief wrought. But all their doubts have been removed by their meeting us. Just mark the dishonesty of Harish Chandra! He has already hindered the work of the publication of the Veda-Bhashya to a considerable extent, and is still hindering it.

"Hence it behoves all Arya brethren to regard him hence forward as one expelled from the Arya Samaj, and never to place any trust in him in future. Be it known that our Rishis and Munis of ancient times were so advances in sciences that, through their physical powers, they could read the secrets of every heart. Just as the material scientist can make external inventions like those of the Railway and the Telegraph (regarded as achievements of 'magic' by the ignorant) by means of physical science, even so the Yogis can do wonderful deeds by the agency of their internal hidden powers.

"There is nothing to be surprised at in this. For that which common mortals can accomplish by the agency of external means, the Yogis can accomplish on a far grander scale by the agency of their internal forces. Just as the application of the external has to do with the outward and tangible, even so the application of internal things (powers) is (with impalpable and hidden).

"A man can see an external result, brought about by the use of external means, with his eyes; but the result brought about by the use of subtler things (forces or powers), he can't see with his external visual organs. This is reason why the achievements of subtle operations excite the wonder of the common people. Of course, it must be admitted that there are many vile persons, who, though unacquainted with this secret knowledge, 'spread the snare of cunning,' and thereby bring discredit on the true sciences.

"Hence, the false one should always be treated with contempt, and the true ones with respect. And as soon as a person is found to be false, he should be given a wide berth. After many days the trickery of Harish Chandra has come to light and hence he has been expelled from the Arya Samaj. Similarly, the moment a member of an Arya Samaj is discovered to be false, he should be deprived of the membership and turned out, be who he may. Have always an eye on the dealer in falsehood, for doing this is identical with regenerating, and persons of truth invariably possess this trait of character. A man is said to have acquired *gyan* (true knowledge), when, on discovering his own untruth, he looks upon *falsehood* as such in the consciousness of his soul, and when the renounces it without delay. For such a man it is the easiest thing to give up the company of others when he finds them false.

Unless a person does so, he can neither reform himself nor others. Now we conclude this letter of ours with the declaration that we have become convinced, on the strength of their previous correspondence, and by, conversing with them for seven days, that the body (tan), mind (man), and wealth (dhan) of these Americans is for the advocacy of truth and destruction of untruth; yet for the good of all, even like those of our own men who are labouring (for their country's good) from conviction.

"Meerut:

"8th May, 1879.

"(Sd.) Dayanand Saraswati

We may be permitted to reproduce another letter of the Swami dated two or three days earlier, and containing, like the foregoing, his opinion about the Americans:

'.....Colonel Olcott and Madam Blavatsky attended the (Meerut) Samaj today; the Colonel will preach in the Meerut Cantonment, and the two are going to leave for Bombay in a say or two. Their beliefs do not differ from those of the Arya Samaj; in other words, their ideas and conduct are in conformity with the teachings of the Samaj. For during the four or five days we have had occasion to talk with them, they have appeared to us pure-hearted. And as regards your saying that our name has been put down as that of a member of the Theosophical Society, we should have shown the Colonel the *patra* (chit), had you sent it to us.

"Yet we did speak to the Colonel orally, and he replied that hitherto the object of the Theosophical Society had been to admit into its fold representatives of all creeds, and to let them hold had express their different views; but that now, having understood the principles of the Arya Samaj, the authorities of the Society should proceed just as we should direct. The former procedure (he assured us) would not be adopted henceforward, and the individual who did not accept the principles of the Arya Samaj, would cease to be a member of the Theosophical Society. When Bhai Moolji returns (to Bombay), he will explain to you the facts more clearly. – May 5th, 1879."

In the year 1880 differences arose, and ugly rumours began to be set afloat. To set the public mind at ease, the Swami thought it advisable to issue the following handbill:

"Be it known to all good men and friends that we have thought it necessary to declare and define the nature of the relations subsisting between the Arya Samaj and the Theosophical Society, for the reason that many people have commenced putting us questions on the subject, and, misunderstanding the nature of the relations, have come to form a wrong opinion about the same, thinking that the Arya Samaj is a branch of the Theosophical Society. Hence, it has become incumbent on us to remove doubts like these. If questions like these (namely, whether the Arya Samaj is a branch of the Theosophical Society, etc.), are not publicly answered, there is the possibility of many people being utterly misled, and of undesirable fruit being the result thereof. This being the case, we will, for the benefit of both Aryas and Un-Aryas, declare the facts, so that by the truth becoming strengthened and doubts being destroyed, happiness may go on ever increasing. Through Babu Harish Chandra Chintamani at one time President of the Bombay Arya Samaj, Colonel H.S. Olcott and Madame Blavatsky, President and Secretary of the Theosophical Society, New York (America), came to know of the principles, etc., of another Sabha (i.e., the Arya Samaj), and shortly after this sent us a letter (Chetra 1935), requesting that we would give them also the primeval Arya Vedic Teaching and Science.

"We were extremely delighted at the receipt of the letter, and answered that we should give the writers all the instructions that our leisure would permit. After this they sent us a Diploma, as they intended to make the Theosophical Society a branch of the Aryavarta. On the Diploma being returned to them, they convened a meeting of their Society. Many of the Members gladly agreed to the change proposed but many said that they would declare assent or dissent mature deliberation.

"When differences thus arose in the ranks of the Theosophical Society, another letter came to us (from the President and the Secretary), enquiring 'What should be done now?' We wrote, in reply, that there were many people in Aryavarta too, who refused to accept the principles of the Arya Samaj, and that consequently there was nothing to wonder at in the Americans doing the same. Whatever persons, we added, gladly accepted the principles of Arya Samaj, the same should be enrolled as followers of the Vedic Faith; but those that did not accept them, they should be permitted to remain members of the Theosophical Society only. Having written this and other things, we sent the letter to Babu Harish Chandra Chintamani, desiring him to translate it into English without delay and forward it to America. But the gentleman did not send the letter to New York. When the answer (to the letter from America) did not reach the authorities there in time, they (of themselves) gave to the members our answer, - namely, that those who believed in the Vedas as pure, eternal and Divine, should be considered as belonging to the 'Vedic Branch,' as such, members of the Arya Samaj, remaining however, at the same time, members of the Theosophical Society also, for they were, so to say, part and parcel of the Society too. In other words, neither the Arya Samaj is a branch of the Theosophical Society, nor the Theosophical Society that of the Arya Samaj.

Even so should it be understood by all good men, and no one should let himself be under a different impression. Is not it, only think, a significant fact that just when the Arya Samaj was established at Bombay, the Theosophical Society came to founded in New York? Even as the principles of the Arya Samaj were framed and accepted, even so the principles of the Theosophical Society were farmed and believed in, and, further, even as our reply for the benefit of the Vedic Shakha (Branch) and the Society directed, even so the Americans (in New York) proceeded (in spite of their never actually having received our letter)? It not the hand of God in all this? Is it not beyond the power of the *alpagya jiva* (conditioned soul) to make such things come to pass? – namely, to ordain, that the things which are being done on this side of the earth, shall be simultaneously done in the region of the antipodese?

"To the Being by whose power all these wonders have been wrought, the Being, who, after the elapse of five thousand years, as once more established a bond of brotherhood between the righteous people of Aryavarta and the natives of America, by making them believe in one and the same eternal, well-tested Vedic Dharma and in what pertains to it, - to this Being, the Almighty Parmatama, we offer innumerable thanks praying to

Him in these words: 'Omnipotent, all-pervading, merciful and just Lord! Even as Thou hast accomplished (for us) this wonderful deed, even so do Thou establish all other righteous people throughout the world in this true Vedic Religion, so that, as the result of this, all men giving up mutual hostility and uniting themselves in friendship, should leave off injuring each other, and labour for the good one and anther.' And our prayer to men is: 'Do ye, in the spirit of the prayer offered to the Deity, bestir and exert yourselves, so that, as the result thereof, we may free each other from pain, and ever enjoy bliss.

"(Sd.) Dayanand Saraswati.

The above handbill was issued on 26th July, 1880 after this, on 10th December, 1880, the Colonel and Madame Blavatsky, on their way to Simla, met the Swami at Meerut, and, after some two years residence in India, thought it was time that the Swami should have an insight into their real belief (about God). In terms that had nothing of the equivocal about them, the learned madam Blavatsky told the Swami that her companion and herself had not faith in God. The Swami was astounded on hearing the confession, and said that atheism was the greatest lie in the world possible, and that he would convince them ere long that it was so. For two years the Swami was trying to hold a shastrarth with the Americans, both in public and private, but would not do, and, at last, disgusted with their evasions and insincerity, he delivered an exhaustive lecture on the "Theosophical Society'," and had the following tract, embodying the substance of the speech, distributed among the people, thus separating the Arya Samaj from the Society, of so-called Theosophists, for ever:

Golmal Polpal of the Theosophists

"Shri Swami and the Arya Samajists had been led to believe from the previous letters and actions of the Americans that the well-being of Aryavarta would, to certain extent, be promoted by them, but that impression of his has proved unfounded, because:

- "They said in their first letters that the Theosophical Society was to be regarded as a branch of the Arya Samaj, but subsequently they changed their mind (and did not declare their Society as a branch of the Arya Samaj).

- "They said that they were coming as students to understand and embrace the Vedic Religion, and to acquire a knowledge of Sanskrit. They have not only failed to keep the promise, but have become disbelievers in any and every Dharma whatsoever. They never studied any Dharma in the capacity of an enquirer, have not yet commenced studying Sanskrit, nor is there any hope of their ever doing so.

- "They gave the Swami the assurance that income from fees, paid by the members of the Society, should belong to the Arya Samaj, and that a good number of books should be presented to the Samaj. They never kept their word: on the contrary, the seven hundred rupees sent to Harish Chandra Chintamani, they pounced upon and never said so much as to a word about the 'engulfing!' They not only did not present any books to the Samaj, but actually went so far as to unblushingly realise Rs. 30 for a book they presented to Babus Chhedi Lal and Shiv Narain, who had spent hundreds of rupees in giving them a reception and in providing for them conveyances, lodgings, etc. (at Meerut): yes, this the Colonel and Madame H.P. Blavatsky did. Again, the Lahore, Amritsar, Saharanpur and other Samajes gave them each a handsome reception, but hey never put an value on the same. And the Swami also benefited them as far as his leisure would permit, but instead of feeling grateful to him, they are barefaced enough to assert that they gave the Swami much assistance.

  "The Swami, however, asserts that the assertion is unfounded. And if they did assist him, why won't they declare, how? As they will not specify the nature of the services they allege to have rendered to the Swami, nobody can be expected to give credence to what they say.

- At the outset they admitted in their letters, and after they had arrived into India' that they were believers in God. But subsequently they, in utter disregard of their previous professions, both declared, in presence of the Swami and many other gentlemen Meerut, that they did not believe in God. Is not this contradiction of what they said at first? Upon this declaration, on their par, the Swami said:

"You prove that belief in God is wrong, and I will prove the contrary. Whatever is found to be the truth, let that be believed in."

They would not agree to this too.

- "When they were about to come into Aryavarta, they got it printed, in the columns of the *Indian Spectator*, dated 14th July, 1878," that they were neither Buddhists, nor Christians, nor Brahmans, believing in the Puranas, but that they were Arya Samajists. Now they have, in contradiction of what they said before got it published that they had been for years Buddhists, and are Buddhists even now. Is not this cunning and trickery? And it is evident from their letter of January, 18880, that they were believers in God. Only eight months after this declaration, they affirmed at Meerut that both of them were atheists. Was not this conduct on their part deceitful?
- "On their arrival here they agreed that the Theosophical Society should be a branch of the Arya Samaj, but subsequently they came to assert that neither the Central Society was a branch of the Arya Samaj, nor the Arya Samaj a branch of the Central Society, but that the Vedic Shakha (Branch) was common, to both. Now, in defiance of their previous declarations, they have got it published that their Society never became a branch of the Arya Samaj, and that theirs is an entirely separate body, having nothing to do with the Arya Samaj. Is not this one of their objectionable freaks?

"When they founded their Society in Bombay, they enrolled the Swami among their members without the Swami having ever asked them to do so, and without their ever having previously consulted the Swami on the subject. When they first met the Swami at Meerut, in company with Moolji, the Swami asked them why they had put him down as a member of their Society without his permission, and requested them to strike his name off. The Colonel assured the Swami, in reply, that such a thing should never be repeated in future, and that they should strike his name off. Afterwards, when they met the Swami at Kashi, it was discovered that they had not struck off his name yet. Then the Swami wrote them a strong letter, asking them to strike off his name. They wired to know, in reply, what they should write (in place of the words – member of the Theosophical Society).

"The answered by wire, telling them to write *Vedic Dharma Updeshak* instead, as desired by him at the very outset, adding that he was neither a member of their Vienna Society, nor of any other similar Society: he was a follower of the Vedic Faith which he could not give up to associate with anyone. But, in spite of that Madame Blavatsky, while at Simla, wrote him such an objectionable letter that no upright man could approve of its tone and spirit. Was this worthy of them? The Swami never wrote to them, nor personally authorised them to make him their member, but, for all that, they did make him one. Was not this shameful?.

- "Their promise at Meerut that they should never henceforward ask any Arya Sabhasad to become a member of their Society, they broke, for only two days after the promise had been given they did their best to persuade, during the journey, Lala Chhedi lal, who accompanied them as far as Umballa, to identify himself with their Society. They further sent him a letter from Simla, advising him to accept the membership of their Society.

"Seeing them having recourse to such deceit and fraud, the Swami delivered a lecture at the anniversary of the Meerut Samaj, declaring, in the course of his remarks, that it was not necessary for a follower of the Vedic Religion to become a member of their Society, for the principles which the Arya Samaj believed in, were not professed and believed in by the Theosophists. It was this remark which made Madame Blavatsky write from Simla the objectionable and untruthful letter she did, and the Swami also answered it as it deserved.

"After that the Swami came to determine that on his visiting Bombay, he should come to an understanding with them on every point. This determination of his was exactly the determination of the Bombay Samaj also. When the Swami reached Bombay, many Arya Sabhasads and the Colonel also received him at the station, and when the Swami had arrived at the place fixed for his residence, he had a long talk with the Colonel, informing him (at the conclusion of the conversational) that there were many things yet to be talked on. The Colonel made no clear reply to this. When he came to the Swami to have a talk about Rev. Cooke, the Swami once more told him that it was high time that a conversation (discussion) should take place between himself and him. The Colonel answered that such a discussion should come on (ere long), but finding that the matter was being delayed, the Swami sent, through Pana Chand Anandji and Rao Bahadur Pandit Gopal Rao Hari Desmukh, word to the Colonel that he (or Madame Blavatsky) should come for a conversation, and that, in the even of his still evading the Swami's request, the real facts should be proclaimed. Pana Chand brought back the answer to the Swami that Colonel Olcott would come for a discussion on 27th March, 1882. The Colonel, however, failed to keep his promise: on the contrary, he left Bombay for Jaipur, from which place he wrote to the Swami that had been unable to see him and that Madame Blavatsky would have a discussion with him in his (Colonel's) place. But Madame Blavatsky too never came.

- "Seeing how matters stood, the Bombay Arya Samaj had a notice issued, announcing that the Swami would deliver, on the *following day*, a lecture on the relations which originally existed between the Arya Samaj and the Theosophical Society, and those that existed at present between the two Bodies, showing, in the course of the lecture, their conflicting nature. Madame Blavatsky had one clear day to come and have a friendly discussion, but she did not come, and so the Swami delivered his lecture.

"Noticing the lecture they write in their paper, the *Theosophists,* that the Swami delivered his lecture without having previously informed them of his intentions. Is not this an untruth? In the lecture, the Swami read out their letters, showing how the former professions and actions of the Theosophists differed from their present; how they said one thing and did quite another. They professed to be trying to promote the well-being of Aryavarta, but they appeared to be only thing it harm. For instance, the Swami dissuaded them several times from writing stories of evil spirits, demons and fiends in the Theosophist, for, as he said, these things were untrue and opposed to science. And what was untrue and unscientific should not be allowed to go into papers, for the great reason that the Theosophist had a circulation in this country as well in Europe, and (if it contained such stories) the Westerns would think that the people of Aryavarta believed in what was foolish and nonsense. They have not heeded the Swami's counsel up to the present time. In their first letters they gave the Swami the Assurance that they would follow and believe in what the Swami should teach them. Can those professions of theirs be regarded as science?

- "The letter addressed to the Rev. Mr. Cooke was written by the Colonel with his own hand, and it was dictated by the Swami. In this he put down, deliberately and of his own accord, the expression, which religion is 'most Divine'? (*i.e., which religion has the greatest connection with the Deity!*) as a translation of the Swami's words. The expression 'most Divine' expresses anything but the Swami's meaning. When, after the Colonel's departure, the Swami had the letter read out and translated to him, he found that it was incorrect. On the Colonel's again coming to the Swami, the letter had the expression expunged and put down, in its place, the words:

'When the discussion between you and me takes place, it will become evident which religion is of *Divine Origin*, and which not' in spite of this the Colonel had the wrong letter printed. Was this worthy of him?

"Among their principles are the following:

'(We are) Theosophists, or believers in God! The Society does not levy fees; no religion is higher than this! Christianity should be always opposed! He who is unborn, Who has been created by none but Who has created all, that is God.' To charge a fee of ten rupees now and to praise whatever 'creed' forms the subject of their lectures for the time being – is not all this after the fashion of flatterers and begging-bards?

"It is not all necessary that any more should be written for the wise. What has been said above will enable everybody to understand the real facts. The object aimed at in issuing this pamphlet is to point out that nothing but harm can come to Aryavarta and to the Arya Samajes by keeping up a connection with the Theosophical Society. For what their real objects is, they alone can tell. Were they pure-minded, why would they do such deeds and write such letters? When they are such dangerous atheists, so unfaithful to their word and so selfish, Aryavarta and the Arya Samajists and other Aryas had better give up the hope that they will do any good to the country.

"A further illustration of their chicanery may be given, one of the many (that may be given). At first they lauded and extolled the Swami, but when the Swami would not be caught in their snare, they commenced talking of Koot Hoomi Lal, a person whom nobody has seen or heard of. If they fail to compass their selfish end through his assistance, they might call him Gotra Koot Hoomi Singh. They assert that Koot Hoomi Appears to them, and works wonders. 'Here,' say they, 'is photograph; letters and flowers fall from above, and things lost can be found.' All those assertions of theirs are wholly untrue. For not to speak of others, Colonel Olcott and Madame Blavatsky themselves, on their arrival at Bombay for the first time, had their clothes, etc., stolen, but could never find them, *in spite of their taking the resources of the Police to the utmost of their power*. Why did not they get the stolen things brought to them by the power of their magic? And when they were unable to recover the same, who can put faith in what they allege they accomplished at Shimla? When the Swami had a talk with Madam Blavatsky on 'yoga,' at Meerut, Madame asserted that she practised yoga as taught in the Yoga and the Sankhya Shastra. On the Swami's desiring her to explain the methods of the yoga recommended by the Shastras, no answer whatever was forthcoming. In other words, it is only *mesmerism* or the juggler's art which they can practice. Those who practice yoga, though but to a small extent, they are always the same externally and internally, and in their dealings they are upright.

"The dealings of these people are marked by deceit and falsehood. If they knew yoga ever so little, they would not be such dangerous atheists, unbelievers in God. That they are wholly ignorant of yoga, is proved by the single fact of their having no faith in God. Hence the certain conclusion from all this is, that their contradictory professions and doings do not deserve to be put faith in, and the best thing is, therefore, to keep aloof from them."

The result of the Swami's lecture and of the distribution of a pamphlet embodying the substance thereof was, that the founders of the Theosophical Society cleared off to Madras bag and baggage. Many Europeans, who had marvelled at their strange feats, now learning that a distinguished teacher, like Swami Dayanand, had exposed them in consequence of which they had fled from Bombay, came to see the Swami. Among these visitors were Colonels and Generals. At the time the Swami sat with his body besmeared with ashes. A conversation ensued, and they were extremely pleased with the interview, praising his profound scholarship and his fearless exposure of the tricks of the Theosophists.

Shortly after this the members of the Lahore Samaj, and other members also, having discovered and thoroughly understood the Nature of so-called wonders and mysteries, made the frauds known to the public. The Madras Christians did the same. One of them won the confidence of the wonder-workers, and, going behind the scenes, saw everything and had the results of his observations and experiences published in the columns of the best-known papers of the country, in a pamphlet form.

Swami Dayanand and the Theosophical Society

In 1875, only some months after the establishment of the Arya Samaj, in India, a society was founded by some gentlemen in America, with the object of studying the hidden and occult forces and powers working, or present, in Nature, in the most comprehensive sense of the term. It had a number of principles to be guided by, and was christened by the "Theosophical Society," or the Society of Seekers after God. While the Society was yet in the very first stages of its infancy, and possessed but a few members, differences crept in its ranks, and it was finally decided that the proceedings of the Society should henceforward be of a strictly confidential and private nature, a decision which pored still more obstructive to its progress, so much so that, in 1878, its existence was entirely dependent upon Colonel Olcott and Madame Blavatsky. So far the members of the Society had no knowledge of the Arya Samaj.

In his voyage of the Atlantic, in 1870, Colonel Olcott had made the acquaintance of a person named Moolji Thakurshi and another Indian gentleman, and their photos were hanging in his room. In 1877, an American traveller, returning from a tour in India, saw Colonel Olcott, and the latter, in the course of conversation that ensued, pointing to the picture of Moolji Thakurshi, enquired from his visitor, whether he had ever come across the gentle man whom it represented.

The reply was in the affirmative, and the traveller, furnishing a complete address of the gentleman in question, the Colonel wrote a long letter to Moolji Thakurshi, telling him therein in all about his Society, and declaring that he (the Colonel) was most friendly dispose towards India, and that he was very desirous of paying it a visit. In answer to the Colonel's letter Mr. Moolji Thakurshi spoke of Swami Dayanand as a reformer who has set, in India, a powerful movement on foot, to revive the ancient Vedic Religion, and he also gave incidentally some particulars about Mr. Hari Chand Chintamani, President, Arya Samaj, Bombay.

On receipt of Mr. Moolji Thakurshi's letter, the Colonel opened a correspondence with Mr. Hari Chand Chintamani, and the latter assured him (so says the Colonel), that the belief of the

Arya Samaj, as regards 'God,' was the same as that of the Theosophical Society; namely, that the Deity was an eternal and omnipotent Principle, which, under many different names, was the same in all religions."

The result of this exchange of letters was, that Mr. Hari Chand became a member of the Theosophical Society, and through him, the Colonel opened a correspondence with Swami Dayanand, the more willingly as Madame Blavatsky (he assures us) had convince him that the soul which tenanted Swami Dayanand's body was one of those of Mahatamas that lived on the Himalaya Mountains, and that the Mahatamas in question not only knew him fully but were, in some measure, in sympathy with his mission.

From the letters received from America, it was perfectly clear that the object of the Theosophical Society was "to oppose materialism," and "to disseminate a knowledge of the sublime teachings," mirrored in the "Oldest Vedas." No one could doubt from the wording and spirit, of what the Colonel, or his principal, had to say to the Swami, directly or indirectly, that they had the highest possible respect for the primeval Scriptures of the Aryas, that they were perfectly convinced of the truth, of the religion which these Scriptures taught, and that they would recognise nothing as true that was repugnant to the tenets of this religion.

Jains and Swami

The first letter, which the Swami received from the Seth Thakur Das, of Gujranwala, was on 3rd July, 1880; it came through the Gujranwala, Arya Samaj. The letter called upon the Swami to quote authorities for his criticism on the Jain Faith, embodied in the twelfth chapter of his Satyarth Prakash. It was evident that the letter had been indited at the instance of somebody else, for the Lala himself was not conversant with the literature of any language, and it was further clear that it was the composition of a man anything but over remarkable for literary tastes.

Press of work did not permit the Swami to answer the letter early, which made the Seth impatient and he served a notice upon the Swami, as well as upon the Arya Samaj, containing the threat that in case the portion objected to was not expunged from the Satyarth Prakash, he should seek redress in a court of law! Many letters passed between the parties, and the Swami in the fullness of time, had an exhaustive reply, dealing with the objections brought forward sent to the Jainis (or Jains), through the Arya Samaj, Gujranwala.

They refused to be satisfied with the answer, and, instead, of discussing the points at issue rationally, commenced indulging in threats afresh. These being unheeded, the Seth had the following notice served upon the Swami, in 1882, through Messrs. Smith and Frere, Solicitors, High Court, Bombay:

Bombay, 13th June, 1882.

To

Paṇdit Dayanand Saraswati Swami

"We are instructed by our client, Lala Thakar Das Moolraj, inhabitant of Gujranwala, in Punjab, and now residing in Bombay, and a follower of the Jain Religion, that you, with a deliberate intention of wounding and offending the religious feelings of our client and other followers of the Jain religion, inserted at pages 402 and 403, Chapter 12, of a book called Satyarth Prakash, published by you, certain *shlokas* (stanzas) belonging to certain other religion opposed to that of the Jains, alleging that such *shlokas* belong to the Jain religion.

That when you inserted *shlokas* in your said book, you were perfectly aware that the principles of the religion to which the said *shlokas* belong were quite opposed to those of the Jain religion.

"We are, further, informed by our said client that although our client has repeatedly asked you either to prove that such *shlokas* belong to the Jain religion, or to withdraw the allegations in your said book, to the effect that such *shlokas* belong to the Jain religion, and apologise to the followers of the Jain religion and our client for having grossly insulted and offended their religious feelings. You have, form time to time, put off our client by various evasive answers.

"Yours truly,
"Sd. Smith & Frere,
"Solicitors, High Court."

To this following reply was sent before a week had gone by:

Bombay, 19th June, 1882
Messrs Smith & Frere,
Attorneys of Lala Thakar Dass Moolraj.

Dear Sirs,

"your letter of the 13th instant, addressed to Pandit Dayanand Saraswati Swami, has been placed in our hands, and in reply we are instructed to state that the *Shlokas* referred to by you are believed to be by our client extracts from works published by persons of great reputation among the Jains, and to contain the principles of tenets of the Jain Religion as propounded by several Jain philosophers. These philosophers have, no doubt, differed from one another and our client in these extracts had no other intention than that of giving a general idea of tenets of the Jain religion as propounded by their several philosophers. Our client emphatically denies that in making these extracts he had any intention of wounding and offending he religious feelings of any portion of the followers of the Jain religion.

"Our client desires yours to refer to the notice published at the commencement of the Satyarth Prakash by the publisher, in which he states the objects of the publication and accepts the whole responsibility in respect of the book. The further sale and publication of the book are entirely under the control of the publisher.

Yours truly,
"Sd., Payne & Gilbert."

The zeal of the Jainis seemed to have cooled down and a judicious silence and reserve was preserved. The reply which produced the sobering effect it did on the champions of Jainism, may be found, in all its entirety, in the work which had so offended them.

Vedantism

- When the report was being assiduously spread by the enemies of reform that Swami Dayanand had refused to hold a shastrarth, some Sadhus elated by the report hastened to the Swami's quarters, and coming into his presence, said that they had sought him out with the view of holding a discussion with him. The Swami, who weakened by dysentery, was laying down, sat up and replied that he was ready.

"Vedantism," was the reply of the leader of the band, a man of learning.

Swami: "To begin with, please explain what do you mean by Vedantism?"

Sadhu: "Vedantism is that which teaches that the world is false and that God is the only true existence."

Swami: "What do you understand by the 'world' (jagata)? What things are included in your 'world' and what do you mean by the term 'false' (mithya)?"

Sadhu: "Whatever there is from atoms up to the sun, is called the 'world' and all that is in it, is false and unreal."

Swami: "Are or are not your body, speech, moving about, updesh, guru, and books included in this world also?

Sadhu: Yes they are."

Swami: "And is your religion also included in this, or is it outside of it?"

Sadhu: "Verily, that too is included in this."

Swami: "When you yourself admit that you and your guru, your faith and your books, your speech and your updesh are false, what can I say to you? The case, according to the statement of the claimant himself, deserves to be dismissed. There is no need of witnesses here."

- One day, a Parmahansa Sanyasi, a man eighty years old, visited the Swami in company with his disciples. At the sight of him the Swami hastily rose, and advancing as far as the door of his *khema*, conducted him into a tent and seated him on an elevated *masnad* (seat). The old saint was a Vedanti, and the discussion between him and the Swami, conducted exclusively in Sanskrit, lasted till 2 pm

All the time the discussion was going on, the Swami would take up one book after another and show his opponent the required *parmanas* (authorities) in support of his position. On the termination of the shastrarth, which had been absorbing enough to make the disputants forget that they were hungry, the two great Sanyasi rose, and the Parmahansa, addressing his disciples, said: "I accept Dayanand's faith, you also do as I do."

7

Ideals and Teachings

Light from Swami

Swami Dayanand Saraswati was always undertaking extensive tours. He was engaged in conversing and debating with scholars, disciples and opponents. The work of establishing and organising the Arya Samaj consumed most of his time, Yet, he never gave up the routine of high thinking and deep study. He made a comparative survey of different religions, namely, Buddhism, Jainism, Islam and Christianity. His knowledge of Vedic scriptures and Hindu mythology was amazingly deep. His opponents found him matchless in the exposition of Vedas, Upanishads, Darshanas, Brahmanas, Manu Smriti and various Sutras. All this is abundantly proved through his famous work, *Satyarth Prakash.*

Swami Dayanand's knowledge of Hindi was not fair in the beginning. His mother-tongue was Gujarati. In conversation and study he was using Sanskrit. Yet, he published *Satyarth Prakash* in Hindi. Its second edition was published again in improved Hindi by the, Swami himself *Satyarth Prakash* remains to this day a correct representative of Dayanand's views on life and religion. We shall make this, and a few other works, the base for this chapter.

In his works, the Swami expressed his ideas on various subjects some of which may be reproduced below.

Education

"When the boys and girls," says Swami Dayanand, "have attained their eighth year, they should be sent to their respective schools. The parents should never permit them to be taught by an immoral instructor (be this instructor a man or a woman). For those alone have the right to teach and instruct children who are themselves profoundly learned and virtuous. The twice-born having performed the *Yajnopavit Sanskar* of their sons, and having also performed a suitable ceremony in relation to their girls, should send them to the seminary of a preceptor who is adorned with the aforesaid qualities and virtues of a teacher.

The schools should be situated away from towns and cities and in localities which are entirely free from every kind of bustle and noise. The schools designed for the girls should be at a distance of four miles (2 koses) from those meant for boys. The teachers in the Girls Schools should be females, and the servants of the same sex also: while the teachers, etc. of boys should be males. Boys, who are more than five years old, should not be permitted to enter a Girls' School, and girls above that age also should not be allowed to set foot in Boys' School.

As long as they are Brahmacharis and Brahmacharinis, they should rigidly and scrupulously avoid indulging in any of the eight kinds of sexual connection, - namely, they should not see each other, should not be alone with each other, should not talk with each other, should not play with each other, should not harbour lust-exciting thoughts, and should not share each other's embraces. It is the duty of the teacher to keep them from indulging in any of these things, so that having obtained the highest kind of education and training, they be adorned with pleasing manners, and, having acquired bodily and moral strength constantly grow in felicity and happiness. The schools should be at a distance of 8 miles (4koses) from cities and towns. The students as regards their dress, their food and drink, and their accommodation, whether they are the sons of Kings or of poor men they should be perfectly self-controlled, so that being free from all worldly cares, they may be in a position to think of acquiring learning and knowledge only.

The parents should not see their children, nor should the latter be permitted to see the former. They should not correspond with each other in any way. When they go out for a walk, the teacher should accompany them, so that they may have no chance of misbehaving in any way, and should not be guilty of negligence and idleness.

"The Government as well as National rule regarding education should be, that no householder should have the power to keep boys and girls above five years of age at home; it should be compulsory for him to send them to school, and if he fails to do it, he should be punished. The full course of study, according to Swami Dayanand, extends over thirty or thirty-one years:

- Ashtadhyayi – to be finished in 1 year six months.
- Mahabhashy – 1 year six months.
- Nirukta of Yaska – six or eight months
- Pingal Chhanda Sutra – four months
- Manu Smriti, Ramayana

Mahabharata, Vidurniti – 1 year.

- The Six Darshanas and the ten Upanishads – in 2 years
- All the four Brahmanas and four Vedas – in 6 years.

After this the student is to complete his study of Medical Science in four years, and that of Military and Political Science in two. The Gandharva Veda of the Science of Music, the Artha Veda, or Mechanics, and other Arts and Sciences are then to be acquired and mastered in 3 or 4 years.

The works whose study is to be eschewed are:- Katantra, Saraswata, Chandrika, Mugdhabodha, Kaumudi, Shekhar, Manorama, etc. (Grammar); Amarkosha, etc. (books of Reference); Vrittaratnakar, etc. (Prosody); Shikshas, as Panini teaches: Shigrabodha, Muhurtta Chintamani, etc. (Astronomy) Nayikbheda, Kuvalayanand, Raghuvansha, Magh, Kiratarjuniya, etc., (Poetry);

Dharma Sindhu, Vratark, etc. (Mimansa); Take Sangrah, (Viashashik); Jagdishi, etc. (Nyaya – Logic); Hathpridipika, etc. (Yoga); Sankhyatattva Kaumudi, etc. (Sankhya); Yogavisisth, Panchdashi, etc., (Vedanta); Sharangdhar (Medicine).

With the exception of Manu Smriti (minus the spurious shalokas), all the Smritis, all the Tantras, the Puranas, the Upa-puranas and works like Tulsi Das's Ramayana are to be entirely ignored.

The Swami shows, on the authority of the Vedas, that women and Shudras, and even those that are below the Shudras, have every right to study the Vedas.

Moral Virtues

Dayanand prescribes eleven virtues to be adhered to; ten being derived from Manu. The one addition is *Ahimsa.* People must never swerve from the right path under the influence of pleasure' or pain, profit or loss, honour or dishonour.

The mind should be driven away from evil and directed to right action. Things belonging to others are not to be coveted in thought even. The body is to be kept clean by water; the soul and mind pure by avoiding feelings of attachment and enmity.

One should have good control of one's senses. Wisdom may be developed from knowledge of the Vedas, sex control, good company and clean habits. One should be true in mind, word and deed. Evil passions such as anger must be avoided.

Character and State

Swami Dayanand saw an important interconnection between the character of the people and the quality of the government. "All forms of governments have been subject to success or failure on account of the high or low character of the people to whom the task of administration was entrusted. Every adult must have the right to vote. Yet, the government formed on such basis would be open to grave danger if the people are unjust, dishonest, cruel and unworthy."

In the sixth chapter of *Satyarth Prakash,* the Rishi discusses in some detail the general principles of statecraft. Its main theme is character. "Political progress is impossible without moral foundation. Political progress is meaningless if it aims not at moral perfection." The rulers must be "learned, virtuous and cultured. A good government raises the level of the character of the people and the character of the people goes a long way in securing a good government."

On the loss of Independence and the value of self-rule, the Swami expresses his clear views. Idleness, vanity and mutual conflicts, according to him, had led to the loss of freedom. Foreign rule, whatever its benefits, could never be preferable to self-rule. He remarks:

> Whatever may one do, the indigenous rule is always the best. Foreign government cannot be perfectly beneficial even when it is free from religious bias, race prejudice and imbued with parental justice and mercy.

With great insight, Dayanand mentions how differences of language, culture and customs were hard to shake off. These differences led to disunity. The remedy prescribed by the Rishi was one common language and due regard to the teachings of Vedas. In his view Hindi alone could be such a language.

Dayanand was against absolute authority "If the ruling class be independent of the people, it will interfere and bring ruin to the people."

On a question: "Who is a true King in the true sense", the Rishi gives an interesting" answer on the authority of Manu:

> Law is the real head, law is the real ruler ...Law governs the King, law protects the subjects, law wakes when men are asleep; therefore, wise men hold that law alone is religion.
>
> Law is very grand, law is a great light, law cannot be sustained by undeveloped souls. Law destroys the King who deviates from the path of righteousness.
>
> Law is worthy of being defended by him alone who is pure of heart....

> *Satyarth Prakash* contains many details of how a country should be militarily prepared and defended; how victory should be achieved in war; and how sometimes it may be desirable to "effect a strategic withdrawal in order to achieve victory."

According to Dayanand, the prisoners of war must be properly treated. A defeated foe should never be ridiculed, scolded or reminded of his fall. He should be provided with the necessaries of life. The enemy's children "should be brought up like your own." The enemy's women "should be looked upon as your sisters and daughters."

In the field of justice, the Rishi felt, a criminal was never forgivable even if he was a close relative or priest. If the criminal is of a higher status, say a minister or a Brahman, the punishment should be proportionately higher. If a person commits a theft, "he should be fined 8 times if he is a Shudra. 16 times if he is a Vaishya and 20 times if he is a Kshatriya. If a Brahman, he should be fined 64 times, a hundred times and even hundred and twenty times."

Similarly, the minister should be punished with a fine 800 times, and the King a thousand times of the fine that may be imposed on an ordinary person for the same crime. The Rishi advocated severe punishments, prompt justice and impartiality in this area of administration. He was in favour of severing of limbs, public exposure to the biting of dogs, burning alive, etc. for certain crimes. Mild punishments are actually "grievous to the nation" and are liable to be administered to a vast mass of lawbreakers. Harsh punishments would mean fewer crimes and eventually less punishment on an overall basis.

The Rishi was interested to see a balanced development of intellect and physique of the nation. The state should not neglect the one for the other. "If only intellectual power is developed and physical side ignored, then one physically strong man can vanquish hundreds of learned persons. If only physical power is developed and not intellectual, then also the work of the government suffers, as no good government can be carried on without brain."

Besides the above subjects, Rishi Dayanand expressed his views on religion, God, celibacy, education of children, truthfulness, meditation, rules of learning and teaching, courses of study, duties of Brahmans and others, Sanyasa and other Ashramas, miracles, etc. He gave his critical comments on religious sects among the Hindus and also on other faiths such as Islam and Christianity.

From the ideas expressed, Dayanand comes out as a man of clear views, critical mind," deep and extensive study, provoking frankness and unrivalled debating talent. He was not prepared to compromise on his ideals. He was not willing to stop proclaiming the truth whatever may be the consequences. His faith in the Vedas rested on rational approach and discerning study. There lies the strength of his ideas. When asked: "Do you believe in any particular religion ?" the Swami replied: "I believe in the faith which can be proved to be true by knowledge and reason."

Yajnas and Blood Sacrifices

Dayanand did not think *Yajnas* need be performed to appease gods and goddesses by sacrificing goats, cows, horses or pigs. *Yajnas* actually meant a real performance of one's duties.

The performance of religious duty by contemplating God and studying holy books was the true *Rishi Yajna.* The purification of air by burning sandal wood, ghee, sugar and other fumigating agents was actually the *Deva Yajna,* Elders and parents must be properly looked after as a duty. This was the *Pitri Yajna.*

Hospitality to the guest was the foremost duty of the householder as *Atithi Yajna.* A person who eats before feeding his guests will endanger the growth, prosperity and glory, of his family. Lastly, a householder, besides being a lover of all humanity, should be humane to all animals. This was the *Bhuta Yajna.*

Thus, according to Dayanand, love for all, cleanliness, respect for elders, regard for one's parents, hospitality, purifying the atmosphere and spiritual meditation were the real *Yajnas* that must be performed.

Brahmacharya and Marriage

The Swami was a firm believer in moral discipline. Sexual control was essential for human dignity. A limit on one's passions must be imposed for the health of individuals and the society as a whole. *Brahmacharya* would impart mental and physical strength to the student. It would bestow sanity and confidence in place of darkness and feebleness. It would give him courage and solidity to face all problems. Once the Rishi was staying with Sardar Vikram Singh of Jullundur.

The Sardar demanded a proof of the fact that *Brahmacharya* could give incalculable strength as emphasised by Dayanand. The Rishi kept quiet. In the evening, the Sardar got into his carriage drawn by two powerful horses. The coachman lashed the horses. The animals lifted their frontal hoofs helplessly in the air. He lashed again. The carriage did not move. The Sardar looked back to find the Rishi holding the carriage. The Sardar got his proof and the Swami released his hold.

Dayanand believed that rules of morality were applicable to all; even the saints. No one could claim that his inner self was pure and the activity of external organs did not matter. Such saints were hypocrites.

The Swami believed in the marriage of fully grown up boys and girls. Regarding choice,, the Swami was in favour of giving full liberty to the boy and the girl. Marriage with mutual consent was more enduring, and helpful in the birth of excellent children. The Rishi was against the marriage of near relatives for medical and social reasons. He was, in fact, in favour of distant marriages for healthy interchange of manners, good progeny and helpful climate for the girls.

The Rishi believed in the equality of both the sexes. Men and women should enjoy equal rights in sexual matters. "There is not one instance in which he has not permitted to the woman that he has allowed to the man."

The Swami criticised the practices of child marriage, sale of girls, female infanticide and *sati* He was conscious of the pitiable lot of the widows. Marriage of grown up partners, marriage through mutual consent and remarriage for the widows were the correct remedies advocated by the Rishi. Since his' times, the Arya Samaj has been promoting and performing widow remarriages throughout the country.

Idolatory

The Rishi advocated the worship of only one God, whom he described as All-truth, All-pervading, Eternal, Holy, the maker of the Universe, and Formless. Dayanand felt that in the Vedas there was not even a word to sanction idol worship. The Rishi expresses his views on this issue by answering a number of questions. Some of them are given below:

Q. God is formless. It is not easy to have its conception in the mind. Therefore, some image is essential. Where is the harm?

A. When God is formless and all pervasive, it is not possible to make an idol of Him. If the mere sight of an idol is a reminder of God, is it not possible to think of God by seeing God-made objects as earth, water, fire, air...which exhibit the wonderful creativeness of the Almighty ? Are not these huge idols, the earth and the mountains ... sufficient to remind you of the existence of that Great Artist, God ?

Q. When God is all-pervading, He is in the idol also. Why is it not then proper to worship Him by supposing him in the object ?

A. When God is all-pervading, then to suppose or conceive Him in one article to the exclusion of others is just like depriving a world-emperor of his vast empire and confining him to the ownership of a small cottage. What a great disrespect !

Q. You can fix your mind at an object which has some form. Idol worship is, therefore, necessary ?

A. The mind can never remain fixed on a gross-object. It grasps that object for an instant and then begins to wander from part to part. But the mind can run to its full capacity in the formless God and His attributes.

Dayanand held that idol worship leads to unhygenic congestion in the temples. Worship of different idols leads to hostility among their worshippers and thus tends to disrupt the country's unity. "They depend upon the idols for the defeat of their enemies. Thus they are vanquished with the loss of their country and liberty." Those who contemplate on the inert substance, themselves become inert and dull. The Swami reminds the questioner of what happened to the idol-worshippers of Banaras, Mathura and Somnath temples when the foreign invaders marched in their troops.

Idol-worship

After this Swami Dayanand, most humbly addressing Kanwal Nain, said: 'I look upon today as a very happy day, inasmuch as it has given me an opportunity to meet you. I assert that idol-worship is not inculcated in the Vedas, and I am ready to prove it. I have delivered lectures and held discussions on this subject in various places. Of which fact you must also be aware. Hence I shall feel obliged if you will be good enough to inform me as to in which Veda the endowing with life, the invoking, the destroying and the worship of idols are spoken of, and what particular portion of the Veda in question. Let us know, further, how the commentators have commented upon and interpreted the passages dealing with these, and what interpretations of the passages the Brahmana of the Veda has adopted as pre-eminently satisfactory and reasonable. This will allay the restlessness of the audience and will be of great benefit to us.

As to *Madhyastha,* there is no need of one between us. If you would have your way, then let the Vedas, the Brahmanas of the Vedas, and similar other works, be nominated as such. They are superior to all, and will be partial to none. They are all lying before you on the table. Whatever there be in the Veda favourable to your contention, bring the same out, and having translated it, make its purport clear to the audience, so that truth may soon come to be known from untruth. And whatever is spoken by yourself or by me, the Pandits will write that down word for word, and the same shall be subsequently published under the signatures of the two gentlemen who got aforementioned document executed between them. The Pandits of the whole country will then be in a position to judge of the merits of the publication, and the entire Arya world will know what is genuine and what is false in the discussion between you and myself.

Kanwal Nain Acharya would not listen to this most reasonable prayer of Pandit Dayanand, and began to talk evasively. Seeing this Seth Mathura Das Logi stood up and thus addressed the audience: 'In company with several laymen I, with the permission of Swami Dayanand, waited upon Kanwal Nain Acharya of 6th June, 1875, and informed him that the knowledge of the fact that the Acharya was in Bombay and was strongly resolved to prove that idol-worship was inculcated in the Vedas, had created in the Swami a desire to meet him.

This being the case, it was desirable (I said) that a public meeting should be held in the house of some layman, or in a garden, or in Framjee Cowasjee Institute, or in a open place, just as it should please the Acharya to direct.

The Acharya, when face to face with the Swami, should prove idolatry from the Vedas. It was his duty to do so, millions of people (Hindus) having faith in idol-worship, and the Swami, on the contrary, having openly and boldly announced that the Vedas did not sanction the worship of idols and images. The Swami maintained that Vedas contained no *mantras* having to do with endowing the images with life, and that the *mantras* employed for the purpose did at all mean what they were made to.

He maintained that the same thing held good in the case of *mantras* pressed into service for invocations, and in connection with the destroying and worshipping of idols. Similarly, he held that no Sankalpa *mantras* were to be found in the Vedas, and those made use of for the purpose did not at all bear the interpretation they were given. The mischief had been wrought by the so-called Acharyas, who, influenced by selfish motives, had created myths.

Dayanand believed that no Acharya or Pandit could have the boldness to come forward and prove the reverse of what he maintained was the truth. It was, under these circumstances, clearly the duty of Kanwal Nain and the other idolatrous Acharyas, I declared, to meet the Swami and to prove that idol-worship was enjoined in the Vedas; as, in case of their failing to do so, the Vaishnav Dharma – our own Dharma – would sustain a great blow. Kanwal Nain Acharya was aware he had a large following. Knowing that and asserting that he was well-versed in the Vedic

Religion, he was, in duty bound, to come forward and to prove idolatry to be in accord with the Vedic teaching. If he did not do it, no other Pandit could be expected to. Consequently said I he must take up the challenge. If he acceded to my request, all necessary arrangements should be made. The problem that faced the Acharya he should solve, he should give an answer to the question, as to in which particular Veda Samhita the mantras employed in connection with the endowing with life, the invoking, the destroying and the worship of idols were to be found. They must be met with in the books of the Acharya's sect, and, if so, he could tell how the commentators had commented upon and interpreted them, and what particular interpretations of the same had been adopted by the Brahmanas of the Vedas as pre-eminently satisfactory.

The answer to the question under reference would end all altercation and would enable everybody to know the truth from falsehood. I assured Kanwal Nain Acharya that in the meeting the might be held, we should so arrange that whatever the Acharya or the Swami should say, the same should be written down at once, and they should run no risk that mere oral speaking is liable to involve one in unquestionably the Acharya should be expected to point out, without delay, in the Vedas and other Granths, whatever passage he might quote professedly from them in support of his faith, and so should the Swami point out, at once, in the Vedas and other books, whatever he might professedly quote from them in support of his faith or against the faith of the Acharya.

All that was spoken by either party should be faithfully reproduced on paper, should be signed by both the parties, should be attested by the Pandits, and then the manuscript, a copy of which should remain separately in the possession of each speaker, should be published, daily, piecemeal, the printed matter, as the public should be daily informed, representing one day's work. The procedure would continue till the discussion was finished, and, on the termination of the discussion, the entire manuscript should be signed by the Acharya and Swami Dayanand, and attested by the Pandits, and, having been published, should be sent to all those principal parts of India, where our brethren in faith were to be found in large numbers. The cost of publishing should be met half- and-half by the two parties.

Kanwal Nain Acharya's reply to all this was that four Pandits, verse in four different branches of knowledge, were wanted, and that these should be examined by him (previous to their attending the would-be meeting). I said that there was no need of such Pandits, fork when the proceedings of the meetings were published, they would be before the Pandits of whole of India, and the Pandits would pass their opinion on the same. And in the publication report of the proceedings it should be stated that whatever Pandits felt disposed to express their opinion on the same. And in the publication (report of the proceedings) it should be stated that whatever Pandits felt disposed to express their opinion as regards the merits of the Shastrarth, the same should kindly forward their remarks, within three months, to such-and-such a person. Such testimony (I presented) would be more useful. And as to the kind of Pandits, of whom the Acharya want those that were well up in Nyaya Shastra, or those who were well up in Vyakarna, or hose who knew the uttara Mimansa, or those who were well-versed in Sankhya, or those who were masters of the Dharma Shastra? The Acharya answered that those who were well-versed in the Vedangas were wanted. I said that such Pandit were difficult to be had. To wish to have such was (under the circumstances) very much like expressing a wish to possess a horned hare, no matter if such a creature was to be had nowhere. The number of books which the Vedas, the Vedangas, the Upanga and the Upavedas made up, was something tremendous, and so was their weight. Where could Pandits well-versed in these be had from?

However, if the Acharya aware of the existence one such, he would kindly say where the man was to be found. The Acharya replied that Rang Jeet Totawari was such a one, and that he was to be found in Nadiea Shanti! I said that I knew none in Nadiea Shanti, but that if he would name any Pandit thoroughly verse in the Vedas and the Vedangas in Banaras, which unquestionably was the seat of our Dharma *par excellence,* and rich in Pandits, I would wire to our agent in that city and find out all about the Pandit, though I was convinced that such a learned man could be had nowhere, yea, even one of an inferior type. Indeed, it was a question whether such Pandits were plentiful evening former times.

The Acharya decline to name any Pandits in Banaras, adding that he would hold a discussion only if the kind of Pandits mentioned in the public notice, issued 4th June, 1875, were forthcoming at the meeting. Upon this I read out the notice to the Acharya saying that the notice mentioned Friday as the day of the meeting, but that his disciple had signed the notice for Saturday and had further entered into a written agreement with a layman, fixing Saturday, as the day of the meeting. Would the Acharya abide by his disciple's announcement, according to which, as the notice said, the shastrarth-meeting should be held in Framjee Institute?

The Acharya answered, he was not aware of this, and he would not abide by the announcement. I remarked that I was sorry that the Acharya shirked a duty whose performance was incumbent upon him – a thing that did not at all reflect credit upon him. There could under certain circumstances, be no doubt that what Swami Dayanand affirmed was true, and indisputable even in slightest degree and were now convinced that the charges which Swami Dayanand has laid at the door of the Acharyas were perfectly well founded. If Kanwal Nain Acharya would free himself form those charges, he should make his word good and prove that the Vedas inculcated idolatry, so that his reputation might be preserved. If he refused to attach any weight to my representations, well, not make Kanwal Nain Acharya pluck up courage to free himself from the charges brought against him.

Now you all see on what absurd ground the Acharya is trying to back out of discussion. This must convince you that the Acharya is utterly powerless to prove the worship of idols to be in accord with the teaching of the Vedas.

When Thakur Mathura Das Loji had done speaking, Kanwal Nain Acharya, without, in the least, furnishing proofs in support of idolatry, rose and prepared to depart in silence. The Chairman, Mr. Bechar Das, turning to the Acharya, said; 'Sir, it is not right that you should leave meeting in silence, without having said anything. All the people that are sitting here, are eagerly expecting you to prove that idol-worship is sanctioned by the Vedas. It does not behove you to depart, all of a sudden, without saying for their conviction that the Vedas do not sanction idolatry.

No reply was forthcoming. For the last time Swami Dayanand addressed him in these words: 'You maintain that idol-worship is allowed in the Vedas, and it was incumbent upon you to prove your assertion. If you are determined not to do this, I must perforce expose idolatry and prove that it is opposed to the teaching of the Veda. You should least hear me.' Kanwal Nain Acharya took his departure. Many idol-worshippers who had flocked to the meeting, eagerly hoping that idol-worship would be proved form the Vedas, were disappointed. Many householders, who had faith in idol-worship, lost all faith in the same, saying to themselves: Our Dharma is so weak and false! That which is the principal article of our faith, even that cannot be proved. How well the proverb applies to it (Hinduism).*Sufficiently capacious throated even to engulf an elephant, but occasionally unable even to swallow an ant.'*

Exactly such has been the case with our Dharma this time. Kanwal Nain Acharya understood his interests too well when he declined to stop to listen to the Swami's speech, being well aware that to hear the exposure in the words of a man like Dayanand, and then to go away without replying to the denunciation, would expose him to the ridicule and contempt of the Believers in the Veda. The meeting was thoroughly satisfied that the Acharya was utterly unable to prove idolatry from the Veda. It was indeed a marvel that he had even gone so far as to put in an appearance at the meeting.

Subsequently, Seth hargobin Das Baba asked the Swami, whether idol-worship existed in Satyuga, or whether it had come into existence only recently. In reply the Swami observed that I had no existence in Sat or any other (of the first three) Yugas: it had been fathered upon the believers in the Vedas by the selfish only in the present Kalyuga, after the birth of the Jain and the Buddhistic creeds. When Shankarcharya exposed the Jain faith, many Jainis put their idols under ground, and it was these that were now and then found in many places where work of excavation was in progress. The worship of idols, the Swami added, was wholly unknown to our sages, and it had no place in the Vedic teachings. After this reply, Seth Chhabil Das Lallobhai commented freely on the unfair move of Kanwal Nain Acharya and Mr. Moolji Thakarshi also expressed his opinion on the subject.

At last Pandit Dayanand, speaking on the want of erudition on the part of Acharya, expressed his regret that so many works should have been brought together for a noble purpose but that not a single page of any one of them should have been turned. To be brief, he commenced his speech, condemnatory of idolatry, by taking, his text, the *mantra - Na Tasya pratima asti yasya anma mahadyasha*, and in support of the truth embodied in the *mantra* he read out many passages from the Vedas, alleged to be concerned with the *avahan, pujan, visarjan* and *pranpratishtha* of idols, and explained what these terms severally meant.

The *Mantras* in question, he made clear, had nothing to do with *avahan* or any other similar function, and the Vedas said nowhere that they should be applies in connection with such functions. Idol-worship had not originated with the followers of the Vedas, he maintained; and he read out passages from the Vedas in support of his position, translating them for his hearers. He demonstrated the fact that idolatry had never been the faith of the followers of the Veda at any time, and that it would never be proved, and ended by exhorting one and all to renounce it without delay."

Cow Protection

A society of this name was founded by Swami Dayanand in 1882, having for its object the protection of animals, especially the cow. The rules of the Sabha:

- The Society shall strive to promote the well-being and comfort of entire mankind, and shall do nothing that might be productive of harm to anyone.
- It shall utilise everything in a proper manner, according to the laws of nature, for the good of all.
- The Society shall not undertake anything calculated to yield little profit and cause great loss.
- The society shall honour all men who should spend their time and money, or otherwise assist it in carrying on its beneficent work.

- The society, having the welfare of entire mankind at heart, shall think itself justified in expecting aid from anyone and everyone (in whatever part of the world he maybe).
- It shall look upon all Societies, whose object is to further the good of humanity, as its helpmeets.
- Society shall have no connection with persons who act against the intent and purport of the law, or do injury to their fellow-beings, who are selfish, the slaves of passion or ignorance, and who do aught detrimental to the interests of the rulers or the ruled.

The Swami was the first who pleaded for protection to the cow on a utilitarian principle. We shall quote from his pamphlet the Gokarunanidhi:

"If 2 seers or 4 pounds be the minimum, 20 seers or 40 pounds the maximum, quantity of milk of two cows, respectively, the average quantity of milk yielded by one cow daily will be 11 seers or 22 pounds. By calculation, the quantity of milk will, in a lunar month of 30 days, amount to 8¼ maunds or 660 pounds. If 6 months be shortest and 18 the longest period during which the cows keep giving milk, the average period, during which one cow keeps yielding milk, will be 12 months. The total quantity of milk yielded by one cow, during 12 months, will 660 × 12 = 77, 920 pounds or 99 maunds. If rice were boiled in this milk, in the proportion of one chhattak or 2 ounce to one seer, the sugar being 1½ chhattaks or 3 ounce per seer, the resulting khir (a kind of frumenty) will be sufficient to give 1,980 persons a good meal, supposing each individual to consume 2 seers or 4 pounds at a meal.

Again, if a cow breed 8 times at the least during its period of existence, and another, 18 times at the most, no less than 13 times will a cow bring forth a young one on the average during her lifetime. Following the calculation, one cow will thus support 25, 740 persons during her lifetime. Suppose that of the 13 young ones, which one cow gives birth into her lifetime, 7 are males and 6 females. Suppose further that one of these is cut shot while yet young. There will be still 12 left to assist man. Carrying on our calculations, the 6 females will be able to maintain 154, 440 persons, since one cow can maintain 25, 740 persons.

"Again, of the 6 males, if a pair of oxen tills as much land as will produce 200 maunds or 1.600 pounds of grain in the two harvests of the year, the 3 pairs or yokes will raise 600 maunds or 48,000 pounds of corn per annum. Let us suppose that he mean working-period of a pair of oxen is 8 years. At this rate the three pairs will help to produce 4,800 maunds or 384,000 pounds of corn during their lifetime.

"Supposing a person to consume ¾ of a seer or 1½ pounds of corn at a time, 4,800 maunds, 384,000 pounds will provide 256,000 persons with a meal. Adding up the total number of persons which milk and corn will feed is 410,000. Similarly, if you proceed to compute the nourishing-power of the progeny of six cows, you will discover that the produce of the descendants of each cow can sustain numerous persons.

"The flesh of one cow, on the other hand, can feed only 80 flesh-eating persons. Now please reflect and say if the slaughter of thousands of animals is not for a trifling gain, and if this starving numerous people is not one of the greatest of sins? This is the reason why the Aryas regard the cow as the best of all the animals on the planet.

Though the camel yield more milk than either the cow or the buffalo, it is yet not so useful. The chief use of the camel or the dromedary is that it carries burdens, and this with speed too.

"Let 1 seer or 2 pounds be the minimum, and 5 seers or 10 pounds the maximum, quantity of the milk of a goat, then the average yield of one goat is 3 seers or 6 pounds a day. If three months be the shortest, and five months the longest, period during which the supply of milk lasts, the goat's mean milk-giving period will be four months. Thus the quantity of milk which one goat would produce in 4 months of 30 days each will be, at the rate of 3 seers or 6 pounds a day, 720 pounds or 9 maunds.

Since, as taken for granted above, and individual consumes 4 pounds of khir at a meal 9, maunds of milk will feed 180 persons. And, since the goat produces offspring twice a year, its milk could maintain 350 during one year, further, suppose the minimum period of the goat's fecundity to be 4 years, and the maximum 8, then by our calculation one goat will support 2,160 persons. Again while some goats produce one kid at a time, others produce 3, hence on the average a goat will produce young ones 24 times during 6 years.

Let us take for granted that 2 of the 24 young ones die early. If of the remaining 22, 12 females, they can fee 25, 920 persons. Of course, these will multiply in their turn, and their offspring can feed an immense number.

"As for he-goats, they are employed for transport purpose. At the same time, the fleece of goats, sheep and the cloth made thereof, proves serviceable to man in may ways.

"Though the sheep yields less than the goat, yet the milk yields more butter and is more nutritious than that of the goat. In the same manner the milk of other lower animals is useful in numerous ways....".

The Swami proceeds to argue his case out on the authority of Medical Science, on that of the Scriptures, etc., and the conclusion he arrives at is, that the cow in particular, and other similar animals in general, deserve protection and should not be destroyed.

The first practical step towards securing the end in view in the Swami's opinion (as he wrote to several gentleman of influence and position in his letters) was that a memorial should be submitted to government on the subject.

But before the requisite member of signatures could be secured (the Swami was of opinion that the petition should be signed by no less than two crores of people), the great worker was no longer in the land of the living.

Caste System

Dayanand strongly condemned the caste system prevailing in his times. He took pains to show that the caste system of the Hindus was just the opposite of the Vedic *Varna Vyavastha,* i.e. class system.

The Vedic *Varna Vyavastha* was in fact a division of labour. It was not birth-based. It had no rigidity. It gave full opportunity of progress to everyone in the society according to his actions or acquired qualifications. It provided a healthy facility of adjustment and placement on the basis of actual performance.

Can the children of non-Brahman parents be ever Brahmans? The Swami replied: "Yes, they have been, they are, and they shall be." He gave the example of sages, Jabali, Vishvamitra and Matange who came from non-Brahman families and became Brahmans.

Dayanand felt, an ignorant person should be called a Shudra. High-born people, if ignorant and sinful, should be reckoned in the low *Varna.* If a person born in a Shudra family possesses merit, and attains the temperament of a Brahman or Kshatriya, he becomes a Brahman or Kshatriya as the case may be.

Dayanand accepted only three principles of classification. These were: (1) aptitude *(Svabhava);* (2) acquired merit (*Guna);* and (3) actual performance *(Karma).* If a person wanted to be a Brahman, he must live accordingly. A Brahman, according to the Rishi was "duty-bound to a life of simplicity, poverty and high thinking. He is to demand nothing, not even fame." Wealth and women must not tempt him. If a person feels inclined to fight and sacrifice his all for the protection of the society, let him choose to be a Kshatriya The same applies to other *Varnas.*

The Rishi advocated cordial relations among the members of the four *Varnas.* They must share each other's grief and happiness. There should be a feeling of genuine companionship among them. The Rishi tried to fashion the Hindu society on the basis of these ideas. In debates, he often criticised the existing caste system as un-Vedic and harmful. The Vedic *Varna Vyavastha* was never based on birth. It was related to real performance.

The Swami was confronted with the 11th verse of the 31st chapter of the *Yajur-Veda* regarding the supposed birth of the Brahman, the Kshatriya, the Vaishya and the Shudra out of the mouth, arms, thighs, and feet of God respectively. Dayanand explained: "The sense you attach to the verse is not correct. Here the reference is to the bodyless God. When God has no body he cannot have portions such as mouth, etc." The correct meaning according to the Rishi was: "Whoever is the most excellent like the month, is thighs, goes abroad and trades is called the Vaishya; and he who is like the lowest limb of the body and is ignorant is called the Shudra."

On the Law of Gravitation

"My own contention, in particular, was, that the law of gravitation was a discovery of Newton, and that nobody was aware of it before. When, after expressing my idea in two words, I had done speaking, the Swami asked me to repeat the whole story. I related how the falling apple had attracted Newton's attention (and led him to make the discovery he had made). Upon this the Swami repeated a *shloka* and translated it. The *shloka* was clear, and I could follow the literal interpretation. I was perfectly convince that the author of the *shloka* thoroughly believed in the law of gravitation. The Swami quoted many Vedamantras also, dealing with the law of gravitation. Although the language of the mantras was too difficult for us to understand, yet we could grasp and appreciate the Swami's rendering of the passages.

On Contemplation of God

Lala Ghanaya Lal, Engineer, observed that in a state of intoxication, the mind became concentrated, and that whatever the attention was directed to, even in that it remained absorbed. This being the case, God could not be contemplated better by a person than when he was in a state of intoxication. The Swami, while admitting that intoxicating liquors did tend to produce a kind of mental fixity, declared that:

"The concentration of attention thus obtained could serve no useful end whatever in reference to God as an object of contemplation. The mental concentration needed for the purpose must partake of the holy nature of the object contemplated, it must be pure, the result of pure action, of righteous practice."

Taking the Bible to Task

"One day Colonel Mansell, Commanding Officer, Roorkee, accompanied by Captain Stuart, Quarter-master, came to hear the

Swami's lecture. When the Swami, in the course of his remarks, began to take the Bible to task, the Colonel was very much excited and, without waiting for the speaker to finish his lecture, commenced asking questions. The Swami to each as soon as it was, put and his answers were so reasonable that the Colonel could not see his way to find fault on them. His mortification was complete, and at last finding that he was unable to carry on the contest longer, he took his leave, remarking that he would reply to the Swami's objections on them morrow, the Captain alone came, and, unlike the Colonel, hear the lecture that was being delivered, with evident pleasure."

Arya Samaj: Ten Principles

As to why the Arya Samaj came to assert its distinctive being in spite of the theistic bodies like the Sat Sabha and the Brahmo Samaj already in existence, the reason is to be sought in their recognising and teaching truth only in part. At the same time, it must not be lost sight of that one of these bodies had, in the lapse of years, degenerated into an eclectic System of Faith which sought for strength and nourishment in the dogmas of an alien creed, and such a System of Faith was bound to give way before an indigenous Faith of an all-embracing character, philosophical and scientific, in the highest degree. The self will prefer its own to what is foreign or but partially its own, and this was the reason why Brahmo Samajists and the Sat Sabhaists, as well as numerous other educated gentlemen, whom these bodies had wholly or partially failed to satisfy, and who were drifting into materialism, gathered under the banner of the Arya Samaj. They saw Dayanand one who was their own, one who offered them once more the legacy left to them by their ancestors.

It will be remembered that the principles of the Arya Samaj proclaimed at the Bombay were a collection of principles and bylaws mixed up. It was evident that they needed a thorough revision before they could be adopted. This was pointed out to Swami Dayanand, and he, in conjunction with the late Lala Sain Das, Lala Mul Raj, M.A., District Judge, Lala Jiwan Das, and few other gentlemen, remodelled and recast them, separating the *niyams* from the *upniyams* (by-laws), and at the inaugural weekly meeting of the Arya Samaj, which tool place on 24th June, 1877, at the *kothi* of Dr. Rahim Khan, had them duly announced. These principles and by-laws were recognised and adopted by the Bombay Samaj, as well as by all the after-coming Arya Samajes, in the whatever part of the country they came to be established, and they remain in force in all Samajes down to the present time. These principles were:

- "The primordial Root – the Eternal Unseen Sustainer – of all true knowledge, and of objects made known by true knowledge, and of objects made known by true knowledge – aye of all these – is the Supreme God.
- "God is All-Truth, All-Knowledge, All-Beatitude. He is Formless, Almighty, Just, Benevolent, Unborn, Endless and Infinite, Unchangeable, Beginningless, Incomparable, Fearless, Eternal, Holy and Maker of the universe. To him alone is worship due.
- "The Veda is the Scripture of true knowledge. It is the paramount Duty of every Arya to learn and teach the Veda, to hear and preach it.
- "We should ever be 'ready to accept Truth, and to renounce Untruth.
- "All acts should be done in accordance with Dharma, after a thorough investigation of Right and wrong.
- "The prime object of the Arya Samaj – Vedic church – is to do good to the world, that is to promote the Physical, Spiritual and Social good of every sentient being.
- "Our conduct towards all should be guided by Love, Righteousness and Justice.
- "We should destroy avidya – Nescience – and promote vidya – Science, spiritual and physical.
- No person should be content with promoting his own good only; on the contrary, he should look for his good in the good of all.
- "All men should abide by the laws of Society calculated to promote the well-being of all; but everybody is free in regard to the laws affecting his individual well-being."

We may be sure that it was no tame affair – that of the establishment of the Arya Samaj at Lahore. We have reliable information that the excitement and enthusiasm created and evoked by the function were at their highest pitch.

The following is the list of office-holders and members elected at the preliminary meeting:

- Lala Mul Raj, M.A., Prem Chand Rai Chand Scholar (at present member, the Anarkali Samaj, Lahore) President.
- Lala Sri Ram, M.A., Headmaster, Normal School Lahore, Vice-President (since dead).
- Lala Sain Das, Translator, Government Gazette, Punjab Secretary (since dead).
- Lal Jiwan Das, Translator, Financial Commissioner's Office, Punjab (at present an Office-bearer of the Vachhowali Samaj, Lahore) – Secretary.
- Babu Sarda Parsad Bhattacharya, Secretary. (The gentleman has ceased to take interest in the Arya Samaj.
- Lala Bishen Lall M.A. Joint Secretary. (Probably member of no Samaj at present)
- Lala Kundan Lal, Treasurer. (Member of no Samaj at present).
- Lala Ballabh Das, Librarian (since dead).
- Pandit Amar Nath, Translator, Chief Court, Member. (Has ceased to be a member of an Samaj.)
- Dr. Bhagat Ram Sahni, Member. (Has ceased to be member of any Samaj.)
- Dr. Khazan Chand, Member. (At present member of the Gujarat Samaj.)
- Lala Madan Singh, B.A., Member (At present member of the Ambala Samaj.)
- Lala Mungoo Mal, Member. (At present a member of the Lahore Arya Samaj, Anarkali.)
- Lala Hans Raj Shani, Member. (At present Secretary, Arya Samaj, Rawalpindi.)

- Lala Dwarka Das, M. A. Member. (At present President, Arya Samaj, Anarkali.)
- Lala Gobind Sahai, Member. (At present member, Lahore Arya Samaj, Anarkali.)
- Dr. Sada Nand, Member.
- Lala Ishwar Das, B.A., Member (deceased).
- Bhai Nihal Singh, Member (ditto).
- Lala Balak Ram, Member. (ditto)
- Lala Ram Sahai, Member. (At present member, Arya Samaj, Lahore, Anarkali.

A gentleman writing to the *Koh-i-Noor* gave expression, in a letter, to the following sentiments regarding the Arya Samaj – sentiments which echo the innermost ideas and feelings of the advanced section of Lahore community of the time.

8

Great Works

Satyarth Prakash

The Satyarth Prakash is divided into two parts, and consists of fourteen chapters in all, the first part comprising ten chapters, and the second four.

The first chapter is an exposition of the word "OM," the highest, the most expressive and most comprehensive name of the Deity in the world's religious literatures. In the course of the exposition it has been proved, on the authority of Vyakarna, that the words Agni, Vayu, Indra, etc., occurring in the Vedas, are primarily the names of the Supreme Being, expressive of His individual attributes, unlike "Om" which expresses the attributes collectively and in their uttermost perfection.

The second chapter sets forth the methods which, if followed, would give parents healthy and strong children, and it further lays down rules regarding their "nurture." The greatest possible stress has been laid throughout on the necessity of the father and mother avoiding or doing or saying aught calculated to weaken the infant's mind.

The third chapter is one Education. It upholds the importance of Brahmacharya and lays down rules which the Brahmacharies and the Brahmacharinies must carry out in the interests of their physical, moral and intellectual development. It refutes the assertion that the Vedas are not for women, and the Shudras, and ends with the following words: "A country in which *Brahmacharya, knowledge* and the Vedic Religion receive the attention they deserve, that country is certainly blessed."

The fourth chapter is concerned with marriage and the *Grihastha Ashrama*. It lays down the rule that the girl a person contemplates marrying should not be within the sixth degree on his mother's side, nor of the *gotra* of his father, that the bride and the bridegroom should be natives of places distant from each other, one of the eight reasons given in support of the injunction being that the word *duhita* (daughter), according to the Shastras, means - *native of a distant place*. The chapter then specifies the marriageable age for the maiden as well as for the young-man, and the manner in which the marriage ceremony should be conducted. No male should marry till he has completed his twenty-fifth year a least, and no female till she is at least sixteen years old. Mutual choice and consent have been declared as indispensable conditions of every marriage.

Early-marriage has been denounced as something positively injurious, being destructive of physical, mental and moral vigour and stamina – as the bane of the individual and the curse of nations. The marriage of virgin-widows has been upheld, and *niyoga*, on the authority of the Shastras, advocated. The end of marriage has been shown to be the procreation of good offspring, and not the enjoyment of pleasure. It has been incidentally pointed out that real sterling worth alone is the determinator of the individual's social status, and not birth. The five *Maha Yajnas* (the five daily duties) have been dealt with, and their importance fully pointed out, in the interest of the house holder. In answer to the question: "Is *Grihastha Ashrama* superior to the other *ashramas*, or inferior to them?" The Swami observes that "each *ashrama* is superior institution when the members thereof faithfully perform their appointed duties," and then adds:

"But as streams, both large and small, keep wandering till they find their rest in the sea, even so the three *ashramas* are dependent upon the *Grihastha Ashrama* for support. No *ashrama* can get on, in any way, without the assistance of this *ashrama* for it is the *Grihastha Ashrama* alone that daily, by making gifts to and supplying the Brahmacharis, the Vanpras this and the Sanyasis with food, etc., contributes towards their maintenance. Hence, one, intensely desirous of securing both worldly happiness and *moksha*, should enter the *Grihastha Ashrama*.....Whoever runs down the *Grihastha Ashrama*, deserves to be denounced himself, but whoever praises it, the same worthy of being praised."

The fifth chapter speaks of the Vanprastha and the Sanyas Ashramas. The duties and responsibilities of both the Vanprasthis and the Sanyasis have been fully explained. It has been pointed out that no Sanyasi deserves the name that does not seek his own highest good in furthering the highest interests of others by preaching truth to them. While the idea that Sanyasis cannot accept gifts has been shown to be erroneous, the fact has been laid stress upon that their attitude towards things worldly, however precious, should be one of perfect indifference. The Brahmans alone can enter the *Sanyas Ashrama*.

The sixth chapter is on "Government." In order that the well-being and prosperity of a government be permanently ensured, there being and prosperity of a government be permanently ensured, there should be three distinct *sabhas* to carry on its affairs - the Raj Sabha, the Dharma Sabha and Vidya Sabha.

The seventh chapter is on 'God and the Vedas.' It proves the existence of God, showing that the Vedic conception of God alone is perfect, and it proves the infallibility and eternity of the Vedas by unanswerable arguments.

The eighth chapter deals with the origin, maintenance and dissolution of the universe. It is a most learned chapter, full of argument.

The ninth chapter explains the nature and character of Vidya and Avidya, Bandh and Moksha and for the learning and intellectual depth displayed in the treatment of the subjects, it is fully on a level with the foregoing two chapters.

The tenth chapter speaks of conduct, approved and reprehensible, of things that may be eaten and that should not be eaten. The chapter forbids indulgence in flesh-diet.

The remaining chapters, containing many more pages than the first ten, embody an intensely interesting account of the various creeds prevailing in Aryavarta, and a complete refutation of whatever there is un-Vedic or false and misleading in them.

A Great Work

A very important contribution of Swami Dayananda is his work, 'Satyartha Prakash' (The Light of Truth). It contains fourteen chapters. It is a great book. It explains the true meaning of the Vedas and therefore is 'Satyartha Prakash'. And it is based solely on the Vedas.

All the teachings of Swami Dayananda are clearly explained in this work. He has shown that his teachings have the support of the Vedas. He has clearly pointed, out the harmful customs and practices not only of the Hindus but also of the followers of other religions. He gave a hero's call to the people of India to shake off their slavery. He declared that it was not sufficient for any religion to teach a man how to attain salvation after death; it must also show a man how to live usefully in this world. The Vedic religion has shown every man the right path, by placing before him the four-fold ideal of righteousness, wealth, enjoyment and salvation.

In those days the people were ignorant of the Vedas. Swami Dayananda strove hard to dispel this ignorance among the masses. His teaching was this: man's main aim is salvation; but if we do not live worthily on the earth we cannot attain salvation. This teaching he supported with passages from the Vedas. And he exhorted people to turn to the Vedas.

Rigveda Bhashya Bhumika

A Sanskrit-Hindi work. It is an invaluable and scholarly Introduction to the Veda-Bhashya, pointing out the lofty and sublime character of the Vedic Teachings and showing how the germs of all sciences are to be found in the Vedas. The Introduction shows how the latter-day commentaries by Sayana, Mahidhar and others, Indians or Europeans, are utterly misleading and false, and justifies the need of a fresh commentary, based entirely on the ancient Niruktak system of interpretation.

We shall give quotations:

Divine Origin of the Vedas

- "From that adorable Yajna have proceeded the Righ and Sama; from Him have proceeded the Chhandansi; and from Him has proceeded the Yaju."
- "He from whom the Rig has sprung, He from whom the Yaju, has sprung, like unto whose loma is the Sama, and like unto whose mouth is the Atharva Angiras, - what is He like? Him thou declare. Reply – Know that He is Skamba." – Atharva.

From Him, the adorable, from Him who is true, all-knowledge, all-happiness, and so forth, - the Perfect Being, who ought to be the object of universal homage, and should be worshipped by all, - yes, from this almighty par Brahma have proceeded all the four Vedas, - the Rig Veda, the Yajur Veda, the Sama Veda, and the Atharva Veda. Even this is to be believed. The term *Sarvahut* may also appropriately be applies to the Vedas. The Vedas are *sarvahut*, for they are worthy of being accepted and received by all men. The object of the two verbs *Jajinire* and *ajayat* (in this mantra) is to show that the Vedas contain numerous sciences, and the repetition of the word *tasmat* is also to convince man that they are of Divine origin. Inasmuch as the Vedas have in them *Gayatri* and the other *Chhandas* the word *Chhandansi*, in the mantra, indicates the Divine origin of the fourth Veda – the Atharva. Even this is to be believed.

"Yajna" is verily the Vishnu."

"Vishnu made this universe, and disposed the things (therein or thereof) in a three-fold order." (This is to be found in the Yajur Veda.) The creation of this universe can be predicated of God only and of none other. "He who pervades both the animate and inanimate creation, He is Vishnu, the Supreme Being." The Almighty from whom the Rig Veda has proceeded, the Great God by whom the Yajur Veda has been revealed, the Being from whom the Sama Veda and the Atharva Veda have sprung, - the Atharva being like unto His mouth, the Sama like unto His lomas (hairs on the body), the Yaju like unto His heart, and Rig like unto His vital airs (figuratively), - He from whom all the four Vedas have come forth:- what is this Deva like? – Declare Him unto me." This is the question. The answer is "He is Skamba," the supporter of the whole universe; other than this Deva (supporter of the universe) the author of the Vedas is none. Even this is to be believed.

"The Rig Veda, the Sama Veda, the Yajur Veda and the Atharva Veda, are the out-breathings of that Great Being".

To make this clearer: "Maitriyi," says Yajnavalkya, "By Him, who encompasses even Sapce, the Righ Veda as the other Vedas – all four of them – are breathed forth, without effort, even as breath is exhaled without effort." Even this is be believed. Just as the vital air issuing from the body is again drawn into it, even so are the Vedas breathed out and (finally) breathed in by God. This is certain.

On this subject many people say:- "How can the Vedas, which are embodied in words, have proceeded from God, who is incorporeal and without parts? We reply: Such an objection cannot hold good when urged against an almighty God. Why? Because, even in the absence of mouth, the pranas (vital airs) and other appliances, the power to do His work is ever manifest in the Supreme Being. And even as in the mind of man, when absorbed in silent thought, words embodying questions in answers are pronounced, even such must be believed to be the case with God also. He who is, beyond doubt, almighty, He never takes anyone's help in doing His work. We cannot do our work without the help of others, but such is not the case with God.

When He, though incorporeal and without parts, made the whole world, then how can a person doubt His having made the Vedas? Yes, how? When in the world itself things extraordinary and marvellous to match the revealing of the Vedas have been done by Him.

Panchmaha Yajnavidhi

The little book deals with the five great daily duties of every householder.

These are:

- *Brahma Yajna*, or the contemplation of, and holding communion with, the Supreme Being, twice daily, morning and evening. After having purified the body, one should seek a clean spot, free from all disturbing influences, and there curbing the wandering tendencies of the mind by means of pranayam (controlling of the in-going and out-going breath) should engage in meditation.

- The *Deva Yajna*, or the burning of odoriferous, nutritive, sweet, curative, and similar other substances, with clarified butter, in the fire. This Yajna is also called *homa*, or the *Agnihotra*. We quote a dialogue from the Satyarth Prakash on the subject of homa.

Q. What good does the homa lead to?

A. Everybody is aware that impure air and water give rise to disease which is productive of pain. The air and water, when impregnated with the articles of odoriferous, and similar substances, destroy disease, and thus conduce to the health and pleasure of sentient beings.

Q. If the sandalwood were applies to an individual's body in powdered form, and the clarified butter were given to some person (to be consumed by him), the act would be productive of much good. It does not become a wise man to waste things by burning them in the fire.

A. If you were conversant with physical science, you would not raise such an objection, for nothing in the world is every annihilated. Did you ever mark what a delicious odour is wafted into adjacent localities from the place where a homa is being performed? But foul and offensive smell only assails the nose when something dirty is near.

Q. If you argue in this way, then I maintain that if musk, saffron, fragrant flowers, attar, etc., are kept in a house, they will impregnate the surrounding air with a pleasant odour, and will thus be productive of pleasure and cheerfulness.

A. The fragrance thus diffused cannot destroy or expel the foul air in, or from, the house and replace it by pure and healthy air for it does not possess the power of penetrating and breaking up. It is only the heat that can penetrate and beak up the foul atmosphere, rarely and expel it, and replace it by pure air.

Q. Well, but why should the homa be performed with the repetition of mantras?

A. The mantras point out the advantages of homa, and their repetition brings the same vividly before the mind. The act also keeps up the reciter's interests in the study of the Vedas, which is thus, as it were, 'protected'.

Q. Is the non-performance of homa, a sin?

A. Yes; for, in proportion a man's body, by throwing out the effluvium, renders the air and water impure and water impure, and thereby becomes a source of suffering to others, in the same proportion does he incur sin. Hence, as an atonement for this sin, fragrance, equal in amount to the offensive smell emitted, or in a larger degree, should be diffused in the atmosphere. Thus it is evident, that while the giving away of the clarified butter, etc., to a person can do good to that person alone, it will, if rightly combusted in the fire, do good to numerous creatures. Of course, nourishing substance ought to be made available for consumption to individuals in the interests of their physical and spiritual advancement, but the gifts should not be made at the expense of homa.

- *The Pitri Yajna* is of two kinds, the *tarpan* and *shraddha*. Ministering to the comfort of the wise and learned, the seers into the meaning of the Veda (rishis) and the elders, is called *tarpan*. And serving the same individuals with *Shraddha* (love and faith), is called *shraddha*. Such service, it must be remembered, can only be rendered to the living, and not the dead, because of their being no longer in contact with us. This is why the Veda speaks of *tarpan* and *shraddha* as institutions for the benefit of the living.

- *The Balivaishva Yajna* which consists in feeding the poor and destitute people.

  "Let food be given to dogs, to unfortunates, to low people, to people afflicted with sin and diseases, and to crows and insects".

- *The Atithi Yajna,* which consists in discharging the obligations of hospitality, especially towards individuals who are wise and learned, whose time of arrival and departure is unknown.

Sixteen Principal Arya Sanskars

This is a treatise on Ritual, and speaks of the sixteen principal Arya Sanskars (ceremonies).

- The *Garbhadhan Sanskar,* or the festal rites performed to announce a conception.
- *Punsavan,* or the festal rites performed in the second or third month of pregnancy.
- *Simantonnayan* , or the festal, purificatory rites performed in the fourth, sixth or eight month of pregnancy.
- *Jat karma,* or the festal rites performed when the child is born.
- *Nam Karana,* or the fetal rites performed on the naming of the child.
- *Nishkraman,* or the festal rites performed when the child is taken out of the house in the fourth month after its birth.
- *Anna Prashan,* or the festal rites performed in connection with the feeding of the child when six months old.
- *Chura Karma,* or the festal rites in connection with the tonsure of the child at the age of one to three years.
- *Karna Vedh,* or the festal rites performed in connection with the boring of the ear or the nose of the child at the age of three or five years.
- *Upanayan or Vearambh,* or the festal rites performed when the child is invested with the 'sacred thread" (in his eight year if a Brahman, in his eleventh if a Kshatriya, and in his twelfth if a Vaishya), the investiture commemorating his commencement of the study of the Vedas, or his second birth.
- *Samavartan,* or the festal rites performed on the return of the student from his preceptor's house (academy) on the completion of his/her studies.

- *Vivah,* or marriage ceremony, which should take place at the minimum age of sixteen in the case of a female, and twenty-five in the case of a male.
- *Grihastashram,* celebration of entrance into the life of a householder and the adoption of a profession.
- *Vanprasthashram,* or retiring from the world on the birth of a grand-child or the coming on of the old age.
- *Sannyas,* or the renunciation of everything in favour of a wholehearted devotion to the preaching of truth and the diffusion of Divine knowledge.
- *Anteshti,* or the ceremony in connection with the cremation of the individual remains.

9

Select Letters

A Letter from Swami Dayanand Setting out the Rules of Conduct

"To those endowed with excellent qualities, actuated with philanthropic sentiments, following the rules of good conduct practised by the righteous, adoring the one only God and devoted to His knowledge, - the Veda, containing his teaching, - even to our dear brethren of America, the honoured Henry S. Olcott and other members of the Theosophical Society (the disseminator of the doctrines of Arya Samaj), our blessing! May it promote their well-being!

"By the grace of God we are her in health, and we wish you to be the same across the waters. The President, the Secretary, and other members of the Samaj and ourselves have been greatly pleased at the receipt, and by the perusal, of the contents of the letters you sent us through the President, Babu Harish Chandra Chintamani.

"Innumerable thanks are due to the Almighty for this noble movement that has been set on foot. For it is He – the One without a Second, the omnipotent Lord, the World's Master and the Creator of the entire universe and its sustainer, who, by His infinite mercy and His justice, has, in order that the false creeds and faiths, which are the outgrowth of vile preaching, and darkly conflicting in their teaching – which are productive of deceit and of pain - may be exposed and blotted out of existence, once more revived, for the good of mankind, through individuals like yourselves and ourselves, a love for His Word – the Vedas – the repository of all sciences. We have all cause to be happy. Being thoroughly convinced of the truth of this fact (namely, of the saving character of the Vedic Religion), we should in the generosity of our soul, pray for the prosperity of this movement, fraught with good to the entire world.

The Diplomas you sent us have been signed and returned to you, and you will get them soon. As to your saying that the Theosophical Society has been named, 'Branch of the Arya Samaj of Aryavarta,' we approve of the change of title; be this known to you.

As to how God should be worshipped and contemplated, we have set forth all this in the Introduction to our commentary of the four Vedas. The same briefly is this:

> All men establishing themselves in a pure locality and having rightly settled the *pranas* and the senses in the *atma* (Soul), should worship and adore God according to the *sagun* and *nirgun-vidhi* (method). Worship has a three-fold aspect - *stuti, prarthana* and *upasana*. Each of these, again, is of two kinds. The praise of the Deity with his positive attributes is termed *sagun stuti*.

As for instance, in the Yajurveda:

> He who is all-pervading, the eternal Creator of the universe, possessing infinite power, endowed with the attribute of justice and other true attributes, the omniscient Being, who knows all hearts, omnipresent and over-spreading all, uniformly permeating all things by virtue of His power to unite; - He, the Lord, imparts real knowledge to men through the Vedas.' In this way should the *sagun stuti* of God be conducted.

"Wherever the Great Architect has bee praised for His skill and workmanship, know that in such places *sagun stuti* is meant.

"Now to speak of the *nirgun stuti*:

> He is formless, i.e., He never becomes corporeal (by assuming a body), He is indivisible, he never becomes unjust by committing deeds of unrighteousness, etc.
>
> "Similarly in the Atharva Veda, Khand 13, anuvaka 4, mantras 16, 17, 18 and 20, which enjoin the worship of the one only God, the previous mantras, from 2 to 9, denouncing polytheism or condemning the worship of many gods at variance with one another. (Even as in the Veda), even so we point out to you. As all things are *sagun* by virtue of their positive attributes, qualities or properties and *nirgun* by reason of their destitute of attributes, qualities or properties repugnant to their distinctive natures, even so is God: the praising of Him as destitute of qualities repugnant to His nature, is termed *nirgun stuti*.

"We speak of *prarthana* now. Yajurveda, Chapter 32:

> 'O Lord, thou illuminator of all, the understanding which the *devas* or the wise long for and possess, the same do Thou bestow upon me.' Praying for knowledge and wisdom and praying for all good qualities in *sagun prarthana*

"The *nirgun prarthana* (Rigveda, 1-104-8 & 1-114-7 & 8):

> 'O rudra! Thou smiter of foul diseases, of fault and of sinful men, do Thou, by Thy mercy, protect us. Do Thou never separate us from Thy blissful Self, from Thy knowledge and love, and from the righteous disposition which is the fruit of the carrying out of Thy commandments, and may we also never cease to think of Thee. Do not, O Lord, separate our good things from us, - our food, our corn, etc. Do not, O Lord, ever afflict us with fear in the womb, and let not the means which promote happiness, be ever be beyond our reach.

'O Rudra! Thou who metest out to the unrighteous the just rewards of their deeds, do not Thou separate us from the society of the good,, who are our superiors in knowledge and in age; do not separate us from our little dwellings; do not deprive us of true teachers and heroes; do not remove us from the company of protectors and *acharyas* (preceptors), and let us not be estranged from the sciences which secure honour and distinction. Do Thou preserve us in perfect health, so that we may ever be engaged in obeying Thy behests.'

'O Lord! Thou destroyer of all ailments do not Thou deprive us of healthy, sound physique, of cows and horses, of fast-going conveyances, and of warriors and heroes who are our well-wishers. We shall, by carrying out Thy commandments, every worship Thee. Thou absolute Knowledge."

"We shall now point out the characteristics of *Sagun upasana*:

"The contemplation of the just, merciful, omniscient, all-illuminating all-pervading Lord, the knower of all hearts, and following His commandments, is called *upasana*. To realise God as a Being who is above the reach of pain, and free from defects; who is indestructible and unconfinable; who is free from birth and death; who cold, heat, hunger and thirst touch not; who is not affected by sorrow, affection, intoxication and jealousy; who has neither shape nor taste, nor smell nor touch, and so on; and to perceive, by a further realisation, that this Being, by virtue of His omniscience, witnesses all our actions, the commission of evil acts., etc., - this is called *nirgun upasana* (in its comprehensive sense) is a mental operation of a three-fold nature - *stuti, prarthana* and *upasna*, each of these being, again, of two kinds, - sagun and nirgun.

The meaning of the word Arya: 'He who is learned, the instructor of others, the practiser of a universally-benefitting *dharma*, the same is Arya. (Ashtadhyayi 26 – 58). He who follows the Divine commandments embodied in the Veda, even the knower of the Veda, is called a Brahman. The exercise of a thorough control over the senses from the 8th up to the 48th year agreeably to the rules laid down (in the Shastras), the hearing of the Vedas and believing in and meditating on their teaching – even this is practising Brahmacharya. After (the expiration of the Bramhacharya period), the enjoyment of the society of one's lawfully-wedded wife (for purposes of procreation), and wholly avoiding the company of strange woman, and doing other commendable thing of the same kind – these constitute the Aryanism of an Arya.

Rigveda, 1-15-8:

> "When the Vedas were revealed in the beginning of creation, God gave a name to everything. Subsequently, in accordance with the character and spirit of the Divinely-appointed names, the Rishis differentiated good men from the bad by designating them Arya and Dasyu, respectively. In this mantra the Supreme Being, speaking to men, says that they are to regard individuals possessing good qualities and of righteous activities and tendencies and of philanthropic instincts as 'Arya', and to look upon those who are the reverse of these, individuals who work evil, as 'Dasyu.' The mantra enjoins upon men the reformation and regeneration of the evil-doer by correcting the same through the agency of knowledge and instruction. The Rigveda, 1-117-21, says the same thing.
>
> "The first scene of creation was the extreme end of the Himalayas. As the population increased, it came to be grouped into tow parties, - the party of the good and the party of the evil-minded. The differences in their dispositions created a feeling of hostility between the two. Those who were Aryas descended into this country, which, in consequence thereof, came to be called 'Aryavarta'.

"It is written in Manu Smriti (2 – 12 – 27):

> "The country lying between the two streams – Saraswati and Drishadwati (The Indus and the Brahmaputra) is called Aryavarta."

The tract enclosed by the Himalayas and he Vindhyachal and extending form the Eastern Sea to the Western Sea, - all this is Aryavarta. The Society of the Aryas is called Arya Samaj, or Arya Samaj is the society of persons who, giving up the evil habits of the Dasyus, assimilate the good qualities of he Aryas. Hence there is not the least harm in giving the name "Arya Samaj" to all good societies: indeed, it is an honour to them, the highest possible, to thus designated.

You should further the well-being of others by giving them the right teaching, by the diffusion of knowledge, by following the dictates of justice in your dealings with them, leading a life of activity, by the adoption of friendly attitude towards all. Girding up you loins, you should make the things named (good instruction, knowledge, etc.) poplar with your brethren, in addition to valuing them yourself. This is the answer to the essence of your question.

"An exhaustive answer to the question can only be obtained by studying the Vedas and the Shastras. And the works I have published, - such as the Veda Bhashya, the Sandhya-Upasana, the Raybhivinai, the Vedavrudhamat khandan, the Vedanta Dhawati Niwaran, the Satyarth Prakash, the Sanskar Vidhi, the Arya updesh Ratanamala, etc., - by the study of these, too, and idea of the Vedic Teaching can be obtained; by this known to you.

The Entity - Soul: That which possess, consciousness, that is, the Jiva (Soul). Yes, consciousness is the characteristic of the soul. Desire, etc., are essential to it. It is formless and indestructible. It was never born, nor will it ever die. This subject has been thoroughly discussed and thrown perfect light upon in the Vedas and in the works by the Aryas...It is by the study of various methods set forth in the Vedas and shastras and by a practical knowledge (yoga) of these methods that the true nature of the Soul was realised in ancient times, can be realised at present, and is possible of being realised in future. When the Soul leaves the body, they say it is dead. But this death mean nothing more than the separation of the Soul from the perishable body.

"The Soul, on throwing off one body, ranges in space, and, in accordance with the Divine law of punishments and rewards, puts on another body to which its merits and demerits entitle it. As long as it floats in space and stays in the womb, - in the baby-state, so long it acquires no special knowledge. The state does not differ in any way from the state of sleep or of stupefaction. While in these, it is exactly as when floating in space.

If the disembodied Soul possessed (as it is asserted, it does) the power of talking, of knocking at doors, and of entering the body of another person, then why cannot it acquire a dearly-loved place, wealth, body, dress, food, etc.? Why cannot it reclaim, or appear to, the beloved wife, the son, the father, the brother, the friend, the servant? Why cannot it obtain cattle, conveyances, etc.? if anyone should assert here that the spirit would come (to the relations specified), if it were summoned with peculiarly concentrated attention, we would ask, in reply – How is it that when the dear one of person dies, the Soul of the departed one does not come to the bereaved individual, in spite of his thinking of it days and night? If anyone should assert that it delights in avoiding its own relatives and in seeking strangers, no would believe him, for while one loves his kith and kin, he does not feel attached to strangers.

The Universe Coming into Being

"The Universe cannot come into existence of itself and without the help of the Deity, for it is the Supreme Being alone who is the real Lord of the Universe, who is just, omniscient, the dispenser of punishments and rewards to Souls according to their merits and demerits; yea, the ever wakeful One.

"And the photo of a dead person you have sent us, we se trickery and vileness at the bottom of the whole affair. Just as a juggler makes, by his cunning, strange and false things appear as real and true, even so has the photo-producer done his work. One who, standing in the light of the sun moon, without opening or shutting his eyes, should steadily look at his likeness placed in front of him, above his neck or head, and, after thus steadily contemplating the picture for some time, look into the clear, blue sky, the same would see, as something distinct from him, the shadow-picture of his own figure, enlarged. The photo sent to us must have come to be, as the result of recourse to some such trickery.

"The embodied Soul, on its separation from the body, is called *bhut,* and so long as the lifeless body is not cremated, it (the Soul) is called *prêt*. In the line - *Ishwarena smah kashchin na bhuto na bhavishyati*as well as in Manu Smriti (5 –65) the words: '*bhut* and *prêt*, occur. In these words '*bhut* and *prêt*' mean the time past and the soulless body.....This (explanation) we have given parenthetically. That which you call *bhut* or *prêt*, that is nonsense, according to the Shastras. For these unrealities, mere illusions without substance. There is not the least doubt that these are mere chimeras of a heated brain, and nothing else.

"The above few hints you can expand for yourself.

- You are desirous of receiving instructions from us, but you have not told us clearly whether the instruction sought after is to be secular or to be of a spiritual nature. We are unable to comply with your wishes in the compass of a letter. The instruction you desire is given in brief in our works, and in a comprehensive form in the Vedas and other Shastras. We have, however, instructed the honoured Harish Chandra to send you an English translation of the Arya Uddesh Ratanmala. You will learn many things from that.
- Two of our letters we have, agreeably to your wishes, forwarded to your address in England.
- When you are thoroughly convinced (the truth of the Aryan doctrine), only then you should change the name of your Society. Such is the rule the wise are guided by. When any new thing is worthy of being done, a meeting of the learned and the thoughtful members should be convened, and, after they have been consulted, the thing should be done. Whatever is obstructive of progress of every description, that should never be done. The desirable

> fruit which the effect in future is to bring, that should be obtained after sustained effort. If an opportunity presents itself for the purpose, the (Theosophical Society) may be called the 'Arya Samaj': there is no harm in doing this, such is our opinion too.

"Innumerable thanks due to the *Parbrahma* (Supreme Being), who is Truth, Intelligence and Happiness, who is almighty, the ocean of mercy, and just to all, for His goodness in having brought about a time when we can unite in friendship in a commendable manner and do good to each other. Having found such an invaluable opportunity, we should, in concert, exert ourselves so that the sinful practices like idol-worship, etc., and the evils like ignorance, jealousy, hate, and so on, should be rooted out from among mankind, and the only true Religion, that which is primeval, based on the Vedas and in agreement with the laws of Nature, be established everywhere. It is but little that can be conveyed through a letter. As along as one does not get a chance to talk with another, being face to face with him, so long full benefit cannot be secured. But by the grace of the very same God, whose goodness has enable us to exchange letters with you, a day will come when we shall meet face to face. A hint is sufficient to the wise.

The 11th of Shravan, Samvat 1935; corresponding to 26th July, 1878.

"(Sd.) Dayanand Saraswati"

The Colonel says that in his letter of 24th September, 1878, addressed to Hari Chand Chintamani he (the Colonel) objected to the belief's of Swami as set forth in the Swami's letter of 21st April, 1878. But, then, what about the letter which the Colonel addressed to the Swami on 5th June, 1878, and which, as the reader will see, clearly refers to the Swami's letter of 21st April, 1878? As regards the Colonel's letters of 24th September, 1878, nobody (except the Colonel and his most intimate friends perhaps) had any knowledge of its existence prior to the year 1882, and when, on the commencement of the dispute between the Theosophical Society and the Arya Samaj, the letter in question was published (by the Colonel), it was, at once, pointed out that this letter had never been received.

On page 397 of his book (The Old Diary Leaves) the Colonel says that the belief which the Swami gave expression to in his letter on 21st April 1878, was "antagonistic to the sentiments, which he expressed in August last in defence of his Veda-Bhashyat" and that he declared his approval of the opinion of Professor Max Muller and other Europeans who hold that the God of the Vedas is an *Impersonality*.

The assertion is clearly without foundation, for the Swami never said in anything he ever wrote that God was an *Impersonality* or a mere force without any individuality. We are assured by the Colonel that Mr. Hari Chand Chintamani wrote to him in his letter of 30th September to come into India, where personal interviews would settle everything, and that it was the assurance contained in this letter which brought Madam Blavatsky and himself from America. Taking for granted that what the Colonel says is true, it is worth enquiring whether Mr. Chintamani could send a reply to the Colonel's letter dated 24th September 1878, on 30th September 1878.

Clearly not, and we have it on the Colonel own authority that he never objected to the Swami's beliefs before the 24th September, 1878. In other words, prior to 24th September, there was no dispute between the Theosophical Society and the Arya Samaj, which should necessitate the writing, on the part of Mr. Chintamani, the letter, dated the 30th September, 1878. The necessary conclusion from this is, that before the Colonel and Madame Balvastsky set foot in India, the Swami had not the slightest suspicion that the gentleman and the lady were disbelievers in God and were believers in some mere force.

A Letter to Maharaja Pratap Singh

"Honoured and valiant Maharaja Pratap Singh unto you be peace!

Kindly show the following to Baba Sahib (Maharaj Gaj Singh) also.

"I am extremely sorry to find that the noble Ruler of Jodhpur is a person of indolent habits, etc., and that you and Baba Sahib both possess deceased Constitutions. You are aware that the burden of protecting and furthering the prosperity of a kingdom inhabited by more than sixteen *lakhs* of people – the elevating or the debasing of these people – is dependent on you three. And yet in spite of the face, you pay but little attention to the work of keeping the body in health, of preserving your manliness, and of doing that which will be conducive to longevity of life.

This is really something painful to contemplate. I wish that you would hear of your daily duties from me, and, by attending to the same, elevate your mode of life, so as to reform, by your distinguished efforts, not only Marwar but the entire Aryavarta itself. Individuals of a superior type, like yourself, are not born everyday in the world, and when they are born they do not live long. Unless you do what I counsel you to, you can never reform and elevate the land. The longer a good man lives, the more useful he proves to his country. It is your duty to seriously think of all this. But, of course, you are free to choose, and can do what you like.

"(Sd.) Dayanand Saraswati

Jodhpur: Ashwan 3,

Samvat 1940;

22nd September, 1883.

Letter to Swami Dayanand from Colonel Olcott in New York

TO THE MOST Honoured PANDIT Dayanand SARASWATI

"Venerated Teacher, - A number of American and other students, who earnestly seed after spiritual knowledge, place themselves at your feet, and pray you to enlighten them. Though natives of different countries and following different employments, their one aim is to become wiser and better. Three years ago, when they founded a Society, calling it the "Theosophical Society," or the *Society of Seekers after God*. As the could find nothing in the Christian Religion which could satisfy their reason or their instincts, they separated themselves from the great mass of its followers, and now turn to the East for enlightenment.

"They have openly proclaimed themselves enemies of the Christian Religion, and have thus deliberately attracted the notice of its followers, who denounce them as infidels, heretics, rustics, and what not. Under the circumstances in which they are placed, they prostrate themselves at your feet, like children kneeling at the feet of their parents, and say: 'Look to us, our Teacher: ell us what we ought to do: give us your aid.'

"There are millions of men here who are destitute of spiritual enlightenment, and are groping in the darkness of sensuality and atheism. Not content with remaining what they are, - perverse, obstinate and comfortless, these people must use their wealth. Their intelligence, and their indefatigable energy in keeping up a constant warfare with the religious literature and philosophy of the East, and in making illiterate persons accept their wrong way of worship. The members of the Theosophical Society have only the newspapers to give expression to their ideas in. It is their desire to disseminate in all Christian lands a correct knowledge of the ideas of the East, and to give the community, denounced as a community of heathens and pagans, an insight into the effects of the creed which the false Missionaries offer for its acceptance. The so-called orientalists, who acquire Sanskrit and other languages, forge and mitilate the Vedas and other sacred books in translating them. The Theosophists wish to print and circulate correct translation made by learned Pandits, with their own commentaries on the text. Should you accept the Diploma of the Society, you would confer a great honour upon the members thereof. Your kindness and sympathy will be a great help to them. They place themselves under you instructions. They might be o some use to you, directly or indirectly, in the accomplishment of the holy work in which you are engaged, for their field of action extends as far as the Himalayas and from the Himalayas down to Cape Comorin. They come to you in humility and not in pride and conceit. Be assured that they are ready to be guided by your precepts, and to discharge the duties that may be entrusted to them. When they write to you in detail, you would know what they really want, and would of course give them what they stand in need of. I subscribe myself on behalf of the Society as,

"Yours respectfully,

"(Sd.) Henry S. Olcott,

"President, the Theosophical Society."

Swami Dayanand's Reply to Colonel Alcott

To the above letter of Colonel Olcott, the Swami replied, in Sanskrit, on 21st April, 1878. The following is a translation of the reply:

"Swami Dayanand Saraswati's blessing on his brethren – Henry S. Olcott and Madame H.P. Blavatsky, the President and Secretary of the Theosophical Society, as well as on other honoured members thereof, endowed with excellent qualities, well-affected towards the ancient true Religion, ready to give up false creeds and desirous of worshipping the only one true God.

"We are here happy, and wish you to be happy also. The letter which you have sent us through Mahashya Moolji Thakur and Harish Chintamani, has given us great pleasure. To the *Jagdhiswara*, the almighty, uniformly all-pervading Being, who is Truth, Intelligence and Bliss, who is infinite, indivisible, unborn, immutable, indestructible, just and merciful, who is the cause of creation, maintenance and dissolution of the universe, whose attributes, actions and tendencies are true, who is above doubt and delusion, incomprehensible and the possessor of knowledge and wisdom – to this Being are due innumerable thanks; for by extreme good luck, traceable to Divine grace, has come, after the lapse of five thousand years, once more the time when we, who are inhabitants of Aryavarta, can correspond with you, the natives of our dearly-loved *Pataldesh*, a thing which must be mutually beneficial, breeding mutual love. We agree to exchange letters with you! Hereafter you may write as you please, and we shall, on our part, write to you, from time to time, through them. We shall help you as far as it lies in our power. Your opinion as to the merits of the Christian Religion agrees with ours. Even as God is one, even so His religion should be one. The adoration of one God and the carrying out of His universally-benefiting commandments, as given in the true, eternal Vedas following the rules of good conduct practised by the most truly wise and profoundly learned sages, and which rules must stand the test of *Pratyaksha* and other *parmanas* - must be in conformity with the laws of nature; obeying the dictates of conscience in a spirit of perfect impartiality, and of duty (dharma): speaking truth – a principle upheld by all religions, - these and other similar other things are conducive to the welfare of all, and be it known, they should be neglected by none.

"What is opposed to this (Vedic Teaching) - the deceitful, delusive, selfish and unrighteous ideas of men, which would have people believe that God can incarnate Himself, that the dead can be brought to life, that the lepers can be (miraculously) healed, that mountains can be lifted up, that the moon can be cleaved in two and so on – things popularly believed in; - such ideas are based on *adharma* (unrighteousness).

"They are productive of differences and disunion among brother and brother, are destructive of happiness of all kinds, - creators of pain of every description, and o this we are certain. When will the true eternal Religion, worthy of being followed by Aryas, become, by the grace of God and activity of men, the religion of the human race? Our prayer to God is, that (this may soon come to pass).

"When your letter came, we were at Lahore in the Punjab. Many gentlemen read your letter, and were pleased by the perusal. We do not always stay in the same place, and hence it would be better for you to send your letters to the former address. Though press of work leaves us but little leisure, yet have we set apart some time to meet the requirements of good men like yourself, who are busy furthering the cause of the true *dharma*, who have girded up their lions to promote the well-being of all to the best of their power, and who are firm in upholding the interests of righteousness and in loving all men. Being convinced that such is the case (i.e., that you are individuals of this type), we shall help you and will exchange letters with you, the honoured ones. These few lines will do for the wise.

{Dated, Vikram Era, 1935, the 5th of Vaisakh, Sunday; corresponding to 21st April, 1878.}

(Sd.) Dayanand Saraswati.

The foregoing letter was, no doubt, written in Sanskrit, but we have no reason to believe that it was faithfully translated into English and forwarded to the Colonel and Madame Blavatsky. If the letter safely reached those for whom it was meant (as unquestionably it did), then one might be perfectly sure that it would effectually remove any misconception that the earlier correspondence of Mr. Hari Chand Chintamani night have been instrumental in giving rise to in the minds of the Americans, in regard to the beliefs of the Swami.

It would appear that with this letter of the Swami, and English translation of the principles of the Arya Samaj, by Shyamiji Krishna Verma, was also forwarded to the Colonel and Madame Blatvatsky. Of course, we cannot say on which particular date the letter in question reached America. This much, however, is evident that Colonel Olcott's letter, dated 23rd may, 1878, addressed to Mr. Hari Chand from New York, was a reply to Mr. Hari Chand's communication, dated 21st April, 1878, to the Colonel.

The Colonel wrote another letter to Mr. Hari Chand on 29th May, 1878, from which it appears that he (the Colonel) had be in receipt of a letter from the Swami before he posted his own letter of 29th May, 1878.

From May 21st to May 30th, 1878, Mr. Hari Chand Chintamani was in receipt of five letters in all from America. Four of these bear the signature of Colonel Olcott, and only one of Mr. Augustus Gustum, Recording Secretary, Theosophical Society.

Letters from the Theosophical Society of America to Swami Dayanand

I

New York

21st May, 1878

"My Dear Brother,

I add a few lines from my own side to my sister's letter, just to inform you that I read the contents of your letter, and heartily sympathise with the various proposals it contains. In suggesting that our Society should make itself known as a branch of the Arya Samaj, subject to Pandit Dayanand's control and myself, I am proud to acknowledge fealty to such an instructor and guide that wise and holy man.

"(Sd.) H.S. Olcott."

II

New York
22nd May, 1878,

To the CHIEFS of the Arya Samaj.

"Honoured Sirs,

I respectfully beg to inform you that at a meeting of this Society held at New York, on 22nd May, 1878, it was, upon motion 00of Vice-President, seconded by the Corresponding Secretary, H.P. Blavatsky, unanimously resolved that the Society accept the proposal of the Arya Samaj to unite with itself, and that the title of this Society be changed to 'Theosophical Society of the Arya Samaj of Aryavarta.'

Resolved, that the Theosophical Society, for itself and branches in America, Europe and elsewhere, recognise hereby Swami Dayanand Saraswati, Pandit, and Founder of the Arya Samaj, as its lawful Director in Chief.

I am awaiting for your consent, and for any instructions which you may kindly send me.

"(Sd.) Augutus Gustum,

"Recording Secretary."

New York
23rd May, 1878

A Letter that Led the Swami to Believe Colonel Olcott and his Companions were Theists

Broadway, No. 71,
New York City:
Dated 5th June, 1878.

To the Most Revered and Distinguished

Pandit Dayanand Saraswati

"Venerated Teacher

The loving letter which you were kind enough to send us in deference to the wishes of Brother Hari Chand Chintamani, reached us safely. All the Members of our Society, as well as the Office-bearers, have been greatly edified at your having blessed them and their efforts, and at your wishing them health and prosperity. In return for this we are, in duty bound, to express the fervent hope hat you will be permitted to stay on earth till your holy work is accomplished, and that you may always find mankind ready to listen to and profit by your wise precepts.

"We perceive! Venerable Sir, in your definition of the nature and attributes of the All-Good, that we humble students at the West have not misinterpreted the teachings of our Aryan ancestors. The Supreme One whom you teach to your disciples to contemplate and lift up their aspirations to, is the very same Eternal Divine Essence as we have been pointing out to the Christians as the proper object of their adoration, instead of their own cruel, remorseless, vacillating Moloch – Jehova..

"I have duly forwarded to Brother Hari Chand Chintamani, the resolution unanimously passed by our Society, namely, that the Society become a branch of the Arya Samaj, and that its name be changed accordingly. As we belong to the Aryan stock, and as our knowledge of things mundane and heavenly, comes from the Aryans, the Theosophists will feel proud to be permitted to call themselves your disciples, and to disseminate in the West a correct idea of he Arya Samaj and its doctrines.

"Permit us to give you the name of Our Teacher, Father and Chief. We shall, by our deeds, try to deserve this great favour at your hands. In respect of the Vedic Philosophy, we are mere children yet. Teach us what we should say to the people, and how. We wait your orders, and shall carry then out. Whatever you may, in your wisdom consider necessary or desirable for us to do, we shall promise be done to the extent of our power....

"What are the rules of the Arya Samaj, and how are they enforced? Who may get themselves enlisted as members of the Body, who may not aspire to the privilege? What should be our policy in our dealings with the various religious sects, both in Europe and America, and with the human race in general? – these are questions which we would request you to throw light upon....

"We gather from you letter that you regard belief, - that the dead can be raised, the lepers healed, the mountains lifted, the moon divide and broken up, and so on, as a sign of impiety, and that you hold miracles as something false, designating them as inferior manifestations, etc., of spirituality."

The foregoing letter unmistakably refers to the Swami's letter dated 21st April, 1878 for it speaks of miracles, etc. the Swami's and it is not clear how the Colonel, who confesses in his reply that the Theosophists were believers in the God of Swami, could over come to assert (as subsequently he actually did) that the Swami was a believer in an impersonal Deity, like himself and his friends!

[The Colonel's letter of 5th June, 1878, was answered as follows on 26th July, 1878.]

10

Golden Words of the Swami

- To the extent you give freedom to others to be what they are, to that extent you are free.
- Inner maturity of a human is not in knowing what is right or wrong, but in knowing what one loses when one does the wrong thing.
- We do not worship many Gods, we do not even worship one God; we worship the only God. We only invoke Him in various names and forms. Every aspect becomes a devata. This is the vision of Isvara of a mature person.
- One who can manage his wants is a successful person and one who allows wants to manage one's life is struggling to be successful.
- There is no failure in life. There are only varieties of experiences. We learn from experiences, not from failure.
- When God is formless and all pervasive, it is not possible to make an idol of Him. If the mere sight of an idol is a reminder of God, is it not possible to think of God by seeing God-made objects as earth, water, fire, air...which exhibit the wonderful creativeness of the Almighty ? Are not these huge idols, the earth and the mountains ... sufficient to remind you of the existence of that Great Artist, God ?

- When God is all-pervading, then to suppose or conceive Him in one article to the exclusion of others is just like depriving a world-emperor of his vast empire and confining him to the ownership of a small cottage. What a great disrespect !
- The mind can never remain fixed on a gross-object. It grasps that object for an instant and then begins to wander from part to part. But the mind can run to its full capacity in the formless God and His attributes.
- "From that adorable Yajna have proceeded the Righ and Sama; from Him have proceeded the Chhandansi; and from Him has proceeded the Yaju."
- "He from whom the Rig has sprung, He from whom the Yaju, has sprung, like unto whose loma is the Sama, and like unto whose mouth is the Atharva Angiras, - what is He like? Him thou declare. Reply – Know that He is Skamba." – Atharva.
- That which possess, consciousness, that is, the Jiva (Soul). Yes, consciousness is the characteristic of the soul. Desire, etc., are essential to it. It is formless and indestructible. It was never born, nor will it ever die. This subject has been thoroughly discussed and thrown perfect light upon in the Vedas and in the works by the Aryas…It is by the study of various methods set forth in the Vedas and shastras and by a practical knowledge (yoga) of these methods that the true nature of the Soul was realised in ancient times, can be realised at present, and is possible of being realised in future. When the Soul leaves the body, they say it is dead. But this death mean nothing more than the separation of the Soul from the perishable body.
- "The Soul, on throwing off one body, ranges in space, and, in accordance with the Divine law of punishments and rewards, puts on another body to which its merits and demerits entitle it. As long as it floats in space and stays in the womb, - in the baby-state, so long it acquires no special knowledge. The state does not differ in any way from the state of sleep or of stupefaction. While in these, it is exactly as when floating in space.

11

Great Life at a Glance

1824: Swami Dayanand Saraswati was born in Kathiawar.

1839: Swami Dayanand opposed the British move to separate Hindus and Sikhs.

1856: Dayanand Saraswati opened a number of colleges and schools to promote women education.

1860: Swami Dayanand came in contact with a blind scholar of the Vedas, Swami Virajanand, who lived at Mathura and who influenced his ideas.

1867: Swami Dayanand, wrote Satyarth Prakash.

1869, Jul.: In the course of his wanderings, Swami Dayananda reached Kanpur and declared that Vedas did not sanction idolatry and that the Puranas were not authoritative books in matters of religion.

1875: Swami Dayanand Saraswati introduced the Arya Samaj ideology and set the mode of operations.

1883, Oct. 30: Swami Dayanand Saraswati passed away at Bhinai House, Ajmer.

Appendix

Teacher's Teacher (the Great Guru of the Swami)

Swami Virjanand belonged to that part of India which has, from times immemorial, been pre-eminently the birthplace of the saints and the sages, which has produced, in the course of the ages and centuries untold, some of the most distinguished thinkers and teachers and representatives of heroic and chivalric impulse and instinct, with whose names the annals of Aryan antiquity are familiar. He belonged to the Punjab, being a native of Kartarpur, a small town situated on the Beas, one of the two rivers which enclose the extensive tract known as Duaba Dist. Jullundur. Long before Virjanand was born, no less than two centuries before that an event took place, Kartarpur had come to be associated with the last years and the death of one of the greatest benefactors of his motherland in her days of suffering and sorrow. Guru Nanak, the founder of Sikhism, the reviver of that pure theism which the primeval Scripture of mankind inculcates, passed the closing decade of his life in this place.

Virjanand was born in 1854 V.E. (AD 1797) at a time when the Maharaja Ranjit Singh sat on the throne of the Punjab, and when the Sikh Empire was in the zenith of its glory. He was Brahman by birth, his father's name being Narayan Dutta. He was hardly more than five or six years of age when he had an attack of smallpox, which left him blind for life. The parents were totally unprepared for the misfortune which had overtaken their younger and favourite child, and their grief was unbounded. But the inevitable had to be accepted.

As will almost always happen in such cases, the helpless condition of the boy only contributed to intensify the parents' consciousness of the claims which he had on their tenderness and care, and he became a greater pet with the than ever. The father, who had already taught him something more than his letters and who had abundant proof that he was a child of remarkable intelligence, eager to learn, came to the conclusion, after much thought and reflection, the best course for him to adopt in regard to his blind son's interests, both temporal and spiritual, was to continue his education. The resolution was carried out, but Virjanand was not to reap the fruit thereof long. He was destined to face another calamity in the near future, and the calamity came, leaving him an orphan at the age of eleven.

By the death of his parents, Virjanand was thrown on the mercy of his elder brother and his wife. The elder brother might not be naturally unkind, but he was weak-minded and entirely guided by his wife, who was cruel to the extreme, hating her brother-in-law with all the hate of a woman. She was always tormenting the poor boy, flinging the most cutting taunts at him, and boldly hinting that he would be better out of the house than in it.

Virjanand would often reply, which rendered he still more savage, and she would beat him unmercifully. At last the crisis came. Convinced that his sister-in-law was bent upon getting rid of him and that his brother also, led and intimated by his despotic spouse, was arrayed against him, deliberately conniving at her faults of omission and commission, he parted company with his father's home and cast himself adrift on the wide world.

God, however, will care for His own, and, in obedience to the promptings of a happy impulse, Virjanand, though no more than twelve years old yet, set off towards Haridwar. It was painful journey, extending over weeks and months and exposing the boy to numberless hardships, but at last it was accomplished. After halting at various places for periods varying in duration, he found himself, in his fifteenth year, at Rishikesh. There he commenced a life of study, more specifically of contemplation. Going to the bank of the river he would sit there for hours together, repeating that noblest of the Veda-mantras, the gayatri and meditating on the nature and attributes of the Divinity of which it so comprehensively speaks. For three years did he thus employ himself, being hunger and thirst and inclemency of weather, and utterly regardless of the dangers which beset a place like Rishikesh in those days. Verily the fiercest denisens of the forest become as lambs when brought into contact with the rue worshippers of the Lord.

At any rate, such worshippers fear naught but the Lord, and they will be loyal to Him under the most trying circumstances. Having reached is eighteenth year, Virjanand returned to Haridwar, to be initiated there into Sanyasa, in response to the summons he thought he had received in a vision he saw in his former place of residence. He sought out a worthy Sanyasni named Paramanand, who, according to his wishes, admitted him to his order, bestowing upon him the name with which we are already familiar, namely, Virjanand (Saraswati). Virjanand now applied himself to his studies with renewed vigour, and had, in a short time, made sufficient progress to be able to compose original verses in Sanskrit. He had real esteem for the Brahman who helped him in his studies at Haridwar.

After a few years spent exclusively in his own improvement, Virjanand began to take in pupils himself, and was pleased to discover that he was a complete master of the Madhyakaumudi, and could teach it with ease. But an occasion now and then arose when a wider and more comprehensive knowledge of Sanskrit grammar was demanded than that which an acquaintance with the Madhayakaumudi, however thorough, places at one's disposal. To make up his deficiency, Virjanand removed to Kahkhal and went through the Siddhantkaumudi with a competent man, teaching it at the same time to his own pupils. As soon as he had finished the book, he left Kankhal and following the course of the Ganges, arrived in time at Kashi.

Here he stayed for over a year, studying and mastering Manorama, Shekhara, Nyayamimansa, and works treating of Vedantic philosophy, astonishing, all around him with his intellectual acumen and the depth of his learning, and gaining from the appellation of Prajnachakshus Swami or the Swami "with eyes of understanding"." On completing his twenty-second year, Virjanand bade farewell to Benaras and proceeded to Gaya. On the way he was set upon by robbers, but before these miscreants could do him any personal injury or strip him of what little he had with him in the shape of money, a Sardar, attracted by the tumult, appeared on the scene and made the fellows take to their heels.

A few moments were sufficient for the nobleman to appreciate the worth of the Sadhu to whom he had been of service, and he kept him in his tent for full five days, showing him every attention and profiting by his teaching. On the sixth day Virjanand resume his journey and reached his destination without meeting with any further adventures of an unpleasant character. At Gaya he continued to live for a considerable period of time studying the Vedanta Shastra (of Vyasa) and other kindred works, and then left for Calcutta. How long he stayed at this place is not known, but certain it is that, on his return from the great city, he resided for some time at the town of Swaron.

It was while Swami Virjanand was stationed at Swaron, that he made the acquaintance of the Maharaja Vinay Singh of Alwar. More correctly, it was the Maharaja (king) that fell in with the Swami and made his acquaintance. While the latter was one morning standing in the Ganges, reciting the Vishnu Stotra of the great Shankara, the Maharaja, who had come to bathe in the river and was actually having a wash at the time, felt as if fascinated by the rich and thrilling tones in which the song was being poured forth. As the melody died away, much to the regret to the listeners in the neighbourhood, and the Swami came out of the stream, the Maharaja approached the Sadhu of marvellous voice and, entering into conversation wit him, was struck with his erudition and with the loftiness and purity of his ideas.

The request was not long in coming that the Swami would accompany His Highness into his dominions, but, to the surprise of the Maharaja, it was refused: "You are a Raja, and I am a recluse," said the Swami; "how can I live with one of your station and surroundings?" The Maharaja, instead of taking the refusal in ill part and turning away, became more determined that ever to have his desire realised, and one day going into the garden where Virjanand was putting up, pressed his request with so much humility and earnestness, that Virjanand at last yielded, but not till His Highness had agreed to the condition that he should read with the Swami fro three hours daily, and that if he missed but a single lesson, unless under circumstances beyond his control, the Swami was at liberty to at once leave his court.

Having reached Alwar, the Maharaja assigned the Swami a palatial building to reside in, and commenced his studies. He proved a very good pupil, taking his lesson regularly and treating Virjanand with all the respect due from a disciple to his preceptor. The courtiers remarking their master's faith in the Swami and perceiving that he was really a man of sterling worth and deep learning - one who could only influence his associates for the better, became his sincere admires and availed themselves of his counsel, and company as of the as they could.

Not so the illiterate and selfish Brahmans around the person of the Prince! They scented in the newcomer an enemy who would spare no pains to weaken the hold of superstition on the Maharaja's mind and to thus render him less liable to be led astray by them. Virjanand heard of their machinations, but caring neither for Prince nor peasant but in the Prince and peasant's own interests, he was, perfectly indifferent as to what they thought of him and as to what plots they formed against him.

Virjanand had been teaching he Maharaja three years, when one day, His Highness, forgetting that it was time for his lesson, joined a party of pleasure and spent several hours in enjoyment. The result was, that it was extremely late when he put in an appearance at the house of his preceptor, whom he found in a temper. "You have broken your promise, Maharaja," said he, "but I will not, and I now think myself absolved from my engagement."

His Highness expressed regret at his conduct and promised a better behaviour in future, but it was in vain. Virjanand set off from Alwar for Bharatpur without so much as informing the Prince that he was going. Possibly, he was convinced that the Maharaja found study no longer pleasant, and this being the case, there was no reason why he should not be strictly uncompromising in adhering to the condition of his engagement in his dealings with His Highness.

Having arrived at Bharatpur, Swami Virjanand stayed there, at the request of Maharaja Balwant Singh, the ruler thereof, for six months, and, when taking his leave of the Maharaja, he prepared to depart to Mursan, a small town, the Maharaja presented him with four hundred rupees in cash and a shawl. At Mursan, the Swami, stopped for some time with a wealthy Raees named Teekam Singh, and then returned to Swaron, where he fell dangerously ill, the physicians actually going so far as to give him up. But the Supreme Healer came to his assistance, for a nobler mission was yet in store for him, and he must live for many years yet to accomplish it!

It is not known how long Swami Virjanand stayed at Swaron after he had recovered his health, or what places he visited after he had left Swaron the second time; but what is positively certain is, that late in the year 1893, V.E., (AD 1836) he arrive at Mathura, and taking up his quarters in a temple resume his work of teaching. As one day after another passed away, the liking of the Swami for Mathura grew stronger and stronger, and finally he became resolved to permanently settle down in the place. Accordingly he rented a suitable building, and, reorganising his classes, formally opened a school.

His fame, as a pre-eminently competent and successful teacher, spread in the city and in its vicinity, and he was ever ready to measure his strength against all who should dispute his learning. Only a single instance would suffice. Rangacharya, the famous leader of the Vaishnovites, came on a visit to Mathura, and his guru, Krishna Shastri, also soon followed him, from the Deccan. The pupils of Virjanand and those of Krishna Shastri met, and a discussion took place between the parties as to the nature of the smasa (combination) in AJATUKTI.

The disciples of Virjanand held that it was shashtitatpursha (Genitive Determinative Compound), while those of Krishna Shastri contended that it was saptamitatpurusha (Locative Determinative Compound). Neither of the two parties would yield, and each referred the question to their guru for a decision. Virjanand assured his disciples that they were in the right while Krishna Shastri told his that truth was on their side. The result of this was, that a discussion was arrange between the teachers,

Seth Radha Krishna being assigned the position of Madhayastha, or of one who was to declare, on the termination of the debate, as to which of the two parties had been victorious. The condition of the Shastrartha was, that the party who should come to be defeated should lose two hundred rupees to the other, the Seth supplementing the amount due to the winner by an additional hundred from his own pocket. The news of the approaching discussion spread through out the city, and the people flocked, in crowds, to the place where it was to be held. The vidyarthis on both sides took their seats, the presidential seat was duly occupied, and the representative youths from each group stood up to have tilting before the principal combatants should arrive and the shastrartha proper should commence.

Several vidyarthis of Virjanand had express orders to come and inform him at once when the Shastri arrived, so that he might be on the spot without delay: but the worthy Shastri never put in an appearance, and the Swami waited for report of his arrival in vain. The Seth being rather partially inclined towards the Shastri and probably well aware how trying it would be to the Shastri to make good his position in an encounter with the prajnachakshus Swami, finally giving it as his judgement that Virjanand has been worsted in the struggle. The bulk of the huge gathering was astonished at such a verdict.

When Krishna Shastri had failed to make his appearance and when no shastrartha had taken place between him and Virjanand, how could the Seth, in justice, declare that Virjanand had been routed? Full of indignation at the conduct of the Seth, the Swami say the Collector, Mr. Alexander, and requested him either to get a Shastrartha held between Krishna Shastri and himself, or, in the absence thereof, to compel the Seth to make the total sum of five hundred rupees to him (Virjanand).

Mr. Alexander counselled the Swami not to bother his head about the money, for the Seth was rich and powerful and could, if necessary, spend thousands to vex and harass him even though he was in the right. In the meantime the Seth had not been idle. He go the Pandits of Agra and Benaras to certify, in writing, that Virjanand had been defeated by the Shastri, and was, of course, the winner of the sum staked on the issue of the encounter.

Virjanand deeply felt this gross injustice, and he wrote to and called upon the Pandits of Benaras (Pandit Kaka Ram Shastri, Gaur Swami, Kahsi Nath Shastri, etc.), to solemnly declare as to who was in the right. These pandits confessed that the right lay on his side, but added: "We have already signed the Seth's paper, and we can do no more?" Pitying these selfish men, the Swami went to Agra, but the reply of the Pandits of that place was the same as that of their brethren of Mathura, and he returned from his fruitless trip utterly disappointed.

To make his assurance doubly sure, he commenced an investigation of the question which had given rise to the shastrartha that never came off, and, while yet busied with his books, he heard one day, early in the morning, a Dakshini Pandit repeating the Panini. He listened attentively, and as the Brahman's recitation progressed, the conviction force itself on his mind that Krishna Shastri was wrong and that he was in the right. From that day, Swami Virjanand transferred his allegiance entirely to the works of the Rishis, and began to instruct his disciples too in the same.

Six months after the Swami had been so shabbily dealt with, Lakshamana Jyotishi (astrologer), a disciple of Krishna Shastri, fell dangerously ill. The astrologer thought it was the Dandi Swami's curse that was at the bottom of his illness, and, being under such an impression, he sent a request to Seth Ram Krishna to see the Swami and, by making him a reparation, to secure his forgiveness. The Seth duly waited upon the Swami and made known to him the Jyotishi's request, adding that he was willing to offer the Swami double the amount he had lost if he would but grant the forgiveness sought for. Swami Virjanand, in reply, bade the Jyotishi and told to disabuse their minds of the impression they were under for man could do nothing and everything rested with God. "You have nothing to apprehend from me," added he; "indeed, I would go so far as to give a thousand rupees from my own pocket to save Jyotishi." The Jyotishi died on the following day. Virjanand had uttered words of truth, for God alone can save.

In the beginning of Samvat 1918, 1861 AD a grand Durbar was held at Agra, in which almost all the leading Native Princes took part. Maharaja Ram Singh of Jaipur was one of those who attended, and hearing that a Dandi Swami of no uncommon type was present in the city, requested him to pay him a visit. When the Swami came, the Maharaja rose to advanced as for as the door to receive him, and conducting him to his own singhasan seated him thereon. After the two had talked a little, the Maharaja expressed a wish to learn Vyakarana (grammar) from the Swami. The Swami replied; " I should be only too happy to accede to your Highness's wishes, provided you would bind yourself to study with me for three hours daily. Works like the Ashtadhyayi are a hard reading, and need sustained application.

On second thoughts, His Highness decided not to read Panini or any other similar book. He would, as the Swami had kindly considerable time daily to be finally mastered, and His Highness doubted if he could stand the strain or regularly spare the time. "If you would kindly prepare an easy book to your own grammar," said the Maharaja, " I should be glad to learn it." Of course, the could not do it, for that would be an insult to the Rishis, and there was an end of the matter.

At parting the Maharaja presented the Swami with two hundred rupees, two gold mohars, and shawl, but he Swami refused to accept the gift, saying that it was not from interested motives that he had accepted the Maharaja's invitation. The Maharaja did not think it prudent to insist, but after six months sent the things back to the Swami from his own dominions, assigning him further an allowance of rupees fifteen monthly. Another Prince allowed the Swami four annas a day and on the income thus accruing the Swami principally lived.

Swami Virjanand was distinguished figure at Mathura, being looked upon, and rightly, as one of the greatest Sanskrit scholars of his time in India and a person of real sterling worth in every respect, whenever any stranger of consequence visited Mathura, he was sure, he be a Native or a European, to call upon the Swami and have a talk with him on advocacy of what he thought right, won him the respect of all but the selfish. If a European or a Native misquoted the Scripture, or did not take care, or was unable, to be correct in his pronunciation of Vedic words, he was snubbed there and then. And as we have seen, the Swami was ever ready to vindicate his views when anyone took exception to them and nothing gave him so much pleasure as a public discussion with the supporters of the false orthodoxy of modern times.

The books which, among many others, he held in the greatest abhorrence, were the Puranas. His contempt for these was so absolute that he would sleep with the Bhagwat placed under one of the legs of the couch. And he was not much to blame for his attitude towards the Puranas. Apart from the fact that they are childish and unscientific productions, they are in many place, as immoral as the Tantras, and hence can produce no effect on the reader's mind.

Is it possible that any moral can tolerate the supremely disgusting and insufferable stuff to be found, for instance, the Linga Purana? The feats of the Linga, though heroic (!) indeed, are a record of shame, a tale of utter indecency and obsenity. Do such books teach religion? If the reply be in the reply be in the affirmative, then we say that they teach a religion which can only debase the people.

Further, a scholar like Swami Virjanand could not but feel that it is the Puranas that have been chiefly instrumental in holding up the true Vedic religion. To the ridicule and contempt of a large portion of mankind. For it is they that evolved a jarring and inharmonious multiplicity out of a perfect, all-embracing Unity.

In a spirit of rivalry and swayed by selfish motives, they relegated the Supreme Being, of whom the Veda speaks, to the background, and set up each of the various names and from under which He appears in the Scripture, as an independent and absolute Deity. Shiva, Vishnu, Brahma, Devi, and so on, are no longer names of the same all-wise, all-powerful and all-pervading Lord, but figure in the pages of the Puranas as separate and distinct personalities perpetually at war with each other and fiercely disputing or ignoring each other's claim to the sovereignty of the universe..

And thus, thanks to the Puranas, idolatry had sprung up where the worship of the one and only God originally existed, the many false gods have come to usurp the place which rightfully belongs, has always belonged, and shall ever belong, to the Paramaatma alone. No genuine follower of the Vedas can help resenting the perfidious concoctions of the authors of the Puranas, and of Swami Virjanand nothing less could have been expected.

An anecdote is told of the Swami, which shows hoe he felt towards the misleading modern compositions. Mr. Priestly, the officiating Collector, and a really worthy European, calling upon the Swami one day, asked if he could do him any service. The Swami replied that the greatest service the collector could do to him was to get hold of every copy of the Kaumud existing in the land and have it thrown into the Jamuna. Such is the value which the jeweller will always place on all false brilliants!

Swami Virjanand was of medium height, sparely built, and fair in complexion. He lived principally on milk and fruits. He would often put some saunf (aniseed) into his milk before drinking it. Once, through mistake, he swallowed arsenic, in sufficient quantity to kill a man.

Prompt measures were taken as soon as the mistake was discovered. By having water, in copious quantities, but slowly and in the form of a thin stream, poured on his head, by lacing the body in a particular position, and by the force of willpower on the internal apparatus he was at last fortunate to escape the great danger that threatened his life.

Swami Virjanand died of colic pains in Samvat 1925, 1868 AD at the age of seventy-one. It is said that two years before his demise, he had foretold his disciples that he should die on a certain day and of such a disease. He left this property worth Rs. 525 to Pandit Jugal Kishore, on of his pupils. When Swami Dayanand heard of his teacher's death, he exclaimed: "Verily, the sun of Vykarana has set!"

Virjanand's entire life passed in teaching, but the only man who came up to his ideal of a pupil, whose heart beat in response to his own, who promised to realised the aspirations of the Blind Swami's great soul, was Swami Dayanand.

Bibliography

Aurobindo Ghosh: Bankim Tilak Dayanand, Calcutta, 1947.

Aurobindo Ghosh: *Lokmanya Tilak also said that Maharishi Dayanand was the First who Proclaimed Swarajya for Bharat,* Calcutta, 1947.

Axel Michaels: *Hinduism: Past and Present,* Princeton, 2004.

Bhawan, Jain: *Jain Journal,* Jain Bhawan, 1977.

David Haslam: *Face to Faith,* The Guardian, 2006.

Dayanand Saraswati: *Commentary on Yajurved,* Lazarus Press, Banaras, 1876.

Dayananda Saraswati: *Founder of Arya Samaj,* Arjan Singh Bawa, Published by Ess Ess Publications, 1979.

Dhanpati Pandey: *Ministry of Information and Broadcasting,* Published by Publications Division, Govt. of India, 1985.

Dhanpati Pandey: *The Arya Samaj and Indian Nationalism, 1875–1920,* Published by S. Chand, 1972.

Dumont, Louis: *Homo Hierarchicus: the Caste System and its Implications,* University of Chicago Press, Chicago, 1980.

Embree, Ainslie Thomas, Stephen Hay, N. William Theodore De Bary: *Sources of Indian Tradition,* Columbia University Press, 1988.

Flood, Gavin: *An Introduction to Hinduism,* Cambridge University Press, 1996.

Ganga Prasad Upadhyaya: *The Origin, Scope and Mission of the Arya Samaj,* Published by Arya Samaj, 1954.

Ganga Ram: *World Perspectives on Swami Dayananda Saraswati,* Concept Publishing Company, 1986.

Ganguly, Rajat, Phadnis, Urmila: *Ethnicity and Nation-building in South Asia,* Sage Publications, Thousand Oaks, 2001.

Garg, Ganga Ram: *Life and Teachings: World Perspectives on Swami Dayananda Saraswati,* Concept Publishing Company, 1986.

Ghanshyam Shah: *Social Movements in India: A Review of the Literature,* New Delhi, Sage India, 2004.

Gulshan Swarup Saxena: *Arya Samaj Movement in India, 1875–1947,* Published by Commonwealth Publishers, 1990.

Hastings, James, John Selbie, A.: *Encyclopedia of Religion and Ethics,* Kessinger Publishing, 2003.

John Nicol Farquhar: *Modern Religious Movements in India,* Kessinger Publishing, 2003.

Johnson, Paul, K.: *The Masters Revealed: Madam Blavatsky and the Myth of the Great White Lodge,* SUNY Press, 1994.

Jordens, J.T.F.: *Dayanada Saraswati,* Oxford University Press, Delhi, 1978.

Kenneth Jones, W.: *Socio-Religious Reform Movements in British India,* The New Cambridge History of India, Cambridge University Press, 1990.

Kripal Chandra Yadav and Krishan Singh Arya: *Arya Samaj and the Freedom Movement: 1875–1918,* Manohar Publications, 1988.

Kumar, Raj: *Swami Dayananda Saraswati: Life and Works,* Essays on Modern India, Discovery Publishing House, 2003.

Lajpat Rai: *The Arya Samaj: An Account of its Aims, Doctrine and Activities, with a Biographical Sketch of the Founder,* D.A.V. College Managing Committee, New Delhi, 1915.

Majumdar, R.C. and Pusalker, A.D.: *The History and Culture of the Indian People,* The Vedic Age, Bombay, 1951.

Mark Juergensmeyer: The Oxford Handbook of Global Religions, Oxford Handbooks in Religion and Theology, 2006.

Mohanty, D.K.: *Indian Political Tradition,* Published by Anmol Publications PVT. LTD, 1964.

Nadkarni, M.V.: *Is Caste System Intrinsic to Hinduism? Demolishing a Myth,* Economic and Political Weekly, 2008.

Nardev Vedalankar, Manohar Somera: *Arya Samaj and Indians Abroad,* Published by Sarvadeshik Arya Pratinidhi Sabha, 1975.

Nitin Mehta: *Caste Prejudice has Nothing to do with the Hindu Scriptures,* The Guardian, 2008.

Pt. Chamupati, M.A.: *Ten Commandments of Arya Samaj,* D.A.V. Publications, New Delhi, 2001.

Radhakrishnan, S.: *Living with a Purpose,* Orient Paperbacks, 2005.

Rajender Sethi: *Rashtra Pitamah Swami Dayanand Saraswati,* Published by M.R. Sethi Educational Trust Chandigarh, 2009.

Robert Graves: *New Larousse Encyclopedia of Mythology,* Hamlyn, Indian Mythology, 1977.

Ruthven, M.: *Fundamentalism: A Very Short Introduction,* Oxford University Press, USA, 2007.

Salmond, N.A.: *Hindu Iconoclasts: Rammohun Roy,* Dayananda Sarasvati and Nineteenth-century Polemics against Idolatry, 2004.

Salmond, Noel Anthony: *Hindu Iconoclasts: Rammohun Roy, Dayananda Sarasvati and Nineteenth-century Polemics against Idolatry,* Wilfrid Laurier University Press, 2004.

Saraswati Shantipriya Pandit: *A Critical Study of the Contribution of the Arya Samaj to Indian Education,* Published by Sarvadeshik Arya, Pratinidhi Sabha, 1975.

Sarkar, Tanika: *Hindu Wife, Hindu Nation: Community, Religion and Cultural Nationalism,* Permanent Black, New Delhi, 2001.

Sarma, Subrahmanya: *Essence of Hinduism,* Bharatiya Vidya Bhavan, 1971.

Satish Kumar Sharma: *Social Movements and Social Change: A Study of Arya Samaj and Untouchables in Punjab,* Published by B.R. Publishing, 1985.

Schouten, Jan Peter: *Goddelijke Vergezichten - Mystiek uit India Voor Westerse Lezers,* Baarn, Netherlands, 1996.

Sharma, J.M.: *Swami Dayanand: A Biography,* USB Publishers Distributors Ltd., India, 1998.

Sinhal, Meenu: *Swami Dayanand Saraswati*, Prabhat Prakashan, 2009.

Steven, Rosen, J.: *The Yoga of Kirtan: Conversations on the Sacred Art of Chanting*, FOLK Books, New York, 2008.

Swami Chinmayananda: *Love Divine – Narada Bhakti Sutra*, Chinmaya Publications Trust, Madras, 1970

Swami Tapasyananda: *Bhakti Schools of Vedanta*, Sri Ramakrishna Math, Madras, 1990.

Vable, D.: *The Arya Samaj: Hindu Without Hinduism*, Published by Vikas, 1983.

Wendy Doniger O'Flaherty: *The Origins of Evil in Hindu Mythology*, University of California, Berkeley, 1976.

Wendy Doniger: *The Hindus: An Alternative History*, Penguin Group, 2009.

Yadav, K.C. and Arya K.S.: *Arya Samaj and the Freedom Movement*, Manohar Publications, Delhi, 1988.

Zavos, J.: *Defending Hindu Tradition: Sanatana Dharma as a Symbol of Orthodoxy in Colonial India*, Religion, Academic Press, 2001.

Index

T

❑❑❑